INNER LIFE
AND
WORLDS OF SOUL & SPIRIT

INNER LIFE
AND
WORLDS OF SOUL
& SPIRIT

Prayer, Parables, Purgatory, The Heavenly Jerusalem, *Revelations*, Holy Places, Gospels, &c.

From the Visions of
ANNE CATHERINE EMMERICH

Selected, Edited & Arranged
With Extensive New Translations from
the Original Notes of Clemens Brentano by
JAMES R. WETMORE

Volume 10 of 12
of the Series: *New Light on the*
Visions of Anne Catherine Emmerich

(With 30 Illustrations)

✣ Angelico Press

First published in the USA
by Angelico Press 2018
Revised Text, New Text, Translations,
and Layout © James R. Wetmore 2018

For information, address:
Angelico Press
169 Monitor St.
Brooklyn, NY 11222
angelicopress.com

ISBN 978-1-62138-379-6 (pbk)
ISBN 978-1-62138-380-2 (cloth)

Cover Image:
J. James Tissot (French, 1836–1902)
The Sower (detail), Brooklyn Museum,
purchased by public subscription: 00.159.119
Reproduced by permission of the Brooklyn Museum
Cover Design: Michael Schrauzer

CONTENTS

Worlds of Soul and Spirit

Jesus

Preface

ANNE Catherine Emmerich was born on September 8, 1774, at Flamske, near Coesfeld, Germany. From early childhood she was blessed with the gift of spiritual sight and lived almost constantly in inner vision of scenes of the Old and New Testaments. As a child, her visions were mostly of pre-Christian events, but these grew less frequent with the passing years, and by the time she had become, at twenty-nine, an Augustinian nun at the Order's convent in Dülmen, Germany, her visions had become concerned primarily with the life of Jesus Christ, although they encompassed also the lives of many saints and other personages (some unknown as yet to history) as well as far-reaching insights into the creation, the fall, a mysterious mountain of the prophets, the spiritual hierarchies, paradise and purgatory, the heavenly Jerusalem, and much besides.

In the context of Anne Catherine's visions, and related conversations, much was said also of spiritual labors, described symbolically as work in the "nuptial house," the "inner chamber," the "garden," and the "vineyard." In this way many teachings on the inner life and prayer came forward, along with detailed accounts of healing work and journeys for "poor souls" in purgatory or in past epochs. Anne Catherine also showed considerable concern for the souls of those around her, especially her later amanuensis Clemens Brentano, in connection with his initial lack of faith.

Owing to difficult political circumstances, Anne Catherine's convent was disbanded on December 3, 1811, and one by one the nuns in residence were obliged to leave. Anne Catherine—already very ill—withdrew to a small room in a house in Dülmen. By November, 1812, her illness had grown so severe that she was permanently confined to bed. Shortly thereafter, on December 29, 1812, she received the stigmata, a manifesting of the wounds suffered by Christ on the cross, and the highest outward sign of inner union with him. Unable to assimilate any form of nourishment,

i

for the rest of her life she was sustained almost exclusively by water and the eucharist.

As news spread that she bore the stigmata (which bled on Fridays), more and more people came to see her. For us, the most significant of these was Clemens Brentano, who first visited her on Thursday morning, September 24, 1818. He was so impressed by the radiance of her being that he decided to relocate nearby in order to record her visions. Anne Catherine had already had a presentiment that someone—whom she called "the pilgrim"—would one day come to preserve her revelations. The moment Clemens Brentano entered her room, she recognized him as this pilgrim.

Brentano, a novelist and Romantic poet then living in Berlin, was associated with leading members of the Romantic Movement in Germany. He settled his affairs and moved from Berlin to Dülmen early in 1819. Thereafter he visited Anne Catherine every morning, noting down briefly all she related to him. After writing out a full report at home, he returned later the same day to read it back to her. She would then often expand upon certain points, or, if necessary, correct details.

On July 29, 1820, Anne Catherine began to communicate visions concerning the day-by-day life of Jesus. These visions encompassed the better part of his ministry, and she was able to describe in extraordinary detail the places he visited, his miracles and healings, his teaching activity in the synagogues and elsewhere, and the people around him. She not only named and described many of these people with astonishing concreteness, but spoke also of their families, their occupations, and other intimate biographical details.

It seems clear that Anne Catherine was called to relate these day-by-day details of the life and ministry of Jesus, and that Clemens Brentano was called to record all she communicated of her visions. They worked together daily until her death on February 9, 1824, except for one period of six months, during which Brentano was away, and several shorter periods when, mainly due to illness, it was impossible for Anne Catherine to communicate her visions.

ENCOUNTERING the visions of Anne Catherine Emmerich can raise the question: how is it possible that this woman, who never left the German region in which she was born and had very little education, could describe in such detail not only the story of creation; heaven, hell, and purgatory; the fall of angels and humanity; the spiritual hierarchies and saints; the Promise and the Ark of the Covenant; the apocalypse; spiritual warfare; and the heavenly Jerusalem—but *also* the geography and topography of Palestine and the customs and habits of people living there at the time of Jesus Christ? To at least partially answer this, the researcher upon whose work the *chronological* aspects of this new edition is largely based, Dr. Robert Powell, undertook an exhaustive analysis of her work, gradually laying bare the historical reality underlying the life of Jesus (see "Chronology" below). But his work was not done in isolation, for others had earlier laid some groundwork.

For example the French priest Abbé Julien Gouyet of Paris, after reading an account of Anne Catherine's visions concerning the death of the Virgin Mary near Ephesus, traveled there and searched the region. On October 18, 1881, guided by various particulars in her account, he discovered the ruins of a small stone building on a mountain (Bulbul Dag, "Mount Nightingale") overlooking the Aegean Sea with a view across to the remains of the ancient city of Ephesus. Abbé Gouyet was convinced that this was the house described in Anne Catherine's visions as the dwelling of the Virgin Mary during the last years of her life. He was at first ridiculed, but several years later the ruins were independently rediscovered by two Lazarist missionaries who had undertaken a similar search on the basis of Anne Catherine's visions. They determined that the building had been a place of pilgrimage in earlier times for Christians descended from the church of Ephesus, the community referred to by St. John (Rev. 2:1–7). The building had been known in those days as Panaya Kapulu, the house of the Blessed Virgin, and was revered as the place where she had died. Traditionally, the date of her death, August 15, was the *very day* of the annual pilgrimage to Panaya Kapulu.

That Anne Catherine's visions provide spiritual nourishment had long been the experience of many spiritual seekers, but the discovery of Panaya Kapulu confirmed that her visions could also (at least in part) be corroborated along conventional lines of research.

Sources

THE visions of Anne Catherine Emmerich have been published in English translation in various editions since late in the nineteenth century. These editions focused primarily on the visions of the life of Jesus Christ and of Mary, with some material drawn from Old Testament times also. However the *original* notes of Clemens Brentano contained material on many other fascinating subjects. Much of this material has not been readily available before now, either in German or in English translation, a gap that this twelve-volume *New Light on the Visions Anne Catherine Emmerich* series is meant at least to begin filling.

Until now the only translations available of some of this latter material appeared in the two-volume biography of Anne Catherine by Rev. Carl E. Schmöger, first published in English in 1885. Rev. Schmöger, who was also instrumental in the selection and arrangement of the visions related to the life of Jesus Christ upon which later English translations were based, included in the biography a selection of the supplemental material mentioned above —but his selection was necessarily limited.

Clemens Brentano himself was only able to compile from his notes a few volumes for publication, and upon his death the notes passed to his brother Christian, who had been an interested participant in Clemens's work with Anne Catherine from the start (in fact, Christian had arranged his brother's first meeting with the visionary). Christian, however, proved unable to coordinate the notes any further. And so the first phase of this seemingly insurmountable task fell in due course to Rev. Schmöger.

Then, in the last decades of the twentieth century, the German publisher Kohlhammer commenced publishing, under the auspices of the *Frankfurter Brentano Ausgabe*, an intended complete edition of Brentano's works, projected to number as many as sixty volumes. Part of this project was the publication of facsimiles of the thirty-eight notebooks of Brentano's notes of the visions of Anne Catherine. (Brentano also noted down details of their conversations in other contexts, as well as his own experiences while attending her.) With the Kohlhammer edition, a wider public would finally gain access to the originals upon which later compilations and translations of the visions had been based. However, this noble project has not been completed, and at present there is no indication whether it will recommence. An additional impediment for researchers in dealing with the facsimiles is the fact that Brentano's notes were penned in a now archaic German script that only specialists can read.

Thus matters stood until Jozef De Raedemaeker, a dedicated Belgian researcher, undertook the enormous task of transcribing the full body of notes from the archaic script into modern German—making it available in printed and digital form in 2009. The combined 38 notebooks exceed 7,300 pages and include many hand-drawn illustrations as well as typographic conventions to identify the contributions of others present at Anne Catherine's bedside, who sometimes took notes or added comments, and sometimes drawings.

ANYONE who does even minimal research on the visions of Anne Catherine Emmerich as depicted in the works attributed to Brentano's notes will soon discover that there are conflicting opinions regarding their fidelity to the words of Anne Catherine herself. This would be a subject in itself, but some remarks may be offered here. First, Anne Catherine, who had little formal education, spoke in a Low-German dialect that even Brentano, at the outset, had some difficulty understanding. Secondly, the material that was eventually fit together into a connected account in the published versions often represents a collation of as many as a dozen or more passages gleaned from visions separated sometimes by months, or even years. This can be partially explained by the fact that the visions were often related to events in the ecclesiastical year, to feasts of saints, to individuals with specific needs or requests, or to the presence of relics.

And so a great deal of work had to be done to organize and knit together related segments of visions, and to then arrange them in a meaningful sequence. Then again, it was deemed necessary to refine the language sufficiently to render it in a more contemporary idiom. There is, then, a legitimate concern that so famous and gifted a literary figure as Clemens Brentano might, even if unintentionally, have introduced some of his own impressions, interpretations, and sensitivities into his renditions. And a similar concern could be raised concerning Rev. Schmöger's subsequent arrangements, as well as those of later editors and translators working at yet a further remove.

Much of the debate on this subject, however, took place without ready access to the original notes, a defect that has now been remedied. At certain points in his transcriptions De Raedemaeker addresses this issue by comparing fragments of the original notes with versions of these same fragments as they appear in Rev. Schmöger's edition, after he in turn had worked, in some instances, with Brentano's own compilations from his original notes—and in some cases there are non-trivial discrepancies. This is an area that requires further research.

Perhaps I myself may be permitted to chime in here, as there are not many who have entered into this vast field, and I can at least appeal to many years of engagement with the visions of Anne Catherine, *including* examining De Raedemaeker's transcriptions of all thirty-eight notebooks. While thus occupied, I inevitably began to identify for myself many of the original sources upon which Rev. Schmöger based his versions well over a century ago, and in such cases could assess the fidelity of the latter to the former. Although such details do not lie within the scope of this series, I can say that, with very rare exceptions—especially allowing for the frequent need to splice together disparate fragments—Rev. Schmöger's renderings remain remarkably true to the original, and any minimal divergences are for the most part quite trivial, insofar as I have been able to investigate.

During this process, however, I *was* struck by the fact that considerable material had been *omitted*. This may well have been owing to the enormity of the task, as also to pagination limits set by the publisher; or also, partly a measure of Rev. Schmöger's personal judgment and concerns. Perhaps some of the excluded material seemed unintelligible to him, or even scandalous. However that may be, in this current series as much as possible of this neglected material has been extracted, translated, and incorporated in the relevant volumes.

It needs to be said also, in response to assertions (made mostly without benefit of access to his actual notes) that Brentano misrepresented Anne Catherine, or, even worse, took advantage of his notes to compile an independent literary work that might embellish his reputation, that in fact, in his notes, Brentano *candidly* reports *exactly* what he heard Anne Catherine say, *no matter* how extraordinary, puzzling, or even apparently contradictory. He himself offers many instances where only later—sometimes years after Anne Catherine had died—he (often with the help of academic experts) finally began to understand previously incomprehensible passages in the visions. He steadfastly refused—according to his own account and that of others—to edit out "difficulties," feeling himself, rather, under a sacred obligation to preserve his record intact and unaltered for posterity. And when the notes passed to his brother Christian, the latter adhered to the same policy.

Even without the benefit of access to the original notes on the part of most researchers, and even in face of an undercurrent of scepticism as to the authenticity of the visions, it may be worthwhile, in drawing this matter to a close for our present purposes, to note that on October 3, 2004, Anne Catherine was beatified by Pope John Paul II, who remarked: "Her example opened the hearts of poor and rich alike, of simple and cultured persons, whom she instructed in loving dedication to Jesus Christ." And in the Vatican's biography of Anne Catherine we read: "Her words, which have reached innumerable people in many languages from her modest room in Dülmen through the writings of Clemens Brentano are an outstanding proclamation of the gospel in service to salvation right up to the present day."

Chronology

PERHAPS the most surprising feature of this new series on Anne Catherine Emmerich will be the inclusion of *historical dates*—and so a brief discussion of this feature is offered below.

As described earlier, Anne Catherine was so attuned to the life of Jesus Christ as a mystical-historical reality that her comprehensive visions encompassed even minute details of time and place—testable "coordinates" in fact. This degree of precision was made possible by the many temporal as well as geographical descriptions and references contained in the visions—as mentioned earlier in connection with the discovery of the house of the Blessed Virgin.

Many chronologies of the life of Jesus Christ have been put forward over the centuries, but the dates offered in this current series differ from previous efforts in that they derive from the application of modern chronological and astro-chronological science to the whole of Anne Catherine's visions—which latter constitute a vast body of data internally consistent as to time and place to an extraordinary degree, so that, taking the generally agreed upon time period of Jesus's life, results of a high degree of reliability can be determined.

Naturally, the overriding value of the visions lies in the additional insight they offer into the life of Jesus Christ, so that for some the dating may represent no more than a convenient framework for study and meditation. Such readers need not trouble themselves about the specific dates, although they may nonetheless find that the chronology offers a useful way to maintain their orientation within any given volume, as also when referring to events in volumes already read. Some, however, will wish to assess for themselves the method by which specific dates have been thought reliable enough to include here. They may read elsewhere[1] the story of the determination of the chronology of the life of Jesus Christ included in these volumes.

---

[1] *The Visions of Anne Catherine Emmerich*, Book III, Appendix I (Kettering, OH: Angelico Press, 2015), which is based on the work of Dr. Robert Powell.

The New Light on the Visions
of Anne Catherine Emmerich *Series*

THE present book is one of the twelve volumes of the "New Light on the Visions of Anne Catherine Emmerich" series published by Angelico Press. This series supplements two earlier Angelico publications: *The Visions of Anne Catherine Emmerich*, Books I–III (1,700 pages in large format, with 600 illustrations and forty-three maps); and the smaller-format, slightly abridged edition: *Life, Passion, Death, & Resurrection of Jesus Christ* (*A Chronicle from the Visions of Anne Catherine Emmerich*), Books I–IV (1,770 pages with 150 illustrations and 43 maps). As described earlier, in 2009 Clemens Brentano's original notes of Anne Catherine's visions became readily available for reference. At that time the above texts were already nearing completion. With the appearance of these notes, however, the editor resolved to pause, and, to the extent possible, research this vast body of notes to ascertain what further light they might shed on what had by then been prepared for publication. While the better part of another decade was devoted to the task, much research, of course, remains to be done (see "Future Prospects" below). But at some point one must call a halt, and so, after the insertion of relevant new translations into the two sets mentioned above and their publication in 2015–2016, the present series was conceived as a means to present in various contexts such new material as has since then been selected and translated from the notes.

In general, the content of each volume of this series consists (1) of material selected by individual or theme from earlier translations—reviewed, supplemented, and revised where necessary, especially for consistency of usage; and (2) of newly selected and translated material germane to the content of that volume. With regard to both individuals and themes, the procedure was to extract every reference thus far located in the notes and in prior translations and weave them together into a connected account. The reader can thus find in one place almost all of what Anne Catherine had to say about any given individual or theme.

Virtually every individual in the biblical visions (approximately 250 in total) is referenced in the five *People of the New Testament* volumes (which include also some figures from earlier and later times). A separate volume, *The Life of the Virgin Mary*, is dedicated to Mary and her ancestry (including much on the Essenes); and another volume, *Scenes from the Lives of the Saints*, treats of fifty-nine saints. Separate volumes cover events prior to the appearance of the holy family: *First Beginnings* and *Mysteries of the Old Testament*. Two further volumes cover a multitude of separate themes: *Inner Life and Worlds of Soul & Spirit* and *Spiritual Works and Journeys*. A final volume represents a condensed, edited, rearranged, supplemented, and retypeset edition of Rev. Carl E. Schmöger's exhaustive biography of Anne Catherine, first published in English in 1885. For clarity of organization, much of this biography in its original form has been redistributed among other volumes of this series. What remains has also been enriched with newly-translated material. A list of all twelve volumes of this series appears at the conclusion of this preface.

Practical Considerations

IN view of the sometimes extensive wealth of material presented concerning certain individuals—especially major characters—a judicious essentializing of scenes has sometimes been resorted to. In some cases, especially those of closely related apostles and disciples (or others regularly treated together in the visions), rather than duplicating material, the expedient adopted was to disentangle scenes to the extent possible, so that the full story could be garnered gradually by reading the separate accounts of each. Nonetheless, since readers may jump around in their selection of individuals to study, some repetition was unavoidable in order to provide enough context to keep the separate accounts reasonably sequential and unified. Put another way, these volumes are conceived primarily as reference works to which one turns for particulars on specific persons or themes rather than as connected narratives to be read cover to cover. Of course, the volumes may be read in the latter fashion also, in which case the occasional repeated material will be more noticeable.

Another consideration was that some individuals play so great a role in the visions (e.g., John the Baptist, St. Joseph, Peter, Matthew, Judas, and the Virgin Mary) that it would be impractical to include every mention in a chronological itinerary. Emphasis in such cases has been placed primarily on more general and newly-translated material. Inquisitive readers can of course turn to the index of the large-format, three-volume *The Visions of Anne Catherine Emmerich* to expand their research on such individuals.

It must be well understood that all the editor could do was work with what Anne Catherine actually said. Some little-known (or even totally unknown) individuals may enjoy longer accounts in these volumes than other, very well known, figures from the gospels or later Christian tradition! There can be no question of assigning relative importance to any individual based solely upon how extensive Anne Catherine's visions of that person may have been. Likewise, stories may have gaps, or sometimes end abruptly. It is indeed unfortunate that (as Brentano repeatedly laments in his notes) so much was lost owing to Anne Catherine's considerable suffering, household distractions, and the many obligations laid upon her—all of which interfered with her visions and her capacity to recall them. And yet withal, how much we have to be grateful for!

To streamline as far as possible a complex text, these usages were established: The voice of the narrator (Rev. Schmöger) is put in italics. Direct citations from Brentano (and a few others) are put in quotes. Anne Catherine's text bears no quotation indicators *except* where references to her words are embedded in the two contexts just mentioned. Parentheses enclose supplemental material from Anne Catherine or Brentano; brackets enclose material from Rev. Schmöger or the present editor. Footnotes from the hand of Brentano are followed by CB; those consisting of further visionary content from Anne Catherine are—for clarity in this context—enclosed in quotation marks; all other unattributed footnotes have been supplied by the present editor, sometimes incorporating what seemed worth retaining from notes by others in earlier editions.[1]

---

[1] The most useful material of this sort has been integrated from notes to a version of *The Life of the Virgin Mary* provided by Rev. Sebastian Bullough, O.P., to whom we express our gratitude.

For convenience, especially in itineraries of individuals, dates are incorporated in what is otherwise purely Anne Catherine's visionary text. It must, however, be well understood that these dates are derivative, as mentioned in "Chronology" above, *not* from the hand of Anne Catherine. As another help, for many major figures, summaries are provided at the outset. These are often in the third person—as they represent a condensation by the editor—but are nonetheless derived directly from the visions.

In such a context as these visions represent, capitalization (a topic upon which there are many and various usages, and often passionate opinions) represented a particular challenge. In the end, after experimenting with progressively increasing degrees of simplification, it was determined—in order not to overly fatigue the reader of what essentially amounts to an extended narrative rather than devotional reading properly speaking—to implement a very spare policy indeed, reserving capitalization to the Deity, and to certain terms that in Anne Catherine's visions assume a unique significance, such as the Ark of the Covenant, and what she calls the Promise, or sometimes the Holy Thing, the Mystery or Sacrament (in this special sense), or even the Germ or Seed. Finally, in cases where more general considerations are followed by chronological extracts forming a connected itinerary, the break is signaled by a row of five typographic crosses.

Prospects for the Future

AS editor of this series I am only too aware of my limitations in the face of the awe-inspiring magnitude of the task. My initial inspiration was solely the *spiritual value* of Anne Catherine's visions as a means to help seekers find their way *back* to a faithful connection with Jesus Christ; or, in the case of so many in our time, find their way *for the first time* to a dawning awareness of what they may thus far have failed to see. Further, there are great, resonant depths in the visions, like choirs of symbolism. As time went on I could only go deeper, entering upon the work that has led now, finally, to completing this series. Along with spiritual benefits and guidance, it was and will ever remain also a thrilling journey of discovery. Now, with Brentano's original notes available thanks to the efforts of Jozef De Raedemaeker, there are further depths to explore, as alas—despite so many years of work—the rich sod has only been broken.

In the visions will be found fascinating indications and hints for archeologists, historians, linguists, theologians, students of comparative religion, chronologists, specialists in symbolism, and more. Over and above the *primary element* of spiritual inspiration, it is my hope that such specialists may in due course take up these visions (including the entire corpus of Brentano's notes) and press further forward. How one would love to see a foundation, a university, a religious sodality, or some private individual or group sponsor so important and propitious a project. If the largely solitary results presented here serve to advance such future research, if hearts and souls are moved and enriched by *The Anne Catherine Emmerich Series* as a whole, the effort will have achieved its primary purpose.

JAMES RICHARD WETMORE

Acknowledgments

IT is difficult to sift out elements from earlier translators of these visions, but our main debt of gratitude for much of the English text taken as a foundation in the current work is owed to Sir Michael Palairet. Incalculable thanks are owed to Jozef De Raedemaeker for his past and present work with the original handwritten notes of Clemens Brentano. Occasional assistance with translation was received from Mado Spiegler, James Morgante, and especially Harrie Salman. A special thanks goes to Robert Powell, who has been a companion at every stage of this journey owing to his dedication to Anne Catherine in every respect: researching, translating when necessary, and, preeminently, applying his skills to the task of establishing the chronology that has been incorporated in this edition (in which connection Fr. Helmut Fahsel should also be mentioned). Most line drawings in the volumes are taken from Brentano's notes; the occasional paintings included are from the hand of James J. Tissot, as are all but one of the cover illustrations.

The New Light on the Visions of Anne Catherine Emmerich Series

Interiority

Differing Manner of Her Visions

ANNE *Catherine tried several times to give the pilgrim some idea of her contemplation, but in vain; she could never satisfactorily explain the spiritual activity of her visions. We quote what the pilgrim was able to write on different occasions:*

I see many things that I cannot possibly express. Who can say with the tongue what he sees not with the bodily eyes?

I see it not with the eyes. It seems as if I saw it with my heart in the midst of my breast. It makes the perspiration start! At the same time I see with my eyes the objects and persons around me; but they concern me not, I know not who or what they are. I am in contemplation even now while I am speaking.

For several days I have been constantly between the state of vision and the natural waking state. I have to do violence to myself. In the middle of a conversation I suddenly see before me other things and pictures and I hear my own words as if proceeding from another, as if coming out of an empty cask. I feel as if I were intoxicated and reeling. My conversation goes on coolly and often more animatedly than usual, but when it is over I know not what I have said, though I have been speaking connectedly. It costs me an effort to maintain this double state. I see passing objects dimly and confusedly like a sleeper awaking out of a dream. The second sight attracts me more powerfully; it is clearer than the natural, but it is not through the eyes.

After relating a vision one day, she laid aside her work, saying:

All this day I have been flying and seeing; sometimes I see the pilgrim, sometimes not. Does he not hear the singing? It seems to me that I am in a beautiful meadow, the trees forming arches over me. I hear wondrously sweet singing like the clear voices of children. All around me here below is like a troubled dream, dim and confused, through which I gaze upon a luminous world perfectly distinct in all its parts, intelligible even in its origin and connected in all its wonders. In it the good and holy delight more powerfully since one sees his way from God to God; and what is bad and unholy troubles more deeply, as the way leads from the demon to the demon in opposition to God and the creature. This life in which nothing hinders me, neither time nor space, neither the body nor mystery, in which all speaks, all enlightens, is so perfect, so free, that the blind, lame, stammering reality appears but an empty dream. In this state I always see the relics by me shining, and sometimes I see little troops of figures floating over them in a distant cloud. When I return to myself, the boxes and caskets in which the shining relics lie reappear.

Once the pilgrim gave her a little parcel into which without her knowledge he had slipped a relic. She took it with a significant smile, as if to say she could not be so deceived, and laying it on her heart, she said:

I knew directly what you were giving me. I cannot describe the impression it produces. I not only see, I *feel* a light like the will-o'-the-wisp, sometimes bright, sometimes dull, blowing toward me as if directed by a current of wind. I feel, too, a certain connecting link between the light and the shining body, and between the latter and a luminous world, itself born of light. Who can express it?—The light seizes me, I cannot prevent it from entering my heart; and when I plunge in deeper it seems as if I passed through it into the body from which it emanates into the scenes of its life, its struggles, its sufferings, its triumphs! Then I am directed in vision as is pleasing to God. There is a wonderful, a mysterious, relation between our body and soul. The soul sanctifies or profanes the body; otherwise there could be no expiation, no penance by means of the body. As the saints while alive worked in the body, so even when separated from it they continue to act by it upon the faithful. But faith is essential to the reception of holy influences.

Often while speaking with others on quite different subjects I see in the distance the soul of a deceased person coming toward me and am forced to attend to it at once. I become silent and thoughtful. I have apparitions also of the saints in the same way. I once had a beautiful revelation on this point, in which I learned that seeing with the eyes is no sight, that there is another, interior sight, that is clear and penetrating. But when deprived of daily communion a cloud obscures my clear inward sight, I pray less fervently, with less devotion, I forget important things, signs, and warnings, and I see the destructive influence of exterior things that are essentially false. I feel a devouring hunger for the blessed sacrament, and when I look toward the Church feel as if my heart were about to escape from my breast and fly to my Redeemer.

When I was in trouble, because in obedience to my guide's orders I refused to be removed to another abode, I cried to God to direct me. I was overwhelmed with trials, and yet I saw so many holy visions that I knew not what to do. In my prayer I was calm. I saw a face, a countenance approach me and melt as it were into my breast as if uniting with my being. It seemed as if my soul, becoming one with it, returned into itself and grew smaller and smaller, while my body appeared to become a great massive substance large as a house. The countenance,[1] the apparition in me, appeared to be triple, infinitely rich and varied but at the same time always one. It penetrated (that is, its beams, its regards) into all the choirs of angels and saints. I experienced joy and consolation from it, and I thought: Could all this come from the evil spirit? And while I was thus thinking, all the pictures, clear and distinct like a series of bright clouds, passed again before my soul, and I felt that they were now out of me, at my side in a luminous sphere. I felt also that although I was larger, yet I was not so massive as before. There was now, as it were, a world outside of me into which I could peer through a luminous opening. A maiden approached who explained this world of light to me, directed my attention here and there, and pointed out to me the vineyard of the holy bishop in which I now had to labor.

But I saw too on my left a second world full of deformed figures, symbols of perversity, calumny, raillery, and injury. They came like a swarm, the point directed toward me. Of all that came

---

[1] This face, this countenance, was the gift of vision, the light of prophecy proceeding from God, by which Anne Catherine conversed with the saints and angels and received their communications.

to me from this sphere I could accept nothing, for the just, the good, were in the pure luminous sphere on my right. Between these two spheres I hung by one arm poor and abandoned, floating, so to say, between heaven and earth. This state lasted long and caused me great pain; still I was not impatient.

The way in which a communication from the blessed is received, is hard to explain. What is said is incredibly brief; by one word from them I understand more than by thirty from others. I see the speaker's thought, but not with the eyes; all is clearer, more distinct than in the present state. One receives it with as much pleasure as he hails a breeze in summer. Words cannot well express it.

All that the poor soul said to me was, as usual, brief. To understand the language of the souls in purgatory is difficult. Their voice is smothered, as if coming through something that dulls the sound; it is like one speaking from a pit or a cask. The meaning also is difficult to grasp. Closer attention is required than when our Lord, or my guide, or a saint speaks to me, for their words penetrate like a clear current of air; one sees and knows all they say.

A Teaching on the Nature of Visions

ONE *day, when the pilgrim drew to Anne Catherine's attention the superabundance of graces she received—but remarking also how the greater part went lost—she responded, with most unselfconscious naiveté, as follows:*

Yes, our Lord said much the same to me just this past evening. Overwhelmed by suffering, when I entreated him to withdraw from me those visions in which I behold so much that I cannot comprehend, he said, "I give you visions not for yourself, but that you may collect and communicate them. The present is not the time for sensible miracles; therefore do I give you visions. I have done the same at all times to show that I am with my Church unto the consummation of ages. But visions alone secure not anyone's salvation. You must practice charity, patience, and the other virtues."

He showed forth before me then a whole litany of saints who have also received visions—and of the most varied sorts—adding

4

that it was only through the manner in which they gleaned profit from such wisdom teachings that they had achieved blessedness. As I beheld in succession these pictures of various saints, I perceived at the same time how often, in their cases also, they had stumbled through their visions, as often as not recording them with not much understanding of their meaning. I saw how on account of all this many suffered greatly, and in particular how long Theresa agonized, on account of the perversity of her father confessor, as to whether her visions were from the devil.

Among those she mentioned were Theresa, Catherine of Siena, Clara of Montefalco, Brigit, Hildegard, Veronica Giuliani, and Maria of Jesus—and as she did so, she spoke of the various sorts of visions each received, which she could only grasp inwardly in a general way. She saw how for the most part the efficacy of such visions was negated either through omissions and alterations introduced later by scholars, or simply through the inability of priests to comprehend them. Many such visions were discarded owing to the difficulty of separating out from the pure visions themselves extraneous elements introduced therein by the visionary herself in connection with her private concerns and devotions. Others tended to regard the visions as astonishingly prolix or overwrought, as though the grace received was immersed in a great stream of flowing words—so much so that it seemed no longer possible to adjudge which portions thereof one might allow oneself to enjoy as credible.

Anne Catherine said that among the sainted visionaries she was shown in this way, Hildegard was the one who transcribed her own visions most truly, for she had been graced also with a great literary gift. Nonetheless, in their published form, even her writings were much changed. The same held true of Theresa's writings. Frances of Rome saw much in vision too, but hers also were poorly presented, largely on account of her anxiety regarding her father confessor's lack of understanding: he could not grasp Frances's manner of understanding the gospel and was at pains to conform her words to rules of his own, controverting much of their content in this way. In this connection she said:

I came to see also how there are different sorts of visions. Some visionaries are simply surrounded all of a sudden with scenes and must quickly commit them to writing while they remain yet present before them. Others are moved in their souls, speak at great length, and transcribe long invectives. Yet others receive through a great inner quickening all manner of allegorical pictures, most often interspersed with historical elements, so that when revisited later it is often no easy matter to distinguish between these two contexts.

In no case however did I see visionary images depict events in the simple, day-to-day manner in which they actually unfold. I mean, last night I must myself have traversed with my guide all the earth, and when we paused at the side of some sick or dying person in order to be of help, I would turn away from my guide and go about my work, for I knew he would remain ever by me. But all the while I could see in the distance—around or past my guide so to speak—many people of my own time and acquaintance, who seemed astonished. It would be well if in future such experiences might be better understood.

Mesmerism

TO *struggle against the dangers arising from mesmerism formed also a part of Anne Catherine's task,*[1] *since both her physician and confessor were the first to resort to it after their vain use of opium and musk. Dr. Wesener tells us:*

"Father Limberg told me that while the invalid lay apparently in a cataleptic state he tried several mesmeric experiments upon her, but without success. Then I determined to make some myself the first chance I should get. I did so a few days later when she lay rigid in ecstasy. I pronounced a few words on the pit of her stomach and the extremities of her toes; I laid the tips of the fingers of my right hand upon the pit of her stomach and spoke some words upon the tips of the fingers of her left hand; I called into her ear. But none of these actions produced the slightest impression upon her. At my request her confessor made the same experiments, though with no better success. But when he

---

[1] A more complete account of mesmerism will be found in *The Life of Anne Catherine Emmerich.*

pronounced the word 'obedience,' she trembled, sighed, and returned to consciousness. He asked what ailed her, and she answered: 'I have been called.'"

Some days after Holy Saturday, April 5, 1817, Dr. Wesener records in his journal:

"Dr. N. has convinced Father Limberg and myself that the science of mesmerism is nothing more than the flowing of certain vital spirits upon the sick. This spirit pervades all nature and the invalid receives it through a spiritual or even corporal communication. It acts upon the recipient according to the nature of the principle from which it springs, enkindling a flame that belongs either to the earth or to the higher or lower regions, and operating accordingly either salutary or pernicious effects. This vital principle the Christian can and ought to kindle by religion and the love of God and the neighbor, in such a way as to render it salutary to soul and body."

The doctor knew however by repeated experience what possessed the power of inflaming his patient, for shortly before he had noted in his journal the following lines:

"I found Sister Emmerich today flushed as if on fire. I asked the cause and received the answer: 'Dean Overberg was here, we spoke only of God! It excited me, but I do not feel sick.'"

But now Dr. Wesener came, supported by her confessor, and full of the new discovery (the mesmeric vital principle) explained it to her with so much warmth that she soon perceived the dangerous ground on which they were both standing. She maintained a prudent silence, listened patiently to their arguments in favor of the new science, and answered only when her angel ordered her to do so. From the doctor's notes we may read Anne Catherine's response:

You have seen how I received what you have all told me about mesmerism. I have not concealed my indifference, though I am pleased that you try to present it in its moral bearing. But now I shall communicate to you what I have been told in vision for the third time concerning it. The first vision presented it in an unfavorable light; the second filled me with terror; and in the third— last night—my angel showed me that almost everything connected with mesmerism is an illusion of the devil. I hope to have the strength to relate it in detail.

For the present I can only say that if we desire to imitate the prophets and apostles in their *works*, we must imitate them also in their *life*. Then we would have no need of a mesmerizer's manipulations—the Holy Name of Jesus would be sufficient. There is no harm in trying to effect a cure by transmitting something from the healthy to the sick, but the juggling connected with such an attempt is both foolish and unlawful. The mesmeric sleep that affords a glimpse of distant and future things comes from the devil, who clothes it with the semblance of piety to gain adherents, and above all to ensnare the good.

Dr. Wesener continues: "Anne Catherine spoke in so impressive a style that I remarked that perhaps I ought to discontinue the mesmeric treatment I had begun on a young peasant girl whose arm was paralyzed. She inquired how I conducted the operation. I told her that I made certain movements of my hands, described circles, and breathed upon the affected part; that the patient drank mesmerized water and wore on her lame arm a band of mesmerized flannel. She replied: 'The breathing upon the arm and warming it with the hands, I think strictly natural remedies; but the passes and circles I condemn as unreasonable and leading to superstition.' When I asked her opinion of the strange physician's views, she answered: 'We must beware of intemperate, ill-advised zeal in his regard, but I feel that he will return to the truth, that I shall be of use to him.'"

The foregoing conversation made so deep an impression upon Dr. Wesener that he forgot his patient's admonition not to make known to Dr. N. her decision too bluntly. He communicated all she had said in the plainest terms, to the stranger's extreme surprise and vexation, as he entertained a high opinion of the piety of a certain somnambulist of Frankfort. Far from losing confidence in his favorite theory, he replied warmly that it could not be thought that men of such consideration as many of its most zealous supporters had anything in common with the evil spirit. He declared that Anne Catherine had looked only on the dark side of mesmerism, but that its bright side might be exhibited with her confessor's assistance by the imposition of hands and the sacerdotal benediction, which he denominated the "mesmeric healing process."

Although Father Limberg had for years experienced his penitent's wonderful sensitiveness to the blessings and prayers of the Church, yet now, strange to say, he was tempted to ascribe their efficacy to the "mesmeric vital principle." He had been accustomed to use the power conferred on him by holy orders only when she was thought to be in extremity, but now—blinded by novelty—he submitted her to the "healing mesmeric process" on every occasion. Anne Catherine was not a little saddened by proceedings so extravagant, and at last—on a formal command from her angel to that effect—she warned her confessor to desist from such folly. It had been said to her in vision: "God wills that you patiently endure your sufferings. Your confessor must do nothing more than hitherto!" She related the following vision:

I was in a spacious hall, like a church, crowded with people. Some grave-looking personages were going around and obliging others to leave the church. I was surprised, and on asking why they sent away people who looked so good and knew how to speak so beautifully, one of the grave-looking men answered: "They have no right here, they are in delusion; and even if they spoke with the tongues of angels, yet their doctrines are false." The stranger, Dr. N., was among those going to be turned out. I felt very sorry for him and I ran to his assistance. Some persons nearby tried to prevent me, saying it would not be proper, but I would not be restrained. I said: "His soul's salvation is at stake'— and I kept him from being expelled."[1]

The following are the visions in which Anne Catherine learned the real nature of animal magnetism, or mesmerism, the degradation into which it plunges the soul, and the dangers thereby incurred:

The first I heard of mesmerism was from the strange doctor.

---

[1] This vision was very remarkably verified, for in spite of their seeming inclination toward Catholicism, in spite of their plausible arguments, most of the members of the circle, bewitched by the mesmeric system, died out of the Church. Dr. N. alone, helped by Anne Catherine's prayers, found another and more solid basis for his faith than mesmerism, to which he had heretofore ascribed the wonders wrought by God in his saints. Father Limberg never after tried any other experiment on his spiritual daughter than that of the Church's blessing, and the doctor also was cured of his enthusiasm for the new theory. His journal contains after this date only the following lines on the subject: "You may make use of the imposition of hands and insufflation when perfectly assured that it will be a cause of temptation neither to yourself nor your patient."

Whenever he mentioned the clairvoyant and her friends, a feeling of repugnance arose in my soul, I knew not why. This clairvoyant was then shown me, and I was enlightened with regard to her state. I saw that it was anything but pure or from God. I saw that sensuality and vanity, though she would by no means acknowledge it, had the greatest share in it, and that without being aware of it, she cherished too great an affection for her mesmerizer. Scattered here and there in the distance I saw as if through a magnifying glass other clairvoyants either sitting or reclining, some having before them a glass with a tube which they held in their hands. The impression produced upon me was one of horror, which arose not so much from the nature of the thing in itself as from the temptations it excited and to which its victims almost always yielded. The mesmerizer's gestures before his patient's eyes, his passes, the stroking of the hand, etc., were so repulsive to me that I cannot express it. I saw the interior of both, the influence of one upon the other, the communication of their nature and evil inclinations. I always saw satan directing the mesmerizer's manipulations and making them with him.

In vision these clairvoyants are very different from me. If on entering into contemplation they have the least impure thought, they see only lies—for it is the demon who presents their visions to them and glosses all over with a fine appearance. If a clairvoyant has formed a desire of saying something to render herself famous, or if she entertains the least sensual feeling, she is instantly exposed to sin. Some do indeed experience bodily relief, but the majority, unknown to themselves, derive results pernicious to their soul. The horror these things excite in me can only be compared to that which a certain secret society and its practises inspire. I perceive the corruption, but I cannot describe it.

Mesmerism is allied to magic. The only difference between the two is this: in the latter the devil is invoked, in the former he comes uninvited. Whoever delivers himself up to mesmerism takes from nature that which can be lawfully acquired only in the Church of Jesus Christ, for the power of healing and sanctifying is preserved only in her bosom. Now, for all who are not in living union with Jesus Christ by faith and grace, nature is full of satan's influence. Persons in the mesmeric state see nothing in its essence and dependence on God—what they see they behold in an isolated, separated condition, as if through a hole or a chink. They perceive as it were a gleam of things—and God grant that this light be pure, be holy! It is one of God's favors to have veiled us from one another, to have raised walls of separation between us, since we incline to sin, are so readily influenced by one another. It is well that we have to act independently before communicating the contagion of our evil inclinations. But in Jesus Christ, the God-Man, we have our Head in whom—purified and sanctified—we may all become one, one single body without our sins and bad inclinations infecting the union. Whoever tries to remove this barrier raised by God unites himself in a most dangerous manner to fallen nature, over which reigns the author of its ruin: the devil with all his seductions.

I see that the essence of mesmerism is true—but there is a thief unchained in its veiled light. All union between sinners is dangerous, but the mutual penetration into one another's interior is still more so. When this happens to an upright soul—when one becomes a clairvoyant only through simplicity and inexperience, a prey to artifice and intrigue—then one of humankind's faculties possessed before the fall, a faculty not entirely extinct, is in a certain measure resuscitated, and we lie helpless in a most mysterious state, exposed to the attacks of the evil one. This state really exists, but it is veiled because it is a poisoned source for all but the saints. I feel that the state of these persons is, in certain particulars, parallel with my own, but springing from another source, tending toward a different end, and followed by very different consequences. The sin of a man in his natural state is an act accomplished by the senses. His interior light is not obscured by it. It stings the conscience, it urges to other acts of the senses, repentance and penance; it leads to the supernatural remedies that the Church administers under sensible forms in the sacraments. The senses are the sinners, the interior light is the accuser.

But in the mesmeric state, when the senses are for the time dead, when the interior light both receives and reflects impressions, then that which is holiest in humankind is exposed to the baneful influence of the evil spirit. The soul cannot fall under

11

such influence by means of the senses—subjected as they are to the laws of time and space. In such a state the mesmeric cannot have recourse to the purifying remedies of the Church. I do indeed see that a pure soul in God's grace cannot be hurt by the devil even in this state; but I also see that if, before entering it (and it may easily happen, especially to females), the individual has consented to the least temptation, satan freely carries on his game in the soul, dazzling it with an appearance of sanctity. Her visions are false, and if perchance she discovers therein a means of healing the body, she purchases her knowledge at the price of her immortal soul; she is sullied by necromantic relations with her mesmerizer.

Females under the influence of mesmerism were often shown Anne Catherine in vision, that she might pray for them and labor to prevent the ulterior consequences of such practises. She was always ready to help them but never willing to be brought into contact with them, either in the natural state or in vision. Once only, when Dr. N. was boasting of his clairvoyant's holy visions, she said:

I wish she were here before me, for her fine visions would soon cease and she would discover by whom she is deceived. I have often seen her in my visions on this subject. I see that when in the mesmeric state satan cast his spells over her while she takes him for an angel of light.

On one of his journeys Dr. Wesener met Dr. Neeff, the mesmerizer of the clairvoyant mentioned above. He pointed out to him her danger, and the latter resolved to go to Dülmen himself to study the resemblance between Anne Catherine and his own patient. On his arrival he informed the sister that his clairvoyant could discern remedies for all diseases, that she was in communication with the blessed, that she was conducted by her own angel and the angel of her mesmerizer through worlds of light, and that she received a species of sacrament from "The Holy Grail!" Anne Catherine shuddered. She tried sweetly and gently to impress him with the immense danger both he and his patient ran (they were Protestants), but she did not succeed. The doctor, completely infatuated by his mesmeric powers, appealed to the good intentions that animated his patient and himself, to the precautions they took before beginning their operations, begging God to preserve them from the snares of the evil one, etc. He declared that his clairvoyant was led by a way that daily became more luminous, more sublime, and he skillfully evaded a closer examination into the nature of his practises. In vain did Anne Catherine protest against the celestial nourishment and luminous worlds, which she stigmatized as diabolical illusions; the doctor turned a deaf ear to her warnings and went his way. In this regard Anne Catherine said:

When such persons are shown me, I see the mesmerizer spinning from the clairvoyant a thread that he knots and swallows. She holds him bound by it and leads him around at will. I see this knot in him like a dark cloud, weighing him down and stifling him. Sometimes he tries to reject it, but without success.

Certain persons, actuated by curiosity—and even by malice—had recourse to a clairvoyant to obtain information concerning Anne Catherine's own state. During the second investigation, of which we shall speak later, they took her head dressing to use as a bond between her and a certain clairvoyant of M—, hoping thereby to hear many interesting things. Anne Catherine said, regarding this:

This person was shown me by my angel, but though she put herself to a great deal of trouble she could never find out anything about me. I always saw the devil with her. When I was released from imprisonment I saw my confessor with her, the devil on one side, another spirit on the other. The devil wanted the woman to say all sorts of infamous things of me in my confessor's presence, but in spite of all her efforts she could see nothing. At last she took Father Limberg by the hand and said: 'Sister Emmerich is in prayer. She is very sick. She is no impostor, but maybe some of her friends are.'

When my confessor returned from M— and told me this, I had another vision on this subject. I was seized with fear at the thought of receiving holy communion from him on the morrow, for I was afraid he had gone to the clairvoyant through curiosity. But I was satisfied when I found it was not by his own choice that he went. I saw that she told falsehoods of other people and that the devil conjured up visions before her.

During the investigation referred to by Anne Catherine when she says, "I was released from imprisonment," an attempt was made to put her in communication with a mesmerizer by making her wear around her neck a magnetic conductor in the form of a little phial covered with silk. So great was the disgust it excited in her that she dashed it from her, indignantly denouncing as a bare-faced lie the assertion that the horrible thing had been sent to her by her director, Dean Overberg.

A woman of Dülmen, having allowed herself to be persuaded to consult a fortune-teller of Warendorf, thought she would try her skill by proposing some questions concerning Anne Catherine. "What is going on near Sister Emmerich?" she inquired. The fortune-teller shuffled her cards uneasily and answered: "Strange! All is exceedingly devout there! There is an aged man, quite stout! There is a younger one! There is an old woman dying! (Anne Catherine's old mother, who died by her). The person herself is sick!" The questioner had heard enough, she departed in fright. When Anne Catherine heard of it, she remarked:

Not the cards, but their faith in them, makes fortune-tellers see! They say what they see, but not what the card shows. The card is the image of an idol, but it is the devil who is the idol. He is often forced to tell the truth, and then the fortune-teller announces it angrily.

In January, 1821, Anne Catherine, while contemplating the public life of Our Lord in a vision of the cure of one possessed, saw again the nature and moral effects of mesmerism. The relation between men and the powers of darkness were shown her in three spheres or worlds. The lowest and darkest comprised those that dealt in magic and openly worshipped the demon; the second, those that indulged superstition and sensual desires; the third was the region of Freemasonry and Liberalism. These three worlds were bound together by innumerable interlacing threads which, like a ladder, led from the highest to the lowest. In the lowest sphere, as also in the middle one, she beheld mesmerism with its various states and bodily remedies. She understood that it was the most efficient means employed by the demon for the destruction of humankind:

In the lowest sphere I saw certain states and relations that in common life are not regarded as absolutely unlawful. Many individuals therein were under the influence of mesmerism. I saw something abominable between them and the mesmerizer—dark, shadowy figures passing from one to the other. I have rarely, if ever, seen persons mesmerized without discovering sensuality in them. Clairvoyance is produced by the agency of evil spirits. I beheld people falling from the upper and brighter sphere on account of their employing magic under the name of science in the treatment of diseases. Then I saw them mesmerizing, and, blinded by their apparent success, they attracted many from the upper sphere. I saw them eager to palm off cures wrought by infernal agency, reflections of the mirrors of hell, as cures from heaven effected by God's favored souls. In this lowest storey I beheld very distinguished men laboring unknown to themselves in the sphere of the infernal Church.

Prayer

THE *following vision on the value of prayer was vouchsafed to Anne Catherine*:

I was in a great, bright place that extended on every side as far as the eye could reach, and there it was shown me how it is with men's prayers before God. They seemed to be inscribed on large white tablets that were divided into four classes: some were written in magnificent golden letters; others in shining silver; some in darker characters; and others again in black, streaked lines. I gazed with delight, but as I thought myself unworthy of such a favor, I hardly dared ask my guide what it all meant. He told me:

"What is written in gold is the prayer of those who have united their good works to the merits of Jesus Christ and who often renew this union; they aim at observing his precepts and imitating his example.

"What is written in silver is the prayer of those who think not of union with the merits of Jesus Christ, but who are notwithstanding pious and who pray in the simplicity of their hearts.

"What is written in darker colors is the prayer of those who have no peace unless they frequently confess and communicate and daily say certain prayers, but who are however tepid and perform their good works through habit.

"Lastly, what is written in black, streaked characters is the prayer of such as place all their confidence in vocal prayers and pretended good works, but who do not keep God's commandments nor curb their evil desires. Such prayer has no merit before God, therefore is it streaked. So also would the good works of a man be streaked who indeed gives himself much trouble to help

15

on some charity, but with a view to the honor or temporal advantage attached to it."

She then related another symbolical vision on prayer:

I was kneeling in my accustomed place in church and I saw by the brilliant light that shone around two beautifully dressed ladies in prayer at the foot of the high altar. With heartfelt emotion I watched them praying so devoutly, when two dazzling crowns of gold were let down as if by a cord over their heads. I drew near and saw that one crown rested on the head of one of the ladies, while the other remained suspended in the air a little above the head of the second. At last they both arose and I remarked to them that they had been praying earnestly. "Yes," replied the second, "it is a long time since I prayed as devoutly and with as much consolation as I have done today." But the first, on whose head the crown had rested, complained that although she had wanted to pray fervently, yet all kinds of thoughts and distractions had assailed her, against which she had to fight the whole time. Now I saw clearly by this that the dear God looks only at the heart in time of prayer.

This vision had been vouchsafed Anne Catherine to teach her that her own prayer, so often disturbed and interrupted by the presence of visitors and other annoyances, was now no less agreeable to God than the tranquil devotion formerly hers in the cloister. We may recognize a similar intention in a later vision, simple apparently and of no great significance, but which is a striking proof of God's constant care over His chosen one:

I had to cross a narrow bridge. In terror I gazed on the deep waters flowing below, but my angel led me over in safety. On the bank was a mouse-trap around which a little mouse kept running and running, and at last it slipped in to get the bait. "Foolish little animal!" I cried, "you are sacrificing your liberty, your life for a mouthful!" "Are men more reasonable?" asked my angel, "when for a momentary gratification they endanger their soul's salvation?"

Her compassion for the poor little mouse was turned by her angel to men blindly rushing to their own destruction, that she might help them from afar by her prayers and supplications. The vision appeared to imply what seemed to her impossible—that the hidden, peaceful life of former years was never to return, and so God willed. That happiness so longed-for was never again to be hers. The time had arrived for the last and most painful part of her mission. As the Church was bereft of her asylums of peace, in which piety could be practiced unmolested and contemplation sheltered from the vulgar gaze, so was Anne Catherine torn from that sacred abode in which she had hoped to end her days, a trial which she shared with Holy Church up to the last instant of her life.

The Rosary

ON *April 12, 1820, in connection with a great vision on ravages against the Church, certain periods of time, and the "twelve new apostles," Anne Catherine spoke also of the rosary:*

I have had another vision on the great tribulation everywhere reigning. It seemed as if something were exacted of the clergy, something that could not be granted. I saw many aged priests, some of them Franciscans, and one in particular—a very old man—weeping bitterly and mingling their tears with those of others younger than themselves. I saw others, tepid souls, willingly acceding to conditions hurtful to religion. The old faithful in their distress submitted to the interdict and closed their churches. Numbers of their parishioners joined them; and so, two parties were formed, a good and a bad one.

As the supporters of the "new lights"—the Illuminati—especially hated the devotion of the rosary, the value of this popular form of prayer was shown Anne Catherine in a very significant vision:

I saw Mary's rosary with all its mysteries. A pious hermit had thus honored the Mother of God, weaving in his childlike faith a garland of leaves and flowers for her; and, as he understood their signification, his garlands were always profoundly symbolical. He begged the Blessed Virgin to obtain for him some favor from her Son, whereupon she gave him the rosary.

Then Anne Catherine described this rosary. But after the vision was over, neither she nor the pilgrim could clearly repeat what had been seen and heard. It seems that the rosary was surrounded by three rows of different-colored notched leaves, on which were represented in transparent figures all the mysteries of the Church from both the Old and the New Testament. In the center of the rosary stood Mary with the child sur-

rounded by angels and virgins, hand in hand—their colors and attributes expressive of the various mysteries. Anne Catherine described each bead, beginning with the coral cross on which is said the Creed:

The cross grew out of a fruit like the apple of the forbidden tree. It was carved, had certain determinate colors, and was full of little nails. On it was the figure of a youth, in his hand a vine that sprang from the cross, and sitting on the vine were other figures eating the grapes. The beads were joined by colored spiral rays, like roots, each possessing some natural and mystical signification.

Every *Our Father* was enclosed in a wreath of leaves from whose center sprang a flower in which was portrayed one of Mary's joys or sorrows. The *Hail Marys* were stars of precious stones on which were cut scenes from the lives of the patriarchs and Mary's ancestors relating to the incarnation and redemption. Thus does the rosary comprehend heaven and earth, God and nature and history, and the restoration of all things through the Redeemer born of Mary. Every figure and color in its essential signification was employed for the perfecting of this divine masterpiece.

This rosary, though inexpressibly profound in signification, was described by Anne Catherine with deep feeling and childlike simplicity. With trembling joy she went from leaf to leaf, from figure to figure, describing all with the eager and joyous readiness of a lively child. She said:

This is the rosary that the Mother of God gave to man as the devotion dearest to her; but few have said it in this way! Mary also showed it to Dominic. But in course of time it became from neglect and disuse so soiled and sullied with dust that she covered it with her veil as with a cloud, through which however it still glimmers. Only by special grace, by great piety and simplicity, can it now be understood. It is veiled and far away—only practice and meditation can bring it near!

The Amen

IN the house used for such purposes at Mallep, a feast was given in which all took part. The poor were fed and presents were given them. Jesus, finally, delivered a grand discourse on the word "Amen," which, he said, was the whole summary of prayer. Whoever pronounces it carelessly makes void his prayer. Prayer cries to God; binds us to God; opens to us His mercy; and with the word "Amen," rightly uttered we take the asked-for gift out of His hands. Jesus spoke most forcibly of the power of the word "Amen." He called it the beginning and the end of everything. He spoke almost as if God had by it created the whole world. He uttered an "Amen" over all that he had taught them, over his own departure from them, over the accomplishment of his own mission, and ended his discourse by a solemn "Amen." Then he blessed his audience, who wept and cried after him.

A Sacramental Gesture

AT the time of the institution of the most blessed sacrament, on Thursday evening, April 2, AD 33, I saw Jesus anointing Peter and John, on whose hands he had poured the water that had flowed over his own, and who had drunk from the chalice in his hand. From the center of the table, where he was standing, Jesus stepped a little to one side and imposed hands upon Peter and John, first on their shoulders and then on their head. During this action they were required to join their hands and crossed their thumbs, thus:

As they bowed low before him (and I am not sure that they did not kneel) Jesus anointed the thumb and forefinger of each of their hands with chrism and made the sign of the cross with it on their head, at the middle. He told them that this anointing would remain with them to the end of the world.

Ways of Healing

JESUS cured in various ways, each one having its own signification. I cannot now, however, repeat them as I saw them. Each had reference to the meaning and the secret cause of the malady, also to the spiritual needs of the invalid. In the anointing with oil, for instance, there was a certain spiritual strength and energy denoted by the signification of the oil itself. No one of these actions was without its own peculiar meaning. With these forms Jesus instituted all those ceremonies that the saints and priests who exercised their healing power would afterward make use of in his name. They either received them from tradition or were used in the name of Jesus through an inspiration of the Holy Spirit. As the Son of God, in order to become man, chose the body of a most pure creature, thus to correspond to the requirements of man's nature, so did he frequently use in effecting his cures pure and simple created substances that had been blessed by his Spirit, as, for instance, oil. He afterward gave to the cured bread to eat with some juice of the grape. At other times he healed by a mere command uttered at a distance, for he had come upon earth to cure the most varied ills, and that in the most varied ways. He had come to satisfy, for all that believed in him, by his own great sacrifice upon the cross, in which sacrifice were contained all pains and sorrows, all penances and satisfactions. With the various keys of his charity he first opened the fetters and bonds of temporal misery and chastisement, instructed the ignorant in all things necessary for them to know, healed all kinds of maladies, and aided the needy in every way; then with that chief key of his love, the key of the cross, he opened heaven's expiatory door as well as the door of limbo.

Immoderate Praise

ABOVE *all, Anne Catherine pitied the poor souls whose friends think to "send them" to heaven at once in reward for natural good qualities, or those to whom relatives bear so soft and foolish an affection as not to be able to endure the idea of their needing the purifying flames of purgatory before their admittance to the enjoyment of God. Such souls she always saw among the most suffering and abandoned. She often said:*

Immoderate praise is a theft committed to the prejudice of those upon whom it is lavished.

Mystery of Pre-Earthly Life

I HAD a singular vision. St. Cunegundes[1] brought me a crown and a little piece of pure gold in which I could see myself. She said: "I have made you this crown, but the right side (where Anne Catherine's great pain was) is not quite finished. You must complete it with this gold. I made you this crown because you placed a precious stone in my crown even before you were born." Then she pointed to a stone or pearl in one side of her crown so dazzlingly bright that one could scarcely look at it—and this I had put there!

I thought that really laughable, and so I said right out: "How can this be? It would indeed be strange had I done that before my birth! To which the saint replied that all my labors and sufferings—as well as those of all humankind—were already portioned out and divided among my ancestors. And she showed me pictures of Jesus working in the person of David, of our own fall in Adam—of the good we do already existing in our ancestors, though obscurely, and other such things.

She showed me my origin on my mother's side up through several generations to her own ancestors, where a thread appeared connecting them. She explained to me how I had put the jewel in the crown. I understood it all in vision, but now I cannot explain it. It was as if the property of patient suffering that sprang from the thread of life connected with my existence had been communicated to her—so that I, or something of mine in her, had gained a victory that was represented by the jewel in her crown.

In the beginning of the vision I saw her in a heavenly sphere or garden in company with kings and princes. I saw Emperor Henry, her holy spouse, in a sphere. He appeared fresh and younger than she, as if she had existed there a longer time in the persons of her ancestors. But this I cannot explain, indeed I did not understand it at the time, and so I let it alone.

There was above all in this vision something unspeakably disengaged from the conditions of time. For although wondering to

---

[1] This account is extracted from a longer article on Cunegundes to be found in the volume of this series entitled *Scenes From the Lives of the Saints.*

find that I had even before my birth labored at a pearl in Cunegundes's crown, yet it seemed very natural. I felt that I had lived in her time—yes, that I was even anterior to her. And I felt myself present to myself even in my earliest origin.

Cunegundes showed me, on her left, her extraction according to the flesh, and on the right her descendants according to the spirit—for she had had no children. Her spiritual posterity was very rich, very fruitful. I saw her ancestors as well as my own far, far back to people who were not Christians. Among them I saw some who had received a merciful judgment. This astonished me, since it is written: "Whoever believes not and is not baptized shall not enter into the kingdom of heaven." But Cunegundes explained it thus: "They loved God as far as they knew Him and their neighbor as themselves. They knew nothing of Christianity, they were as if in a dark pit into which light never penetrated. But they were such as would have been perfect Christians had they known Christ. Consequently, they found mercy in his sight."

I had a vision of my being before my birth, or that of my forefathers—not like one genealogical tree, but like numerous branches spread over all the earth and in all sorts of places. I saw rays extending from one to another which, after uniting in multiplied beams, branched out again in different directions. I saw many pious members among my ancestors, some high, some low. I saw a whole branch of them on an island: they were wealthy and owned large ships, but I know not where it was. I saw very many things in this vision. I received many clear lights upon the importance of transmitting to the world a pure posterity and of maintaining pure, or of purifying in ourselves, that which our ancestors have handed down to us. I understood it to refer both to spiritual and to natural posterity.

Parables and Allegories

The Lost Sheep

REGARDING *the parable of the lost sheep,*[1] *Anne Catherine reports on one occasion*:

On a level area in the land of Palestine I saw a long rectangular building that looked rather like a school. Many people were gathered there, among them tax collectors and many who had given offence, when I saw Jesus and several of his disciples enter. It seemed to me they had just come from a banquet at the home of a Pharisee. Many had stationed themselves outside the window and doors to hear Jesus speak, but some among them were false and only lurking there, mumbling against Jesus because he kept company with what they regarded as such lowly people. But Jesus spoke with great calmness as all listened—including the disciples. That was when the following vision came to me.

I was looking out upon a beautiful meadow of flowers bounded by thickets, when I saw of fine flock of sheep, and among them a winsome shepherd I recognized as Jesus in shepherd's garb. Then a number of sheep broke away, making for a thicket along a descending path that ended in a copse of worthless alder trees, before which lay a swamp like a deep dark fen. However the shepherd, looking careworn, entered the thicket and then joyfully returned bearing a sheep upon his shoulders, which he carried back to his flock.

But another time I saw the shepherd troubled, having returned without a sheep he had set out to save.

In my vision this sheepfold seemed to be in the promised land. The shepherd came and went many times, looking very worried. When finally he came back with a sheep, he called out to his fel-

---

[1] Luke 15:3–7; Matthew 18:12–14.

low-shepherds, who once they had been shown the rescued sheep entered an edifice like a school, where with raised arms they sang praises, as at a church festival.

Lost Sheep in Our Own Time

IMMEDIATELY thereafter I beheld in a series of scenes what seemed to me successors of these shepherds as well as images or likenesses of the lost sheep—as though these things pertained to our present time and place. I saw individuals, like children, lost in sin—quarreling, drinking, impure and darkened through irreverence, lost to the Church through taverns and dance halls, and so forth—and priests seeking to rescue them. Those that were saved I saw contritely confessing and receiving communion, and the priests joyfully thanking God. I beheld many such beautiful images of such good and pure priests, and also some bishops exercising the same care and concern over the priests in their charge—though not so many of these latter.

The Lost Coin

REGARDING *the parable of the lost coin,*[1] *Anne Catherine says:*

I saw a house as though in the promised land. It was dark inside, but still I could make out the figure of Jewish woman. A man approached and said something to her, and it seemed to me it was the same shepherd I had earlier seen save the lost sheep. The shepherd was a likeness of Jesus, and as he took his departure I saw the woman light a lamp, and how as she did so she herself began to shimmer with light. She commenced sweeping the floor, and in the light she cast soon discovered a coin. The coin shone also, and of a sudden it was as though the shining coin was at the center of her breast. Then she herself waxed ever brighter —as also the lamplight and the coin—until her own light, and that of the lamp and the coin, were become all one within her, so that she was all brightness, and the house also.

Then another woman came to her, and she grew bright also, as

---

[1] Luke 15:8–10.

though from the light of the first. And then more came, and the same brightness arose in all—so that all present in full, shining clarity joyfully praised God.

The Lost Coin in Our Own Time

I SAW now in many examples how good priests, and also lay people—some of whom I knew, others not—through hearing confession (or even by no more than a good word) awoke in some an inner awareness of their failings and a resolution to better themselves. I saw then how these efforts were communicated to others who were awoken similarly. This was an image of how through good spiritual direction we can awaken.

Further on the Lost Coin

THE woman was in outer darkness, but darkness was within her also. She was troubled and restless. I saw the man enter by the door. She went up to him, and hardly had he begun speaking to her when it seemed she held in her hand a lamp. It was as though this man had brought her the lamp, or the fire.

She set the lamp on a tall post or lampstand in the middle of the house, and as she did so a brightness spread all around, and she herself grew brighter, purer—transparent even. She took a broom —not one of hair, but of long fine straw bound around the shaft— and commenced sweeping the house from all sides toward the shining lamp in the midst, gathering the dust and rubbish into a pile there. Then, as she was sifting through the pile, she came upon a large coin; and as she did so both she and the coin lit up brightly— she, the light, and the coin were all one. When a neighbor woman came in, she grew bright also, as did those that followed (that is, the coin could now shed its light in the proper way), after which all praised God.

The Prodigal Son

REGARDING *the parable of the prodigal son (Luke 15:11–32), Anne Catherine says:*

I saw an ancient Hebrew family—their home, children, and livestock. The father had two sons: the younger insolent and disagreeable, the elder close to his father and quite like him. I did not much like the elder; he had a certain self-assurance based more upon his father's achievements than his own. In consequence the younger was contesting the matter of their inheritance. His having set all this motion, and not letting the matter drop, troubled his father, but delighted his elder brother.

I saw the prodigal son take leave of his father without his blessing and head down a mountain. He journeyed on until he came at length to a region of marsh and mist. Along the way he passed many a hall of dance and gaming full of women of ill repute. He went from one such house of pleasure to the next, descending ever deeper into a dark land, until finally—by now poor as a beggar—he was thrown out of a brothel. He made his way then into a forest riddled with swamps and fens, where I saw him among swine eating fruits and husks scattered about. He was sitting on a stump, sadly supporting his head upon his hands, when suddenly he looked around him, then up toward heaven, and then went down upon his knees. I thought to myself: "Thank God, he is kneeling!"

Afterward the prodigal son hurried back to his father, who rushed to greet this son whom he had so longed to see again. The son went down on bended knee. The father embraced him and then called out to the household servants, who came promptly and in a most friendly way, bringing with them clothing, shoes, and a ring. A calf was slaughtered and guests arrived. A meal followed at which, after the custom of the Jews, the diners reclined at table. The guests sang praises and played upon flutes. All was joyous.

When the elder son (who was out in the fields) heard all the commotion, he stealthily approached the house. I saw him address a servant, and then go no further. His father came out. The elder son had gone pale with jealousy and chagrin. The father answered him something.

Inside at the meal I saw all standing around the table eating a lamb. The lamb was lying humbly upon a large plate, its head upon its forelegs!

The Prodigal Son in Our Own Time

ACCORDING to the spirit of this parable it seemed to me that the elder brother had now many more siblings upon the earth— and the younger also. I beheld in pictures the destiny of both types, in particular cases and also more generally—sometimes in connection with people known to me.

I saw how some turned away from the good and, notwithstanding their capacities and talents, gave way to living the "good life," waltzing to the tune of depravity. But in the end they found no peace, and hungered for grace. Indeed, they would have been happy to return home as servants. The loveless ones who stayed put were all the more angered by those who thought to make amends and return.

In vision I saw some clergy as shepherds who had abandoned their fields and flocks in order to gain a better position. Their downward path led toward a land beckoning brightly from a distance—an ever deeper distance—where they hoped to be seated at a richly-laden table. But when they arrived, of a sudden the table was transformed into a trough of slops, and they were dining among swine! I understood all this to mean that they had chosen to nourish themselves with carnal pleasures and impurity.

Among the prodigal sons I saw many who had gone astray out of inexperience or recklessness, and others who had left the Church out of intellectual arrogance. But when their destiny called them back to their father's house they often became far worthier—and were better received—than those brothers who had remained ever true, but who it seemed were the sort who, though supported by others, held their noses in the air and were ever jealous.

The pictures that came to me were uncommonly numerous and diverse. Among prodigal sons I saw some give way to blasphemy, succumb to so-called rational enlightenment, or fall into heresy. A few I saw lost among schismatic churches and religious teachers, and others quite convinced that they alone were the chosen ones.

Whenever I beheld clergy who had secured for themselves the choicest benefices, or lay persons who wanted nothing more than rationalism and a less arduous life, a picture of Lot's separation from Abraham was given me.

The Unjust Steward

EVEN as a child, I saw the parable of the unjust steward [Luke 16:1–13] and the other parables passing like living scenes before my eyes, and I used to think that, here and there, I recognized occasional figures from them in the life around me. And so it happened also with this steward whom I have always seen as a hunchback with a reddish beard, a receiver of revenues. I used to see him running briskly among the undertenants, making them sign their contracts with a pen.

I had seen him thus many times, when one day, on the way to a church in a nearby town, I stopped at a small shop to purchase some wares and noticed that the shopkeeper had the look of the unjust steward as I always saw him—so that whenever I saw that man I was reminded of the unjust, deceiving steward. Indeed, I would often chuckle to myself when I saw him!

On another occasion Anne Catherine saw more regarding this parable of the unjust steward from the gospel of Luke. As before, it was as though she saw it in the distance. What further she remembered regarding this parable follows:

I saw the unjust steward living in a tent castle in the desert of Arabia, not far from the place where the children of Israel murmured against their leaders. The steward's lord, who dwelt far away across Mount Lebanon, owned here on the frontiers of Palestine a corn and olive plantation. On either side of the field lived a peasant to whom it was rented.

The steward was a diminutive, humpbacked fellow, very cunning and full of expedients. He thought: "The lord will not come for some while yet," and so feasted freely and let things go as they would. The two peasants were pretty much of the same stamp, and spent their time carousing.

Then, all of a sudden, I saw the lord coming. Far over a high mountain range I saw a magnificent city and palace from which a most beautiful road led straight to the plantation. I saw the king and his whole court coming down with a great caravan of camels and little low chariots drawn by asses. I saw all this very much as I see paths coming down from the heavenly Jerusalem. The king was a heavenly king who owned a wheat and olive field on this earth. But he came in the manner of the patriarchal kings, attended by a great retinue. I saw him coming down from on high, for that little fellow, the steward, had been denounced to him for dissipating his revenues.

The lord's two debtors wore long coats buttoned all the way down, while the steward himself wore a little cap. The castle of the latter was nearer the desert than the wheat and olive plantation, on either side of which the peasant-debtors lived. That was more toward the land of Canaan, and formed a triangle with the castle.

And now came the lord down over the cornfield. The two debtors had squandered the fruits of the field with the steward, although toward their own dependents they were hard and exacting. They were like two bad parish priests, and the steward like a bishop far from good—or again, like a worldling putting his affairs in order.

The steward, having espied the coming of his lord while he was yet a long way off, fell into the greatest anxiety. He prepared a grand feast, and became very active and servile. When the lord arrived, he thus addressed the steward: "Why, what is this I hear of you, that you squander my property! Render an account, for you shall no longer be my steward!"

Then I saw the steward hurriedly summoning the two peasants. They presented themselves with scrolls, which they unrolled. The steward questioned them as to the amount of their indebtedness—for of that he was utterly ignorant—and they showed it to him. With the crooked reed that he held in his hand, he made them quickly alter the sum to a lesser amount, for he thought: "When I am discharged I shall find shelter with them and have whereon to live, for I cannot work."

I saw now the peasants sending their servants to the lord with camels and asses laden with sacks of corn and baskets of olives. They that had charge of the olives carried money also, little metal bars done up in packages, larger or smaller according to their sum, and fastened together with rings.

But the lord, glancing at the packages, saw by what he had before received that these were far too slight, and from the false account rendered he understood the designs of the steward. Turning to his courtiers he said with a laugh: "See how shrewd and underhanded is the steward, who hopes to win friends with what he holds back from what is owed. The children of this world are indeed more clever in their dealings than are children of light. It they applied themselves as much to the good as they have done to what is evil, they would receive as much reward as they must now, rather, suffer the loss in punishment."

Then I saw that the hunchbacked knave was discharged from his office and banished into the desert. The soil there was metallic (yellow, hard, unfruitful ferruginous sand, ocher), its only vegetation being the alder tree. He was at first quite confounded and troubled, but I saw that he afterward set to work to chop wood and build. The two peasants also were sent away, though to them somewhat better places amidst the sand of the desert were allotted. But the poor underservants, formerly the victims of cruel extortion, were now entrusted with the care of the choicest fields.

The Cross and the Winepress

AS I was meditating upon these words or thoughts of Jesus when hanging on the cross: "I am pressed like wine placed here under the press for the first time; my blood must continue to flow until water comes, but wine shall no more be made here," an explanation was given me by means of another vision relating to Golgotha.

I saw this rocky country at a period anterior to the deluge. It was then less wild and less barren than it afterward became, and was laid out in vineyards and fields. I saw there the patriarch Japhet,[1] a majestic dark-complexioned old man, surrounded by immense flocks and herds and a numerous posterity: his children as well as himself had dwellings excavated in the ground and

---

[1] Japhet (or Japheth) was one of the sons of Noah.

covered with turf roofs on which herbs and flowers were growing. There were vines all around, and a new method of making
wine was being tried on Golgotha in the presence of Japhet. I saw
also the ancient method of preparing wine, but I can give only
the following description of it.

At first, men were satisfied with only eating the grapes; then
they pressed them with pestles in hollow stones, and finally in
large wooden trenches. Upon this occasion a new wine-press,
resembling the holy cross in shape, had been devised. It consisted
of the hollow trunk of a tree placed upright, with a bag of grapes
suspended over it. Upon this bag was fastened a pestle surmounted by a weight, and on both sides of the trunk were arms
joined to the bag through openings made for the purpose, and
which, when put in motion by lowering the ends crushed the
grapes. The juice flowed out of the tree by five openings and fell
into a stone vat, whence it flowed through a channel made of
bark and coated with resin into the kind of cistern excavated in
the rock where Jesus was confined before his crucifixion. At the
foot of the winepress, in the stone vat, was a sort of sieve to stop
the skins, which were put to one side.

When they had made their winepress, they filled the bag with
grapes, nailed it to the top of the trunk, placed the pestle, and set
in motion the side arms in order to make the wine flow.

All this very strongly reminded me of the crucifixion, on
account of the resemblance between the winepress and the cross.
They had a long reed at the end of which there were points, so
that it looked like an enormous thistle, and they ran this through
the channel and trunk of the tree when there was any obstruc-
tion. By these, I was reminded of the lance and sponge. There
were also some leathern bottles, and vases made of bark and plas-
tered with resin. I saw several young men with nothing but a
cloth wrapped round their loins, like Jesus, working at this winepress.

Japhet was very old. He wore a long beard and a dress made of
the skins of beasts, and he looked at the new winepress with evident satisfaction. It was a festival day and they sacrificed on a
stone altar some animals that were running loose in the vineyard:
young asses, goats, and sheep. It was not in this place that Abra-

ham came to sacrifice Isaac; perhaps it was on Mount Moriah. I have forgotten many of the instructions regarding the wine, vinegar, and skins, and the different ways in which everything was to be distributed to the right and to the left; and I regret it, because even the least trifles in these matters have a profound symbolical meaning. If it should be the will of God for me to make them known, He will show them to me again.

A Wonderful Parable of Marriage

BRENTANO *writes that on the occasion of a teaching regarding marriage, a great parable was given Anne Catherine, much of which she was unable to retain. His initial note reads:*

"Marriage of the blood ends at death, but marriage of the spirit endures. Sometimes, however, a couple married upon earth do not find each other again in the hereafter—for the one may rise high, the other remain down lower. On the other hand, sometimes a couple who did not know each other (while living upon the earth) find each other and come together in the life after death."

In this parable Anne Catherine was pointing to the degeneracy that befell human beings in their (originally) pure state—as first proceeding from the hand of God—when they succumbed to fleshly sin; to ejection from paradise and (procreative) multiplication in the wilderness; to obscuration through mixing darkness with the holy, original light in humankind; and to the time when, finally, the promise of salvation would come, the time when the pure grain of wheat and the noble grape would have developed and found one another—when the heavenly wedding-banquet will be celebrated, offering mercy and strength again to poor, fallen humanity.

Contained in this parable is the whole story of the fall and the resulting dissemination and dispersal of humankind in their fallen corporeality, as well as God's subsequent provision to save them by gathering all together in one body—the body of the Bride of Christ, the Church—in order that they may be reborn as children of God. According to Anne Catherine:

This is the story of marriage, both as among fallen humankind and as a great sacrament in Christ and in his Church. All these things were presented with such simplicity and beauty that a child could have understood. And so did I also understand, when I received this parable. But now that I am present here once again in the dark desert of this world—filled as it is with pain and suffering—I can recall no more than the broadest brush strokes. But these at least I shall seek to convey.[1]

I beheld a world, and set at either side a king and a queen. They were luminous and transparent. They longed for one another—were truly meant to be together—but were unable to meet. In due course the king took to himself a bride, and the queen a bridegroom, and they lived full well, and begat children. Then both passed away and rose up to a heavenly place.

The king and queen were brilliant and transparent, but separated and solitary. Behind the king, upon a hill, was a garden; and the queen had a garden also, though hers grew upon a hill before her. Between the two stretched a wasteland, a region that lay in darkness.

The king held a scepter formed at the top like a lily, or scalloped calyx, while the queen held a branch covered with a row of yellow flower buds. The two longed for one another, as has been said, for they were indeed each other's intended. Their longing streamed out like rays that intersected, meeting in their midst. However, I understood that they did not know one another, and that a bride had been given in marriage to the king, and a bridegroom to the queen. They (the bride and bridegroom) had come from a third place in the middle between them, but lying off in a far corner.

---

[1] The wonderful, comprehensive imagery of this parable cannot unfortunately be presented in a complete form. Much must remain forever missing, for the solution to the mystery surely lies largely in the proper order of events. Still, enough remains to warrant its inclusion here. Anne Catherine later supplemented her description as follows: "I understood from the teaching on marriage that the marriage of flesh and blood ends upon death, but that marriage of the spirit endures in the hereafter; that often a man and woman joined in earthly marriage fail to find each other again after death—for it may happen that one of them stands higher [in that world], and the other lower—whereas often two come together in the hereafter who were not joined in their earthly lives.

This third place was like a dark swamp overspread with a vile mist in which those present seemed to be held fast up to their necks. In any event, everything but the hills and gardens of the king and queen lay waste, all mire and muck and uprooted trees—it was like a destruction of the world.

I saw the king and queen plant something, and beget children, and how everything continued to multiply—plants, growth, propagation—always in a circle, so that their two realms grew ever closer together. The plants kept sending forth into the ground new shoots, from which new stems would grow—and so it went.

Then, when these two ever-propagating plant circles finally grew together, from their union rose up a great tree. On one side it bore the small leaves of the luminous fruits of the queen's garden, and on the other the great leaves of the fruits of the king's garden. The tree grew to a great height, and upon its branches I beheld ascending and descending generations. Above the tree hovered a world of light, like a beautiful garden, within which I beheld a table oriented to the four cardinal directions. Higher still was the Holy Trinity (just as we often see it represented in pictures), as also the twenty-four elders and the choirs of angels. At table I saw seated kings and queens, but on one side only.

Yes, they were in a beautiful, lustrous garden in which had been set a long table. Upon a heavenly meadow angels were busy collecting dew, like manna gathered in the wilderness. From what they gathered they kneaded a long, ribbed loaf of bread, which was then placed at the center of the table, at which were seated many guests.

Then I saw the queen floating upward all-shining between the north and east sides of the table, and the king just so between the west and south—it was as though they had quit the earth, though I cannot say whether they had died.

They passed by one another as they proceeded toward the unoccupied side of the table and met in the middle, where each took a morsel of the heavenly bread and placed it in the other's mouth—which act established them in marriage, in fulfillment of the longing they had had for one another upon the earth.

The question was raised why the bread had not been set at the ends of the table, to which an angel answered that it must needs

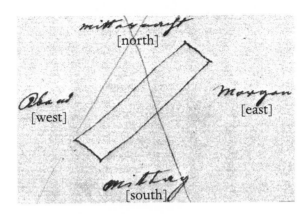

be stationed at the center. But as for the reason, I have forgotten it, as I have so many other details. It had to do with the passion of Christ; that in some way the bread of the wilderness, the manna, had been baked in Christ's passion. I no longer recall exactly the sense, only such dim images as I have here offered.

Now I saw another picture of what I had left behind in the wilderness (on earth). I saw the dark (repentant) wife of the king and the dark (repentant) husband of the queen take leave of the beautiful gardens (which had grown into woods) and also of their progeny—for all was gone rampant: no fruits, flowers fallen to the ground; all now dust and dark decay.

Then I saw the wife of the king and the husband of the queen approaching either side of a desolate, dilapidated, and overgrown stone structure resembling the buildings of Egypt. They seemed not to know one another, and as though they wished—both of them—to retire there into an eremitical life of penitence. Each built, from their own side, a little garden around an old thorn- or rose-bush, which however sent forth no roses but only stems and leaves.

In consequence of their penitential labors I beheld the heavenly king send down to the repentant man a garland, as did the queen likewise to the repentant woman.

The two penitents received many mystical gifts, always as garlands or fruits. Between them came to stand the hidden mystical chalice—guarded by the thorn-bush. Ears of grain and grapevines waxed ever closer to it, in varying proportion to each other

35

as time went along—and finally out of it grew the Holy Thing of Redemption.

Because it took on this character, Anne Catherine then saw the Holy Thing repeatedly assailed. This she beheld in images of warriors and chariots of different sorts, armored in particular ways, which she described in much the same way as does John in the Apocalypse. She continued:

Among these assailants was an army of soldiers with stiff arms. I do not know whether these stiff arms represented a sort of weaponry, or bore some other signficance. It was as though the warriors were instruments of darkness whose object was to destroy, to rip to pieces, or to take possession of the penitents' Holy Thing, which was their pledge of security.

But then I beheld in another stream of images how carefully the penitents hid the Holy Thing—keeping it secure, well-guarded, and ever-victorious—until it appeared to me no longer as the Ark of the Promise in the Temple in Jerusalem, but as the most holy Virgin of this present parable, until finally she—the small grain of wheat—became so clear and pure that, through the overshadowing of the Holy Spirit, she came to bear the Son of God, who then, as both Godhead and Man, offered his holy body and blood as a most holy sacrament to all who repent.

This was truly the most holy of humankind, and the parable a symbolic story of how repentant, fallen human beings had worked together with the merciful God to bring to fulfillment the moment of redemption in the course of time. [*Or as Anne Catherine more briefly puts it elsewhere*]: The mystery became gradually more hidden and secure, until finally it passed from the Ark of the Covenant into the Holy Virgin, and thence, through the Savior, into the sacrament. [*Or again:*] The mass is the hidden history of redemption—redemption become a sacrament.

✝ ✝ ✝ ✝ ✝

ON *another occasion, in connection with a vision of Adam and Mount Golgotha, the place of the skull, Anne Catherine says:*

On this occasion I was given special insight into the recently received vision regarding the parable of the king and queen. I saw that the place where their gardens came together, where rose up the tree upon which the differing fruits of the king and of the queen united, and over which stood the heavenly table at which the two bound themselves together by sharing angelic bread—that this place was no other than Mount Golgotha.

A Picture of Stars at Birth
(Prayer-Work with Birthing Women)

THROUGHOUT the night I found myself occupied with pregnant women, some already in childbed. How did this come to be? There must have been at least a hundred, all in the land of Münster. I remember the wife of Dr. Wesener; the others I do not now know. Each of these women had a garden, and each garden was different, with varying figures, plants, and overall shape. Some were triangular, some round; others octagonal, pentagonal, rectangular. All sorts of forms were represented.

I was at work in these gardens. I had to pick and prune among the shrubs and herbs. In the garden of one of the women [the wife of Dr. Wesener, Anne Catherine's physician], which was rectangular, I crawled about between the beds searching among the plants for all sorts of treats and trinkets scattered about—pretzels and rings, among other things—which I was to gather up. She herself was unable to bend over. She received much in the way of such treats, which she consumed. When she came to the end of the garden, she moved off to the side, after which I had nothing more to do with her: her time was up. The gardens with their beds signified the given womens' remaining time. Mrs. Wesener's time was nearly finished.[1]

For other women I had to crush the herbs in their gardens, some of them very bitter—particularly myrrh and aloe. Many misfortunes, affrights, and snares were to be found in the gardens as well, so I had much to clear away and pray for; saints helped me with this task.

While I was among these gardens I looked up at the stars and found them different than I customarily saw them. They seemed situated within a kind of figure, and each such figure appeared to

---

[1] Presumably referring to the due date for her child's birth.

be related in some way to one of the gardens. Rays from the various stars shone upon and interpenetrated each other, and within them all sorts of pictures could be seen. The stars as I then saw them were like discs, and within each disc was a primary figure of a certain form and attire expressing a specific influence.[1]

For instance, in one such star-disc was a gentle male form to which seven other figures were offering peaceful service. This image presided also over the ending of Mrs. Wesener's garden. I beheld how the spirits of individual stars breathed into those of other stars. Such streams of breath were red, or sometimes other colors. Then I saw how the spirits of some stars would on occasion come together at a separate place where they struggled and retched—and from such a scene light-rays with particular colors and powers would descend to the ends of the gardens where the women delivered. These rays had to do with the moment—that is, the essence and nature of the time—when the newborn babe would first enter the daylight.

In other instances I beheld figures seeming to be intoxicated, or quite at peace, or groups of figures occupied with counting and measuring—indeed, this latter I saw quite often. All such spiritual figures had much to do with various instruments. Sometimes I also saw figures that were ill. I saw bandages being prepared; it

---

[1] "On the occasion when the twelve-year-old Jesus was teaching in the Temple, a physician asked the young Jesus whether he could tell whether a man was of a dry, matter-of-fact nature or of a phlegmatic disposition, under what planets such a one was born, what simples were good for this or that temperament, and how the human body is formed. Jesus answered him with great wisdom. He spoke of the complexion of some of those present, their diseases and the remedies thereof, and of the human body—all with a depth of knowledge quite unknown to the physician. He spoke of life, of the spirit and how it influences the body, of sicknesses that could be cured only by prayer and amendment, of such as needed medicine for their cure—and that in language so profound and yet so beautiful that the physician in astonishment declared himself vanquished and that he had never before heard such things. I think he afterward became one of Jesus's disciples.

There was an astrologer present who spoke of the course of the stars. Jesus explained how one constellation ruled another, how different stars possess different influences, and he discoursed upon comets and the signs of the zodiac. His hearers were transported by his wisdom."

seemed as though such bandages and other medical items would then descend. All the stars I am speaking of seemed to have a relation to our earth. Again, these stars did not appear to me as stars usually do when I sometimes look into a whole world. Today I saw them as images of the meaning of various sorts of influences. I saw many of these stars especially toward the end of my journey, on a mountain from where I looked into a region of swamps, moors, and peat-mounds.

Anne Catherine's
Elucidations Regarding the Above Vision

ANNE *Catherine at first spoke of the whole vista of the preceding vision in a childish, confused manner—even making light of the amusing treats she had seen, and in such quantity. Only after the pilgrim quite casually brought up the subject of how many comets had recently been discovered did she further treat of aspects of the foregoing vision of which she had been reluctant to speak at first owing to an initial aversion and incomprehension:*

At first I thought to myself, what nonsense! Of what use can all this be? Anyway, the spirits of these stars will be destroyed together with the earth upon the day of Judgment. These [spirits] are not devils and fallen angels, who in my visions are in other, deeper and darker, spheres. These [latter] devils are at work in the qualities that the spirits of the stars pour down upon those children born under their influence, holding them back from other, healing influences that break the yoke of fallen nature, keeping and provoking them in the evil dependencies of this nature. The influence of the stars is at the moment of birth, when the child becomes free, whereas the nature of the parents works at the conception.

Through baptism man is born again and enters into another, holy world, receiving therefrom rays and influences from other stars, from—so to speak—the redeemed, liberated heavenly world. But these influences partly pass through the will and blessing and prayer of the parents—or later through their own will or effort, collaboration with grace in and through Christ, the center of this victorious world, of heaven, in which the saints are the various expressions of the content and of the forces by which we are nourished in the varying ways he succors us. It cannot be said how that is—all is a garden, a nature, a fullness of grace and love, but every individual is a separate flower and herb from a specific bed, each working in a different way. In the blessed supernatural world everything works in harmony, all becomes one. In the natural world everything is separated more and more, each wants to be alone and push away the other, everything is struggle and destruction and separation. By the Church and the life in her, the dependency arising from the influences of the natural stars is broken and healed through the appropriation of the influences of the emanating merits of the saints from and through Jesus; in this way do we become free, reaching our goal in struggle.

In secret relationship with this rests also the merit of abstinence at holy times, the abstinence or long period of infertility before the conception of saints, the refraining from intercourse at certain holy times set by the Church. All this also plays into the secret influence of the protection of grace and of the Church against the influence of nature, in which we are imprisoned because of sin, and from which we are redeemed through faith. The economy of the procreation and birth of saints is a great secret, and even as it is superstitious to consult the stars, so is it a matter of faith to follow grace.[1]

A Heavy-Set Woman and a Child She Stole

WITHOUT *in the least making the connection with yesterday's vision, Anne Catherine related the following somewhat sporadic account, adding that it was difficult to say what it all meant, though in the end it was evident she had been occupied with the miracle at Saragossa [in Spain], which she hoped to again behold. She found herself wondering how it was that in her visions she saw everything in a different—a simpler, more natural—way than did others,[2] and also who the broad person*

---

[1] The force of the original German of this final formulation is difficult to preserve in translation, for the root *Glaube* (faith) is found also in the word *Aberglaube* (superstition).

[the heavy-set woman mentioned below] might be who appeared in her vision.

Her guide led her into the following wonderful story. What she was shown was not, however, a so-called tangled dream confounded of motifs received the preceding day, but rather a formal teaching cast as an allegory, dressed as a fairy tale, regarding what she so wished to know—and on this night the fairy tale took the place of her more accustomed "helping journeys," during the course of which (after she had earlier received her usual pictures of the life of Jesus) she was taken in pictures, as usual, through various landscapes to the region where was what she needed to see. It is unfortunate that so little of this vision could be retrieved, as also that the order of its episodes is so uncertain:

Today I received a most curious vision of a child with one eye whom I found, and of an emperor and a king, which you [Brentano] will know nothing of, and of which I can recall only what follows.

My guide took me from my home, through France, to a seacoast in Spain, where we were to take ship. But there we came upon a pair of the most unusual people. The one was an earnest elderly man who was good and well-composed; the other, a broad woman, was haughty, long-winded, dotty, and full of compliments. The dress she wore was hilariously wide and its hinter parts looked rather like some old town. [This analogy was apparently drawn from the many folds and staggered ornaments of the crinoline.] Not only this, but, all laced up as she was—and bedecked with bows and frills—she never ceased moving and talking.

These two had with them, lying just now in a bush by the sea, a most wondrous child. In fact this child was not theirs; rather had they gotten their hands upon it in some way, having either stumbled upon it or stolen it, or perhaps overpowered those to

---

[2] Anne Catherine was referring more specifically to Mary of Jesus of Ágreda (1602–1665), a Franciscan abbess, spiritual writer, and visionary from Spain, whose extensive visions were published under the title *The Mystical City of God*. She was known also for bilocation, specifically her appearances among the Jumano Indians of New Spain (Texas and New Mexico), which in turn had a profound effect on missionary activities in that region, as also more generally.

whom it belonged and got hold of it that way, with a view to putting it on display in exchange for money. I am uncertain just how this was—only that it was a foul affair, what they intended for him, the woman especially.

I had also a side image of how the broad women made herself appear very pious. She was headstrong and wanted to enter the church through the very narrow corridor with the child pressed tightly against the folds of her voluminous dress, but to no avail, as she became stuck fast each time she tried, though she kept at it obstinately, as she did not want to give up the vain appearance of her efforts [this being a symbol of aberrant efforts to introduce into the faith of the Church the rudimentary visions of persons to some degree enlightened in this way though not in the best of taste. No better image of this can be imagined than that just given here, especially in considering such visions as those presented in the works of Mary of Ágreda].

At the time he appeared to me, the child was five weeks old. I took him to me. I knew him already. I took him into my apron, but he wanted nothing from me. I fed him, and the broad Madam had to leave—I do not recall why—but the good man remained by me.

The little one was the child of a heavenly king and an earthly empress. But I do not recall that part of the story. Most strange it was, how in my presence the child grew so quickly. In no time he was five months old and could already speak and walk! And all this while there were, along with me, many others on the pilgrimage to Spain—James and his disciples, and in the distance all sorts of people from our present time. Wherever we passed by, many saints who had once lived there would step forward, astounded by this child, who would stand and teach, point out all things, remaining always by my side.

The extraordinary thing about the child, though, was that its eyes were closed, but on its forehead was an eye like a sun, like the eye of God. Thus did it travel along with me throughout Spain, where James had once been, pointing things out and explaining all to me.

Again I beheld the image of Mary's apparition to James at Saragossa, and all appeared so natural. Wherever we went, we found ourselves in a great company of saints descended from on high, among those in particular who had themselves experienced visions. All were in awe of this child, who pointed the saints out to me, describing to me what each had beheld and prophesied, from which I came to appreciate the multiplicity of the kinds of visions [that may be received]—encompassing all the earth and all times, leading back through the Old Testament prophets all the way to Adam.

In their variety, the visions were beyond counting and infinitely varied. Yet was there such an order to them that it was possible to gain an overview of them all. I recall how [for example] Samuel's mother prayed before the Ark of the Covenant, and how Heli wanted to drive her away because she was so inflamed with longing that he thought her inebriated. I saw how from the Ark there fell upon her a ray within which was a child, and Heli said to her that she had been heard and would conceive a son. He pressed against her something like a little box as he blessed her [presumably the holy Mystery of the Ark].

Thus did I behold in inconceivable measure the nature of the different sorts of vision and prophecy as manifested among all the prophets; and yet in face of all this they too stood in wonder of this child, as if none had ever had such a one [with them] as did I. At the same time I beheld a prophecy emanating from the realm of darkness of that part of nature that is connected therewith. I beheld this realm as large, round, world spheres in darker, lighter, and turbid colors. Indeed, all things one sees as a totality appear in this way as world spheres. In their center I saw spirits and their effects [as though] interpenetrating each other.

Within such dark circles I saw magnetized somnambulists partially contained, but also partially influenced from these circles, for in front of the magnetizer I usually saw a dark spirit coming out from these dark realms, entering into the somnambulists, and taking possession of them. I saw that their prophesying was mostly earthly, lowly, and fraught with danger—though to varying degrees.

I saw that even some monastics—especially particular nuns with visionary gifts—were partially illuminated by rays from these dark spheres. Many of these were from Spain, among them even some who beheld spiritual things, images from the life and passion of Christ. Some of these were much given to self-mortification, yet influences from the nether spheres nevertheless penetrated into their experiences, deforming them through influences coming from the natural and demonic spheres, to which their weaknesses had brought them into contact; also, the being [the dark spirit]—and the realms to which this commanding authority belonged—influenced them. Some I saw who stood wholly in the thrall of such evil powers, for instance Magdalene of the cross. I perceived the connection between spirits and demons among the pagans of old, among the Moors and the primitive peoples. If I were to recount all I beheld on this occasion regarding such things, it would make a very big book indeed.

Finally, then, I awoke from these images and—startled to discover the child lying beside me—returned to sleep and was again a child myself in my Flamske home, going about my chores driving the cows to pasture, whereupon, finding the boy as a small child in bush, I ran to bring him some porridge, which I then fed him. And now I experienced in vision my whole life up to the present in pictures, and beheld how throughout the boy kept appearing therein, coming and going. In this way I experienced a repetition of my whole destiny, with all the consolations and pains I had endured, which completely crushed me. I experienced again also both the horrible investigations [into the stigmata she bore] that I had had to endure.

In vision I saw the boy also in Rome, where he pointed out all sorts of things [to me], though unfortunately I can no longer recall anything clearly other than that it seemed to me that after the [present] pope another had replaced him, though for only a brief time, rather like our own bishop;[1] however his papacy was soon over and the legitimate pope returned.

I saw the boy in a different time teaching in Münster. Where the castle stood, much had been cleared away. I beheld another life. Some men of the present time, old and vexed, went around complaining of all the inconvenient changes. I saw the bishop, who should really help, in the form of a child. He is still a boy

---

[1] Ferdinand von Lüninck.

now. He was not from the countryside but the son of a noble family. At the time from which these last pictures were drawn, I must already have been dead.

In the course of these visions, in my vicinity I often saw the pilgrim, with whom I was not shy; neither was the boy, who went around him quite contentedly and with no great surprise. I saw also my father confessor, who often could not understand the boy, whom he would chase away, or try to cover up—but all in vain, for the child would soon return and stay by me. Often he kept himself at a distance from the boy, but would then be again confidential with him—though he never did fully understand him, and so ever and again shrank away. I saw also how Lambert[1] sometimes suppresses him, and all the damage done in that way to the boy.

I saw also many people who took much joy in this boy and held him in awe, later for example some great men, even kings, and many others, especially [in my time] Overberg, Mrs. Hirn, the old Diepenbrock, Windischmann, Appel, and Melchior,[2] as well as many others all around the world.

From the partial and somewhat confused record of this vision, one can appreciate the contrast between what Anne Catherine often beheld, and to what degree details went lost on account of her situation and the difficulties entailed in bringing her experiences into some order.

An Allegorical Tale of Five Upraised Birds

ANNE *Catherine told this story with particular relish, as though bringing it through her childlike side—as though it were nothing but childishness—despite the fact that she knew so well from such long experience that many times the case would prove quite otherwise. But she is quite difficult to instruct, for what with her continual sufferings and visionary state, her waking conversation sometimes had an uncertain*

---

[1] Fr. Lambert was chaplain to Anne Catherine during her time in the convent and is described by her biographer, Fr. Schmöger, as "the only one who treated her kindly [at that time], the only one to whom she could make known her sorrows."

[2] Apollonia and Melchior Diepenbrock.

quality to it. *She found her way straightaway to this tale, and had the pilgrim kept her to it, she might well have introduced confusions into the scenes of the life of Jesus that she had also just been relating. Her corporeal life is indeed well-ordered, as is also her unself-conscious spiritual life—but the same cannot be said of her more personal conversation and communications:*

As I was wandering around the huts of the poor people on the mountain, I came suddenly upon a bush in which was a nest with five young, unfledged, but quite large birds. They were quite ungainly in appearance, with what seemed thin filaments dangling from their heads. The parents had been caught by a bird of prey, and the nestlings' beaks were opened quite pitifully wide with hunger, but I had nothing to offer them. So I gathered up some worms and lady bugs with which to feed them, and as I was doing so was astonished to discover how in so short a space they grew in size, their feathers came in, and they fluttered from the nest. Then I espied a poor youth in a long shirt who seemed to be wandering around in some confusion, and called out to him that he might put to some good use for himself the birds, which were still running around near the nest.

The youth was quite joyful at these words, collected the birds, both gray and colored, and happily said: "I can put these birds to splendid use. I shall carry them to the city. For they have nothing, and can nothing receive, till it is brought to them.[1] You don't seem to be from these parts, but still I thank you—indeed, you will still feel my thanks even when are have returned to your home." And therewith he hurried to that city, which from the way it appeared to my view, seemed a holy city.

A Somewhat Confused Elucidation of the Tale of the Five Birds

THE *following day Anne Catherine followed up on this story in a somewhat scattered way, as follows:*

I was shown the signficance of this tale, but can no longer hold it all together. I saw the youth again, full of joy and much grown,

---

[1] This is unclear in the original.

on a green, spiritual mountain [elevated, a better state or condition]. He thanked me. He was a soul from olden times who had incurred some debt in connection with that city, on account of which until now he had been unable to find any rest, but, entirely forgotten, had had to wander hither and yon without cease.

The five young birds so rapidly fed, grown, and fledged represented graces which, through various small victories—and through prayer—I had quickly gained in reference to the lady bugs,[1] and wherewith I could make recompense for at least some portion of debt to that place. The orphaned nestlings signified the youth's guilt, when, as a man in that former time and place, he had brought others into slavery—this latter represented as the bird of prey that had carried away the parent birds. And so the birds, in making reparation, represented both the youth's guilt (in his former life) as well as graces he had been gifted, with which then he was able to redeem his debt.

At this point Anne Catherine said she could no longer recall more of the explication she had received of the tale, other than that involved was something to do with interest that needs paying on debts.

Of the city in the tale she added that it was set out in most holy way and that it seemed to her it played a role in some event in the life of Abraham. At the time of the vision, however, she saw it populated with men and women striving to live holy lives after the fashion of the Essenes. The place was already Christian, so that the guilt or debt of which the tale told must have stemmed from a later time. The graces in the story, then, she would have gathered from the service to Christ current at that time.

Anne Catherine and the "Little Boy"

THREE *days before Christmas, Anne Catherine cried out in ecstasy: "There I see all the children for whom I have ever made anything! They are so merry, they have all the things, they all shine—my little boy is there, too. Come here, dear little one, sit there," and she pointed to a*

---

[1] Called in German *Herrgottstierchen*, that is, "little creature of the Lord God," literally translated.

seat. After this she had a vision of how the "little boy," had been the constant companion of her life:

What I now saw in vision, once really happened; for the little boy used to work with me when I was a child. When I was ten years old, he said to me: "Let us go see how the little crib looks that we made years ago!"—"Where can it be!" I thought. But the little boy said I had only to go with him, and we should soon find it. When we did so, we saw that the flowers[1] of which we had made it had formed garlands and crowns, some only half-finished. The little boy said: "The pearls are still wanting in front." Only one small circlet of pearls was entirely finished and I slipped it on my finger. But to my great distress and fright I could not get it off. I begged the little boy to do so, for I was afraid I should not be able to work with it on. He succeeded, and we put everything back again. But I think it was only a picture; I do not remember it as a real event. After I had grown up I got sick. I wanted to go to the convent; but as I was so poor, I became sad. The little boy said that that was nothing, his father had enough, the Christ child had nothing either, and that I should one day enter a convent. I did indeed enter, and it was a joyful time! As a nun I was sick and in distress because I had nothing. I used to say: "Now, see how it is! You were to have care of all, I was always to have enough; and now you go away, and I get nothing!"

Then the little boy came that night with gold, pearls, flowers, and all kinds of precious things. I knew not where to put them all. Twice again I received such things in vision, but I know not what has become of them. I think they were symbolical of the gifts I was to receive and which were miraculously multiplied; as for example Herr von Galen's present and the coffee on St. Catherine's day. I used to be sick all the time; well for a couple of days, then sick again, and in this state I saw many things with the child Jesus and many cures. Then I was out of the convent and very ill, often in intense agony and distress; but the little boy always came with help and advice.

Lastly, I had a vision of the future. The little boy took me again

---

[1] Symbols of suffering. CB

to see the garlands and flowers of the crib in a kind of sacristy, where they lay in a casket, like golden crowns and jewels. He again said: "Only some pearls are wanting, and then all will be used in the Church."—I understood that I am to die as soon as all the pearls will have been added.

Worlds of Soul and Spirit

Purgatory

ANNE *Catherine always showed great compassion for the souls in purgatory. We shall here give those visions that refer to them particularly, as also the various good works undertaken by her for their relief. The first feast of All Souls that the pilgrim spent in Dülmen, Anne Catherine noticed in the pilgrim that general indifference toward the dead, that comforting assurance with which the living look upon their deceased relations and friends as no longer in need of special assistance. Consequently she often repeated with a sigh:*

It is truly sad to think how few help the poor souls in purgatory. Their misery is so great! They cannot help themselves, though they may be so easily relieved by prayers, alms, and suffering offered for them! O how joyful they then are!—as happy as a thirsty man to whom a cool drink is given.

When she saw that her words produced a deep impression, she went on to say how powerful are meritorious works offered for the poor souls; for example, acts of self-abnegation and mortification of self-will, victories gained over evil inclinations, acts of patience, meekness, humility, forgiveness of injuries, and so forth:

Ah! how many poor souls are left to suffer in consequence of lukewarmness, want of zeal for God's glory and the salvation of the neighbor! What can help them except satisfactory works—acts of those virtues they themselves neglected most on earth? The saints in heaven can no longer do penance, they cannot satisfy for them. Help can come only from the children of the Church Militant. And how the souls long for it! They know that no good thought, no earnest desire to help them, is lost. And yet how few trouble themselves about them! A priest who says his breviary devoutly with the intention of supplying for the failings the poor souls have still to expiate can procure for them incredible consolation. Yes, the power of the sacerdotal benediction penetrates even into purgatory and, like a celestial dew, refreshes the souls to whom it is sent in the spirit of faith. One who could see all this as I see it would certainly try to relieve them as far as he is able.

Above all, Anne Catherine pitied the poor souls whose friends think to "send them to heaven" at once in reward for natural good qualities, or those to whom relatives bear so soft and foolish an affection as not to be able to endure the idea of their needing the purifying flames of purgatory before their admittance to the enjoyment of God. Such souls she always saw among the most suffering and abandoned. She used to say:

Immoderate praise is a theft committed to the prejudice of those upon whom it is lavished.

One day, after a conversation on the relations existing between the survivors and the deceased, the pilgrim wrote down the following, which embodies the salient points of their discourse:

All that man thinks, says, or does has in it a living principle for good or evil. He who sins should hasten to efface his faults by the sacrament of penance, otherwise he will not be able to prevent the full or partial consequence of his crime. I have often seen such consequence even in the physical sickness and sufferings of many individuals and in the curse attached to certain places. I am always told that a crime unpardoned, unexpiated, entails an infinity of evils. I have seen such chastisements extending to posterity as a natural and necessary consequence—for instance the curse attached to ill-gotten goods—and I have felt involuntary horror in places where great crimes were once perpetrated. This is as natural, as necessary, as that a benediction should bless, and what is holy sanctify.

I have always had an intuitive perception of what is sacred and of what is profane, of what is holy and what unholy. The former attracts me, the latter repels, disquiets, and terrifies me, forcing me to resist it by faith and prayer. This impression is especially keen near human remains—nay more, near the smallest atoms of a body once animated by a soul. The feeling is so strong that I have always thought there exists a certain relation between soul and body even after death, for I have felt the most opposite emotions near graves and tombs. Near some I have had a sensation of light, of superabundant benediction and salvation; by others a sentiment of poverty and indigence—and I felt that the dead implored prayers, fasts, and alms. By many others I have been struck with dread and horror.

When I had to pray at night in the cemetery I have felt that there brooded around such graves as the last-named a darkness deeper and blacker than night itself—just as a hole in black cloth makes the blackness still deeper. Over them I sometimes saw a black vapor rising that made me shudder. It also happened sometimes that when my desire to render assistance urged me to penetrate into the darkness, I felt something repulsing my proffered aid. The lively conviction of God's most holy justice was then for me like an angel leading me out from the horrors of such a grave. Over some I saw a column of gray vapor, brighter or darker; over others one of light more or less brilliant. And over many others I beheld nothing at all. These last made me very sad, for I had an interior conviction that the vapor—more or less brilliant—issuing from the graves was the means by which the poor souls made known their needs, and that they who could give no sign were in the lowest part of purgatory, forgotten by everybody, deprived of all power of acting or communicating with the body of the Church.

When I knelt in prayer over such graves I often heard a hollow, smothered voice, as if calling to me from a deep abyss: "Help me out!" and I felt most keenly in my own soul the anguish of the helpless sufferer. I pray for these abandoned, forgotten ones with greater ardor and perseverance than for the others. I have often seen a gray vapor slowly rising over their empty silent tombs, which by the help of continued prayer grew brighter and brighter. The graves over which I saw columns of vapor more or less bright were shown me as those of such as are not entirely forgotten, not entirely bound—who by their own expiatory sufferings, or the help of their friends, are more or less consoled. They have still the power to give a sign of their participation in the communion of saints, they are increasing in light and beatitude, they implore that help they cannot render themselves, and what we do for them they offer to our Lord for us. They remind me of poor prisoners who can still excite the pity of their fellow-men by a cry, a petition, an outstretched hand.

A cemetery, such as I have described—with its apparitions, its different degrees of light and darkness—always seemed to me like a garden all parts of which are not equally cultivated, but some allowed to run rank. When I earnestly prayed and labored and urged others to the same, it seemed as if the plants began to revive, as if the ground were dug and renewed, as if the seed sprang forth under the beneficent influence of the rain and dew. Ah! if all men saw this as I see it, they would surely labor in this garden with far more diligence than I! Such cemeteries speak as plainly to me of the Christian zeal and charity of a parish, as do the gardens and meadows around a village proclaim the industry of its inhabitants.

God has often allowed me to see souls mounting joyously from purgatory to paradise. But as nothing is accomplished without pain and trouble, so too when praying for the dead, I was frequently terrified and maltreated by lost spirits, even by the demon himself. Loud noises and frightful specters surrounded me. I was pushed off the graves, tossed from side to side, and sometimes an invisible power tried to force me out of the cemetery. But God strengthened me against fear. I never recoiled one hair's breadth before the enemy, and when thus interrupted I redoubled my prayers.

O, how many thanks I have received from the poor, dear souls! Ah! if all men would share this joy with me! What a superabundance of grace is upon earth, but forgotten, despised, while the poor souls languish for it! In their manifold sufferings they are full of anguish and longing, they sigh after help and deliverance; yet however great their distress, they still praise our Lord and Savior, and all that we can do for them is a source of unending bliss.

WHAT *follows brings together numerous visions and experiences received by Anne Catherine during the time of All Saints and All Souls, 1819, on the theme of purgatory:*

I made a great journey with my guide, how I know not. At such times I neither know who I am nor how I exist. I follow unquestioningly—I look, and I am satisfied. If I happen to put a question and receive an answer, well and good; but if not, still I am satisfied.

We went over the city of martyrs [Rome], then across the sea and through a wilderness to a place where once stood the house of Anne and Mary, and here I left the earth. I saw innumerable cohorts of saints of endless variety, and yet in my soul—in my interior—they were all only one, all living and revelling in a life of joy, all interpenetrating and reflecting one another. The place was like a boundless dome full of thrones, gardens, palaces, arches, flower-gardens and trees, with pathways sparkling like gold and precious stones. On high in the center, in infinite splendor, was the throne of the Godhead.

The saints were grouped according to their spiritual relationship: the religious in their orders higher or lower according to their individual merits; the martyrs according to their victories; and laics of all classes according to their progress in the spiritual life, the efforts they had made to sanctify themselves. All were ranged in admirable order in the palaces and gardens, which were inexpressibly brilliant and lovely.

I saw trees with little yellow luminous fruits. They who were associated by similar efforts to sanctify themselves had aureolas of the same form, like a supernatural spiritual habit, and they were otherwise distinguished by emblems of victory, crowns and garlands and palms—and they were of all classes and nations. Among them I saw a priest of my acquaintance who said to me: "Thy task is not yet finished!" I saw, too, legions of soldiers in Roman costume, and many people whom I knew, all singing together. I joined in a sweet song with them. I looked down on the earth, which lay like a speck of land amid the waters; but where I was, all was immense. Ah! life is so short, the end soon comes! One can gain so much—I must not be sad! Willingly and joyfully shall I accept all sufferings from my God!

I went with my guide into a gloomy prison for souls, where I consoled on all sides. The souls were buried in darkness, all more or less so—some to the neck, others to the waist. They were in separate though adjoining dungeons, some tortured with thirst, others by cold, others by heat, unable to help themselves, sighing in uninterrupted torments. I saw numbers delivered, and their joy was inexpressible. They went forth as gray figures. They received for their short passage to a higher region the costume and distinctive marks of their state upon earth. They assembled in a vast place above purgatory enclosed as with a thorn hedge.

I saw many physicians received by a procession of physicians like themselves and conducted on high. I saw numbers of soldiers liberated, and the sight made me rejoice with the poor men slaughtered in war. I saw few female religious, still fewer judges; but led out by blessed nuns were numbers of virginal souls who had wanted only an opportunity to consecrate themselves to the religious life. I saw some kings of the olden times, some members of royal families, a large number of ecclesiastics, and many peasants, among whom I saw some of my acquaintance and others who, by their costume, seemed to belong to foreign lands. Each class was led on high and in different directions by souls of their own condition in life and, as they ascended, were divested of their earthly insignia and clothed in a luminous robe peculiar to the blessed.

I recognized in purgatory not only my own acquaintances but also their relatives whom, perhaps, I had never before seen. I saw in the greatest abandonment those poor, dear souls who have no one to think of them. Among those who forget them are so many of their brethren in the faith who neglect prayer! It is for such souls that I pray the most.

Now began another vision. All at once I found myself a little peasant girl just as in my childhood, a band on my forehead, a cap on my head. My guide took me to a luminous troop of blessed spirits coming down from heaven, shining forms with crowns on their heads. Above them hovered the Savior holding a white staff surmounted by a cross and banner. There were about one hundred spirits, most of them maidens, only one-third of them youths, all in royal robes sparkling with the various colors of their aureolas and presenting a most lovely spectacle. Among them were some conspicuous by their wounds, which shone with a rosy light.

I was greatly abashed when my guide led me to them, for I—poor little peasant girl—knew not how to act before kings and queens. But my guide said: "Thou canst be like them," and then, instead of my peasant dress, I was clothed in the white habit of a religious. I saw all around those who had assisted at my clothing in the convent, especially the deceased members of my own community. Then I saw many of the poor souls whom I had known in life, with whom I had had dealings, looking wistfully after me from purgatory, and I understood the difference between true and false sympathy. They followed me with sad eyes, repenting of many things now that I was forced to leave them. They were citizens of the little city.

Between Purgatory and Heaven • Work for Souls

FOR *some time previously to the feasts of All Saints and All Souls, 1820, Anne Catherine suffered in every member for the souls in purgatory, sitting up in bed whole nights and counting every hour. Like a child she was unable to help herself. Consumed with thirst yet unable to drink; ardently desirous of assisting the souls, yet feeling herself bound as it were in chains; tortured until she lost consciousness, yet preserving the utmost patience and tranquillity—thus she prepared for the feast of All Souls. On November 1, she said:*

I have had an indescribably great and magnificent vision, but I cannot well express it. I saw an immense table with a red and white transparent cover. It was laden with all sorts of dishes. They were all like gold with blue letters around the rim. Flowers and fruits of every description lay there together, not broken from their stems, but living, growing, and though consumed, eternally renewed—the mere sight of them gave strength.[1] Bishops and all their clergy who had had charge of souls appeared at the table as stewards and servers. Around it, seated on thrones or standing in half-circles were troops of holy ones in their choirs and orders. As I stood at the immense table, I thought the innumerable choirs around it were in one garden; but on looking more closely I saw that each choir was in a separate garden and at a separate table. All received, however, a part of everything on the great table. And in all the gardens and fields and borders, the plants and branches and flowers were living as on the great table.

---

[1] That is, one was nourished by merely gazing upon them; but the strength, the nourishment they imparted lay in the interior perception of their essence, in their signification. CB

The fruits were not eaten; *they were received by conscious perception of them.*

All the saints appeared with their various distinctive characteristics: many bishops had little churches in their hands, because they had built churches; and others, croziers, as they had only discharged their duties as pastors. By them were trees laden with fruits. I wanted so badly to give some to the poor that I shook them.[1] Quantities fell upon certain regions of the earth.

I saw the saints in choirs according to their nature and strength, bringing materials to erect a throne at one end of the table, and all sorts of garlands, flowers, and decorations for it. All was done with indescribable order, as is proper to a nature exempt from defect, sin, and death; all seemed to spring forth spontaneously. In the meantime, spiritual guards watched over the table.

Twenty-four old men now seated themselves on magnificent seats around the throne with harps and censers, praising and offering incense. An apparition like an old man with a triple crown and widespread mantle descended from on high upon the throne. In his forehead was a three-cornered light-mass in which was a mirror that reflected everything: everyone could see his own image therein. From his mouth issued a beam of light in which were words. I distinguished letters and numbers quite distinctly, but I have now forgotten them.

Lower down, in front of his breast, was a dazzlingly bright crucified youth, from whose wounds streamed forth arches of rainbow-colored light, which surrounded all the saints like a great ring and with which their own aureolas mingled and played in unspeakable order, freedom, and beauty. From the radiating wounds I saw a rain of many-colored drops fall upon the earth, like a shower of precious stones, each with its own meaning. I received then the knowledge of the value, virtue, secret properties, and color of precious stones, as also the properties of all colors in general.

Between the crucified youth and the eye in the forehead of the old man, I saw the Holy Spirit under a winged form, and rays streaming to it from both. Before the cross, but a little lower

---

[1] Her earnest prayers drew down to earth the fruits of heaven. CB

down, was the Blessed Virgin, surrounded by virgins. I saw a circle of popes, apostles, and virgins around the lower part of the cross.

All these apparitions as well as the myriads of saints and angels in circle after circle were in constant movement, mingling together in perfect unity and endless variety. The spectacle was infinitely richer and grander than that of the starry heavens, and yet all was perfectly clear and distinct—but I cannot describe it.

As has been said, Anne Catherine at this period was weighed down by sufferings for the poor souls. Fever produced in her violent thirst, which she refused to allay by a drop of water, that by this act of self-denial she might alleviate the pains of those poor sufferers. Although weak and exhausted to a degree, she exerted herself to relate the following:

I was taken by my guide, I knew not where or in what direction, but it was over a very difficult road, the ascent becoming steeper, the path narrower, until it led like a bridge of light to an immense height. Darkness lay to the right and left and the path grew so narrow that I had to go sideways. Below was the earth, shrouded in mist and obscurity, and humankind wallowing in misery and mire. Almost the whole night was passed in this painful ascent. I often fell, and I should certainly have been dashed to pieces had not my guide given me his hand and helped me continue on. It may be that we journeyed toward some point on the globe, for my guide pointed out certain places on our way wherein were accomplished various mysteries connected with the deliverance of God's people. I saw the countries over which the patriarchs and later on the children of Israel traveled. They seemed to spring forth from the darkness and grow distinct as my guide pointed them out, appearing as deserts, great ruined towers, huge bending trees, marshes, etc. He told me that when these countries shall again be cultivated and inhabited by Christians, the end of time will draw nigh.

Souls accompanied by their guides floated around us over the road, looking gray in the surrounding darkness. It was as though they appeared out of a broad stretch of night, moving toward this narrow, illuminated path upon which I was ascending with such difficulty, praying and entreating all the while. The souls did not come on the path itself but fluttered by on both sides and behind me the whole length of the way. They were souls lately deceased, for whom I had had to suffer and pray for some days past, as Saints Teresa, Augustine, Ignatius, and Francis Xavier had earlier appeared and exhorted me to prayer and labor, promising that on this day I should know for what end.

My road led to purgatory proper, which lay below us, and I saw the souls entering for a purgation of about eight days, some more, others less. This they owed to my prayers, which I still had to continue for them. I saw the planetary spirits, not yet damned, teasing and tormenting the poor souls, reproaching them, trying to make them impatient, etc.

The part I entered was an immense, skyless region covered with foliage as with an arch. There were indeed some trees, fruits, and flowers, but the place breathed an air of melancholy; in it there was neither actual suffering nor real happiness.

There were innumerable other sections separated by vapors, mist, clouds, or barriers according to the different degrees of isolation to which the souls in them were condemned. This region was one between purgatory proper and heaven. On my arrival I saw a number of souls flying out three by three, each set accompanied by an angel, to a place on which a glimmering of light descended from on high—all were uncommonly joyous. They shone with colored light which, as they mounted, became clearer and brighter.

I received an instruction on the signification of their colors: ardent love, which they had not practiced purely in life, emitted a red light that tormented them; the white light was that of purity of intention, which sloth had led them to neglect; green was that of patience, from which their irritability had led them far astray; but the yellow and blue I have forgotten.

As they passed me in threes, the souls saluted and thanked me. I knew many of them, mostly people of the middle class and peasants. I saw indeed some of the higher ranks, but only a few. Though one can scarcely speak of rank in the other world, yet those who have received a more polished education are easily recognized. There is an essential difference between races, as may be detected in these apparitions, as also between the sexes: strength, vigor, decision, distinguish the male sex, while the female may be known by something soft, receptive, impressionable—I cannot express it.

There are angels here who nourish the souls with the fruits of the place. These souls exercise an influence over purgatory and the earth and have too a consciousness of heavenly beatitude. Their longing and eager waiting for this forms their last purification.

Further on I came to a brighter region with more beautiful trees. There were angels going to and fro. I was told that this was the abode of the patriarchs before Christ's descent into hell, and I saw where Adam, Abraham, and John had been. I returned home by a fatiguing road to the left and passed by the mountain where I had seen a man tormented by dogs; but he was no longer there, he was now in purgatory.

The planetary spirits act in purgatory. They reproach the sufferers with their sins. The poor souls are informed by angels of what goes on in heaven and on earth relative to the affairs of salvation, and are visited also by souls from Abraham's bosom. The soul of a daughter who called me to comfort her mother was one of the latter. They cannot act themselves. In purgatory there are no natural productions, no trees, no fruits—all is colorless, brighter or darker according to the different degrees of purification. The abodes are disposed in order. In Abraham's bosom it is like the country, like nature. A soul in Abraham's bosom already possesses the faint colors of its future glory, which become resplendent on its entrance into beatitude.

Judgment takes but a very short time. It is held the instant the soul leaves the body and just over the place where death occurred. Jesus, Mary, the holy patron, and good angel of the soul are present. Mary is present even at the judgment of Protestants.

Some days later: I was thinking this evening that, after all, the poor souls are sure of what they hope for, but sinners are in danger of eternal damnation; and so I would pray for them rather than for the souls. Then St. Ignatius stood before me, having on one side a proud, independent, healthy man whom I knew, and on the other a man sunk to the neck in mire. This last uttered piteous cries, being wholly unable to help himself. He reached to me one finger. It was a deceased ecclesiastic, but a stranger to me. St. Ignatius said to me: "For which will you intercede—for this proud, wicked fellow who can do penance if he pleases, or for this poor, helpless soul?" I trembled and wept bitterly.

I was then taken by a painful road to purgatory, where I prayed for the souls, and afterward into an immense house of correction in my own country. There I saw numbers whom misery and seduction had drawn into crime. I was able to soften their hearts, but the wretches who had ruined them were hardened in their guilt. I went to other similar institutions, also to subterranean dungeons wherein were confined long-bearded men. Their souls were in a good state and they seemed to be doing penance. I consoled them. These places were shown me as terrestrial purgatories. Afterward I visited some bishops—one, a very worldly man, was giving a banquet to which even females were invited. I calculated the cost of the feast as well as the number of poor people it would have fed, and held it up before the bishop. He grew indignant, but I told him that it was all being recorded by an angel holding a book and a rod above him. He replied that it was nothing, that others did still worse. I saw that this was indeed true, but the chastising angel is everywhere.

In the midst of her painful spiritual labors for the suffering souls Anne Catherine had at the close of the octave a consoling vision in which she saw the effects of all the charitable works she had ever performed for them:

I was again in my father's house, and it seemed to me that I was going to be married. All the souls for whom I had ever prayed came with gifts of various kinds and placed them on the nuptial car. I could not make up my mind to take my seat in the coach and await the moment of departure, for I was confused at the sight of so many things; therefore I slipped under it and ran on before to the house in which the ceremony was to be performed. But in creeping under the car I soiled my white dress, which however I did not perceive until I had reached Martinswinkle. I was dreadfully annoyed when I caught sight of the stain. I knew not what to do. But Blessed Brother Nicholas [of Flüe] came to my aid and took it every bit out with a little butter.

The house of the marriage was none other than the school house to which I had gone in my childhood and which was now greatly enlarged and beautified. The two holy old nuns were to be my bridesmaids. Then came my Affianced and the bridal coach.

When I found myself in the school house, I thought: Here I am for the third time. The first time I was brought as a child to school, and on the way the Mother of God, with the little boy, appeared to me, promising that if I studied hard he should be my bridegroom; the second time was when, going to the convent, I was espoused in a vision in this same house; and now for the third time I was come to it for the marriage celebration. It was now magnificent and full of luscious fruits. The house and garden were elevated high above the earth, which lay dark and desolate below. I was told that my creeping under the bridal car signified death incurred by impatience before the completion of my task, and the consequent loss of much merit.

Some days later: I have had to go into several neglected vineyards and cover up the grapes from the frost. I went also to three vineyards in the neighborhood of Coblentz, where I worked hard. As I was thinking of applying to the poor souls for help, nine figures suddenly appeared around me with loads upon their backs, and a tenth laid down his and retired. I had to take on my shoulder and under my arm the long, heavy bundle and mount with the nine toward the east. The road was not an ordinary one; it shone with light and ran straight on in the midst of fog and darkness. I soon fell, unable to support the load, when a bank suddenly appeared on the roadside whereon I rested it. The bundle contained a great human form, the same that two days previously St. Ignatius had shown me sunk in the mire. I understood by the elector's cap fastened to his arm that he was one of the last electors of Cologne. The nine others were his running-footmen. Not being able to keep up with them, the elector had been dragged along by one of his men who, however, had grown weary of the task and handed it over to me.

Continuing our ascent we arrived at a large, wonderful place at the gate of which were spirits on guard. The nine entered without difficulty; but after my burden was taken from me and deposited in a safe place I was shown to the top of a rampart surrounded by trees. I could see all around upon an immense expanse of water full of hills and fortifications on which multitudes of souls were working. They were kings, princes, bishops, and people of other ranks, principally servants. Some of the kings had their crowns on their arms, and others again—the more sinful—had them fastened to their lower limbs. All were obliged to labor at the works, digging, hauling, climbing, etc. I saw some continually falling and climbing up again. The servants drove on their former masters. As far as one could see there was nothing but ramparts and waters, excepting the few sterile trees near me. I saw the elector, whom I had carried, working hard. He was condemned to dig continually under the earth. The nine spoke to me. I had to help them in something, but in what I cannot now remember. There were no females in this place. It seemed to be less dreary than purgatory, for here there was movement and life; here the souls labored, leveling and filling up. I was surprised to see no horizon, only the sky above, the laborers below, and to right and left a boundless expanse of space and water.

Opposite the last, another region, or sphere, was shown me peopled only by females. My guide bade me cross over the water to it, but I knew not how. He said: "Obey by thy faith!" and at once I began to spread my cloak on the water to cross on it, when lo! a tiny raft appeared that bore me over without rowing. My guide floated by me just skimming the waves.

In the sphere to which I was now introduced was a huge square dwelling full of females of all classes, even nuns, some of whom I knew. They had numerous gardens to cultivate, and here too the former mistresses were ordered about by their maids. The souls dwelt in bowers, and at the four corners of the abode floated four spirits on guard; they had little watch houses hanging from the branches of high trees. All kinds of fruit were cultivated here by the souls, but on account of the clouds and fog it does not ripen.

What the souls here gained was handed over to some little, deformed creatures whom I saw wandering around in another region among huge icebergs. Rafts laden with this fruit were sent to them. They picked it over and, in their turn, passed on the best of it to souls in another place. Those on the iceberg were the souls of barbarians, of nations never Christianized. The women asked me what year it was and how affairs were progressing on earth. I told them, and also that I thought very few would join them in the future on account of the great sins committed on earth. I cannot remember what else I did there.

I returned by a narrow descending path and saw the mountain of the prophets, on which everything seemed even more flourishing than usual. There were two figures occupied under the tent with the books: one laid aside the fresh rolls of parchment, the other erased certain passages from them.[1] As I glanced down I saw the tops of the highest mountains on the globe, the rivers looking like silver threads, and the seas glistening like mirrors. I recognized forests and cities. I descended at length near the Ganges. The road behind me looked like a slender beam of light which, like a lambent flame, was soon lost in the sun's bright rays. The good Hindus, whom I saw recently praying before the cross, had constructed for themselves in wicker-work a very beautiful chapel covered with verdant foliage in which they met for divine service.

Thence I went to Persia, to the place where Jesus taught shortly before his crucifixion. But nothing remains of it now, excepting some fine fruit trees and the traces of a vineyard which Our Lord himself had planted. Then I went to Egypt through the land in which Judith dwells.[2] I saw her castle and I felt that she sighs more ardently than ever to become a Christian.

I pursued my wonderful journey over the sea into Sicily, where I found many places laid waste and deserted. I crossed a mountain chain not far from Rome and saw in a sandy plain near a forest of fir trees a band of robbers about attacking a mill. As my guide and I drew near, one of them was seized with fright and cried out to his companions: "Such fear comes over me! I feel as if someone were behind us!"—and with that they all took flight. I am so worn out by this journey, especially with dragging that heavy soul, that I am aching all over. I saw and did extraordinary things, but many of them I have now forgotten.

On the last day of the year: I settled up accounts with myself for the closing year. I saw how much I have lost, how much I have to repair. I saw my own misery and wept bitterly over it! I had also many pictures of the poor souls and of the dying. I saw a priest

[1] See "The Mountain of the Prophets" in *First Beginnings*.
[2] See "Judith" in *Scenes from the Lives of the Saints*.

who died yesterday evening at nine o'clock, a most pious, charitable man who nevertheless went to purgatory for three hours because he had lost time in jesting. He was to have remained for years, but numerous masses and prayers had shortened his punishment. I saw his sufferings during the three hours. When he was delivered I almost laughed to hear him say to the angel: "Now I see that even an angel can deceive. I was to have been here but three hours, and yet I have been so long! so long!"—I know this priest very well.

On June 29, 1821, the pilgrim, unknown to her, attached to Anne Catherine's dress a little parcel containing the hair of a deceased woman and that of her two children, one having died without baptism a few hours after its birth, the other at the age of two months after receiving the sacrament. Next day she spoke, as follows:

I have seen the life of Peter and scenes from that of Mary Mark. At the same time I had another picture of some poor souls to whom I was powerfully drawn, but whom I could not reach. I wanted to help a mother and her two children, but I could not. The mother was in a deep abyss to which I could not approach, and she spoke in a hollow, smothered voice scarcely intelligible. The children were in another sphere, to which I had access. One was baptized and I could speak to it; it belonged to a higher sphere and seemed to be only on a visit in the place in which I saw it. When I tried to go to the mother it seemed as if I became too heavy, I sank down unable to move. I tried every means of assisting her by prayer and suffering but I could not go to her.

I saw into a vast, dark region, a world of fog in which are many spheres. The souls here confined are in restraint, pain, and privation, the necessary consequences of their earthly imperfections and transgressions. Some are in bands, others solitary. Their abodes are dark and foggy, more or less dense, damp or parched, hot or cold, with various degrees of light and color—the whole lit up by a glimmer of morning twilight. The children are nearest the entrance. The unbaptized suffer chiefly from their connection with sin and with the impurity of their parents; the baptized are free and purified. One can approach the souls only by grace, meditation, prayer, good works, the merits of the saints, and sometimes by some good trait in their (the souls') own life on earth. The clearest idea one can form of their state is from those houses of correction that are conducted according to rules of perfect justice, in which the punishments inflicted in satisfaction exactly correspond to the faults committed.

Let us imagine our corporeal separation set aside, so that one can act in and for the other, and we may possibly gain some idea of the manner in which one can satisfy for, can deliver, another. The poor captive can do nothing but suffer; he is what a diseased or paralyzed member is to the body. But if the veins and nerves that connect it with the body are not entirely dead, the suffering of the affected part awakens a sympathetic chord in the other members, which immediately seek to relieve their afflicted neighbor. As one enters such a house only by the intervention of friends and officials, and yet can by his own petitions, labor, payment of debts, etc., obtain pardon and again lead a happy life; as they who are confined in deep dungeons can make their voices heard at a distance, though the sound be dull and muffled—so in some respects can the same be done by the poor souls in the other world.

On earth all is mingled with sin, lying, and injustice; but in purgatory's abodes of purification whatever tends to console and assist the poor inmates is executed with the most rigid and impartial justice. There is as much difference between the two as between the currency of earth and that of heaven. I made many attempts to understand the soul and to help her and her children; but, when I thought I was about raising her up, something always prevented me. At length I persuaded Mary Mark to go with me (for the vision of these souls was always accompanied by another of the feast of St. Peter and Mary Mark). She did so, and by her merits I was enabled to draw nearer to the poor souls. I received also information respecting a poor unburied child whom I must have interred at the pilgrim's expense. The woman's soul stands in need of this good work. She told me also what else was to be done for her besides continual prayer. I shall notify the pilgrim of it in good time.

Next day, a poor woman of Dülmen came begging money to bury her child, aged three years. The pilgrim gave the necessary sum and Anne Catherine furnished the linen, which good work was offered for the benefit of the soul mentioned above:

I was again with the poor mother and her little child, the latter of whom I had to clothe; but it was so weak as to be unable to sit upright. I put on it a little dress given me by a lady, the Mother of God, I think. It was white and transparent and seemed to have been knit in stripes. I felt much ashamed, I know not why, unless it was of those who so neglected the little one. Before this, the poor little thing could not stand, but now it went to a feast and played with the other children. The place in which this scene was enacted, and in which the mother then was, was better, brighter, than the one in which I had first seen them. (This vision took place after the burial of the child above spoken of.) The mother thanked me, but not as we do in this life. I did not hear, I merely felt. Great trouble is necessary to reach such souls, for they can do nothing of themselves. If one of them could spend only a quarter of an hour on earth it could shorten its punishment by many years.

Some days later: I had to work in the cathedral cloister of Münster, washing with great fatigue altar linen brought me by the priests of the whole country around. Clare of Montefalco, Frances of Rome, Louise, and other deceased nuns of our convent helped me. My share of the work was the starching and bluing. As my fatigue was great, I was continually running to look at the clock. Then came a poor soul whom the pilgrim had recommended to my prayers. She gave me a little hourglass that she took from her side, saying that she found it frightfully heavy. When I took it from her she seemed unspeakably relieved and overjoyed to get rid of it. It did not seem to me to be so heavy, and I returned to my work thinking I could sell it for the benefit of the poor, when lo! my washing was all spoiled! I began to feel impatient, when the soul hastily returned and whispered in my ear: "Gently, gently! you have still time enough!" She begged me earnestly to go on quietly with my work, as if my impatience would do her much harm. She left me, and I contentedly returned my washing. I made over the spoiled starch so that I was able to use it. Again, I felt my eagerness return and a desire to look at the time, but I repressed it. The clocks were symbols of time and patience. The poor soul was relieved by my quietly continuing my work, and when I took her hourglass, her time no longer seemed so heavy.

During the first week of July, 1821, a poor woman of Dülmen in the pangs of childbirth sent to implore Anne Catherine's prayers; the latter beheld the woman's alarming condition and ceased not her supplications that the unborn babe might receive baptism. The nurse hesitated, but at last baptized the child, which next day came into the world lifeless; the poor mother died about a week later. The child appeared to Anne Catherine on the 8th, lovely and radiant with light. It greeted her familiarly, thanked her for its baptism, and said: "Without it I should now be with the pagans." Some time later, Anne Catherine said:

All sorts of people, long since deceased and whom I once knew, came to beg my help. They took me to dark corners of fields where they had various tasks to perform but which they never could finish, as certain tools were wanting. All cried to me to help them. With great fatigue I had to do this or that piece of work for them, mostly field labors, whereby they were relieved. After each task I returned home, but only to set out again for another. I worked also for the clergy in their vineyards, which were so full of sharp stakes that one could not move without hurting one's self. I slipped and a stake ran into the calf of my leg, which bled profusely.

Concerning Some Jews

LAST night I worked hard for the poor souls and also for the Jews, both living and dead. My first assistance was given in a case of great misery. The soul of one of my country-women claimed my aid. I saw her being horribly scourged and maltreated. I heard her cries but could not go to her. It seems she had had a good, pious, but rather simple daughter whom she had been in the habit of abusing cruelly; and for this she was now being punished. I suffered long for her. I must now find some means to rouse up the daughter, who is still alive, to pray for her mother's soul.

Yesterday, I saw a Jewish wedding, but I cannot now recall it. (There had been one in the city.) Last night the soul of a poor Jewess came and took me around to exhort her brethren to be converted and amend their life.

Then Anne Catherine recounted various scenes in which Jews —living and dead, known and unknown—figured, and whom she visited in far-off lands even in Asia and near Mt. Sinai.

Anne Catherine entered the store of a Jewess of Coesfeld. She was busily arranging her goods, mixing up laces and linen of infer-ior quality with the superior in order to deceive customers. This fraud Anne Catherine prevented by perplexing the woman in such a way that she could not find what she was seeking, could not open the drawers, etc. Greatly disquieted, she ran in tears to her husband who on hearing her trouble decided she had committed some sin—yielded to some bad thought perhaps—for which she must do penance. Then Anne Catherine received a certain power over her. She spoke to her conscience and made her feel so sensibly the wrong she was about to do that the woman cried out to her husband for assistance and consolation. He ran to her, saying: "Now, do you not see that you did something wrong?"—and the wife resolved to give a quantity of old linen and other alms to poor Christians in expiation of her fraud. She thus obtained pardon for many other sins. Anne Catherine continued:

I was taken by the soul of the old Jewess to the abode of Jewish souls to help and comfort many poor creatures belonging to Coesfeld, some of whom I knew. It is an isolated place of purgation, quite separate from that of Christians. I was deeply touched at seeing that they are not eternally lost, and I beheld their various pitiable conditions. I saw a poor but uncommonly pious Jewish family who used to trade in old silver and little crosses—as goldsmiths do—and who now had to work incessantly, melting, weighing, and filing. But not having the implements necessary, they could never finish anything and so were obliged to continually begin all over again. I remember making a bellows for them, and I spoke to them of the messiah, etc. All that I said, the old Jewess repeated and confirmed. I saw some of them swimming in blood and entrails, which produced an ever-abiding loathing; others running without a moment's rest; some dragging heavy loads; others constantly rolling and unrolling packages; and others, again, tormented by bees, wax, honey—but it is inexpressible!

I visited all the Jews of this city. I went by night into their dwellings. The rabbi was perfectly inflexible, petrified as it were. He possesses no bond of grace. I could in no way approach him. Mrs. P. is chained down by the firm, fundamental principle that it is a sin even to think upon Christian truths. One must repel such thoughts at once, she thinks. The nearest to Christianity is the big

Jewess who sells meat. If she were not such a cheat, she would receive still more grace. But no one sympathizes with these people. I stood at her bedside and tried to influence her; I told her many things. She awoke in fright and ran to her husband, saying she thought her mother had appeared to her. She was in great agony of mind and she resolved to give an alms to poor Christians.

I was also among some Jews in a large street where none but their race reside. Very many of them are good and pious. Some are quite rich and distinguished. They have quantities of gold and jewels concealed under their floors. I could do them no good. I went also to Thessalonica. In another great Jewish city I met many pious Jews whom later I saw assembling together and speaking as if the messiah had come. They communicated to one another their various emotions and projects. I was also among some Jews who lived in caves near Mt. Sinai and committed numerous robberies and cruelties in the country around. I had to frighten them—perhaps for the sake of the Christian pilgrims as well as for that of the inhabitants of the place.

A Gray, Sad-Looking Soul

I SAW a peasant woman returning from a village fair and a soul approaching and whispering something into her ear. The soul was a gray, sad-looking figure. The woman shuddered, seemed annoyed, and tried to believe it all imagination. She went into a room to speak to her servant, the soul still pursuing her with its remonstrances. Next morning she went again to the fair. Then the gray, sad-looking soul came and addressed me in a hollow, deep voice that sounded as if it came from the depths of a well, but in few words full of meaning. I understood that he was the peasant woman's deceased husband, who was detained a captive because he had been in a fold in which the sheep went not to true pasturage; they knew not their pastor, they could receive nothing from him.

It is a terrible thing to live in such misery and blindness through the fault of one's ancestors, and to see it clearly only after death! He had been commissioned by God to remonstrate with his wife and warn her not to follow the advice of false friends and enter into a lawsuit that would only result in the loss of her house and farm, and reduce her daughter to poverty. She had married her son to the sister of a widow with whom she had so entangled her affairs that she was about to begin a suit fatal to her credit and property. The soul could find no rest until he had dissuaded her from such a course; but unhappily, he was in so restrained a state that he was unable to do more than disquiet her by interior reproaches. He continued his efforts, but as yet with little success, for his wife attributed her uneasiness to imagination, disclosed it to no one, sought distraction in weddings, baptisms, and festivities, and harkened to domestics cunningly urging her on in her false step rather than to her honest neighbors. No blessing fell on her household, since she stifled the voice of conscience and confessed not her sins. Grace comes to such a soul only by the way of penance.

"For a long time," said her husband, "I have disquieted my unhappy wife, but she yields more and more to the influence of the widow who is leading her to ruin. She will not listen to me and when she cannot restrain her anxiety she runs to the stable or meadow, visits her flocks, or engages in some manual labor. You have prayed lately for my poor wife, you have prayed so fervently that God has heard you, and in virtue of the cruel sufferings you offered for her today I have been allowed to come to beg you to help me. I shall now take you to my son, that you may speak to him—for I am bound, I cannot do it myself. He may perhaps be able to change his mother's mind, for he is good and simple-hearted, and he will believe us."

Then I accompanied the soul, first to the fair, where his wife was sitting with her companions. He went up to her, whispered into her ear that she must absolutely free herself from all connection with the widow and not risk body and soul, goods and property, in an unjust lawsuit. She grew uneasy, left her companions abruptly, and sought to divert herself elsewhere. The husband told me that the foolish woman was on the point of beginning the suit, but that he would not desist from his efforts, since his sufferings and privation of light in the other world would be greatly prolonged by his wife's perversity; for through his fault the affairs of the family had often been very badly administered.

Then he took me to his son by a long dreary way over a broad pool of raging waters. The danger was great, anguish and peril encompassed us, and I was worn out by fatigue and alarm. The soul was at my side but his voice sounded hollow and as if far off in the distance. As we passed certain fields and cottages, he told what danger threatened them and on account of what sins. He urged upon me the necessity of prayer and told me what to do.

When we had crossed the water, the road ran north through a desolate region until we reached the son's cottage. We entered and went straight to his room. He was seized with fright (I think he saw his father's spirit) but he soon recovered himself. I exhorted him to pray more earnestly and pointed out what he should do regarding his mother's business affairs. I explained to him that his father's soul was not at rest, that he, the father, could not himself actually address his mother, but that he, the son, should do it and tell her the cause of his father's disquietude. I told him other important things that I now forget. The son is a good, simple-hearted young man with a round face and slightly turned-up nose. He was much affected, very desirous of doing right, and distressed at his mother's state. His simplicity was truly touching.

Then I saw the effect of my words in a far-off picture. The son called his wife from her spinning and she came, ungraciously enough, still holding her distaff. He told her what had just happened and begged that his mother might be released from the lawsuit. I heard the wife remark: "We shall take from her even the gown on her back!"—whereupon the young husband went on his knees, begging that they would at least leave her two fields, or farms, that I saw hanging like islands in the air. Then I heard the wife reply: "Since you are so good and honest, I shall leave your mother one gown if I can."

From that moment things took a turn: the widow's affairs inclined to the dark side with herself, and the peasant woman was freed from her evil influence. The latter remained poorer indeed than before, but in far better dispositions among the peasants of the parish, against which the widow had begun the iniquitous suit. I shall often have to accompany the poor soul of the husband in whose distress and unavailing efforts there was something truly affecting. I could not approach the woman; she seemed to be surrounded by a lake in whose waters she was about to be engulfed.

Clothing for Souls

DURING *the first week of October, 1821, Anne Catherine labored hard and unremittingly for the poor souls, suffering at the same time intense pains in the abdomen:*

I was in a dark place with souls of non-Catholics who were in need of something I had to supply. They entreated me to make and have made for different poor people some articles of clothing, the materials for which I was to beg. The articles were shown me and I was told where to get materials. At first I declined, but the poor souls were so pressing that I consented. It has proved a very difficult task.

For several days Anne Catherine was very busy cutting out clothes for the poor in the midst of excruciating pains and incessant interruptions and annoyances from visitors. But she calmly overcame every feeling of impatience, as the pilgrim tells us in his notes for October 4th:

"Although suffering intense pains in the abdomen, Anne Catherine has been all day cheerful, patient, and kind. Visits that could not be declined have greatly fatigued her, without however ruffling her serenity. She speaks kindly of all that have wearied and annoyed her."

She herself says: Again I have been busy with the poor souls, and I know exactly what articles are needed—I have seen their shape and size as well as the materials required. I have been told to ask the pilgrim to contribute to the work. I went to the poor souls on my journey to the nuptial house, in one of whose fields I had to weed. I found there the big cook with an iron girdle around her waist from which hung spoons, ladles, and other kitchen utensils. My pains were intense, but as my confessor had ordered me to bear them, I kept quiet. Toward midnight they became still sharper, and I saw something like a horrible figure casting itself upon me. I sat up in bed and cried with simple faith: "Be off! What do you want with me? I have no need of you! My confessor has given me my orders!" Instantly the pain ceased, and I rested quietly till morning.

On October 10th, the clothing demanded by the holy souls was finished and Anne Catherine received instructions regarding its disposal. On October 7th, the pilgrim had made the following entry:

"Anne Catherine prepared all the articles requested by the holy souls, although she knew not as yet for whom they were destined. When she sent to purchase the materials, she knew exactly where they could, or could not, be procured."

Other Works for Souls

FOR *several nights [says the pilgrim toward the close of October, 1821], Anne Catherine has had, on account of the approach of All Souls, to work hard for the poor souls—some known, others unknown to her. She is often requested by them, or by their guardian angels, to do such or such a thing in satisfaction for their shortcomings, and sometimes she is commissioned to exhort the living to certain good works. The soul of a woman appeared to her begging her to inform her daughter that some of the property she then possessed had been dishonestly acquired by her grandparents. To do so, Anne Catherine had to take a long journey through the snow. She remembers also a wonderful spiritual church in which she had to serve mass and distribute the holy communion to some souls. She says:*

I was very much frightened, although I took the host in a linen cloth. I felt that I, a woman, dared not do it, and even the serving of mass gave me great uneasiness, until the priest turned around and told me very earnestly that I must do it. In him I recognized the deceased Abbé Lambert. He was perfectly luminous. I do not remember the vision very well, nor do I understand it.

On the morning of October 25th, the pilgrim found Anne Catherine greatly distressed and terrified:

Last night I had a frightful vision that still haunts me. As I was praying for the dying, I was taken to the home of a wealthy lady who I saw was about to be damned. I struggled with satan by her bedside, but in vain; he pushed me back—it was too late! I cannot express my grief on seeing him carry off the poor soul, leaving the body a distorted, frightful carcass—for so it looked to me. I could not approach it. With the angels I could only gaze upon it from on high.

The woman had a husband and children. She passed for a worthy person according to the world; but she had maintained illicit communications with a priest, and this sin of long standing she had never confessed. She had received the last sacraments. All praised her edifying preparation and resignation; and yet she was in mental agony on account of her concealment in confession. Then the devil sent to her one of her friends, a miserable old woman, to whom she expressed her anxiety; but the friend urged her to banish such thoughts and beware of giving scandal. The old woman told her not to worry over the past, that she had received the sacraments to the great edification of her friends, and that she must not now excite suspicion by sending again for the priest, but go in peace to God.

After this harangue, the old woman left the room and gave orders that the dying woman should not be disturbed. The unhappy woman, so near her end, still dwelt with pleasure on the thought of the priest, the accomplice of her guilt. As I drew near I found satan under the form of this priest praying by her. She herself prayed not, for she was dying full of bad thoughts. The accursed one prayed in the words of the Psalms: *Let Israel hope in the Lord, for in Him is mercy and plentiful redemption,* etc. He was furious with me. I told him to make a cross over her mouth, which I knew he could not do; but all my efforts were useless—it was too late, no one could reach her, and so she died!

It was horrible, satan carrying off her soul! I wept and cried. The miserable old woman returned, consoled the relatives, and spoke of her beautiful death. As I was crossing the bridge on my way from the city, I met some people going to see the dead woman. I thought: Ah! had you seen what I did, you would fly far from her! I am still quite sick, I am trembling in every limb.

A Dying Nun and a Dying Author

SCARCELY *had Anne Catherine finished the above when she begged to be left alone. They were calling her, she said; she saw something, she must pray—and the pilgrim, seeing in her countenance that look of abstraction he so well knew, drew the curtain in front of her bed and left her. That afternoon, she related what follows:*

76

This morning when I asked to be left alone, I saw a dying nun who could not receive holy viaticum, as the sacristy key was lost. She was in a suppressed convent in which some members of the community still remained, but in secular dress. The others lodged in the neighboring town, which had a mixed population of Catholics and Protestants. They often visited their former companions and gossiped and drank coffee at the bedside of the sick one, who now lay at the point of death and longing for the blessed sacrament. Divine service was still held in the church of the convent and the blessed sacrament kept there.

At the time of which I speak, some careless nun had mislaid the key of the sacristy. The priest came to administer to the dying sister, but there was no admittance! The whole house was thrown into confusion, a general search was instituted, the nuns ran talking here and there, and at last the priest went away. I saw it all, and I also saw that the nun was absolutely dying, though none knew it. My guide ordered me to pray, and I remember not how, but the key was immediately found in a crevice near the fireplace, where a sister had laid and forgotten it. The priest was recalled, the sacraments administered, and the nun died. I did not know the religious, nor do I now remember where it all took place.

In the same city in which the unhappy lady died I attended the deathbed of an author. The good man had written some things against his conscience, but of which he had quite lost sight. He had confessed and received all the last sacraments and was now left alone by the advice of some individuals inspired by the enemy of souls. Then satan suggested to him all kinds of thoughts calculated to drive him to despair, filling his imagination with images of people who reproached him with the harm done by his writings. He fell into an agony of despair, and so was about to die abandoned by all.

Then it was that my guide took me to him. I had by my prayers to disquiet his confessor and make him hurry back to the dying man. The latter recognized him, but begged not to be disturbed, as he had business with the people present. The priest, seeing that he was delirious, sprinkled him with holy water and made him kiss something that he wore around his neck. The dying man recovered his senses and told the priest the mental anguish that had so suddenly come upon him. This time the Accursed One was caught in his own net, for had he not driven the man to despair he never would have recalled what now troubled him. He had his papers hunted up, the priest put them in order before witnesses, and the man died in peace.

Journey Through Purgatory

I CANNOT say exactly where purgatory lies. But when going there I generally journey northward for awhile when leaving the earth by a gloomy, difficult road of water, snow, briars, swamps, etc. I descend by dark, aerial paths, as if far under the earth, to dismal places of different degrees of cold, fog, and obscurity. I go around among souls in higher or lower positions, of more or less difficult access. Last night I went among them all, consoling them and receiving their commissions for various labors. I had to say right off the *Litany of the Saints* and the *Seven Penitential Psalms*. My guide warned me to guard carefully against impatience. The other morning I almost forgot his admonition and was on the point of yielding to impatience, but I repressed it. I am very glad I did so, and I thank my good angel for helping me. No words can say what immense consolation the poor souls receive from a little sacrifice, a trifling self-victory.

For fourteen days, Anne Catherine had been constantly occupied with the poor souls, offering for them prayers, mortifications, alms, and spiritual labors, and arranging numerous things to be given away on the feast of All Souls. She related the following:

I went again with the saints to purgatory. The prisons of the souls are not all in the same place, they are far apart and very different. The road to them often lies over icebergs, snow, and clouds; sometimes it winds all around the earth. The saints float lightly by me on luminous clouds of various colors, according to the different kinds of help and consolation their good works entitle them to bestow. I had to travel painful, rugged paths, praying the while and offering it all for the souls. I reminded the saints of their own sufferings, and offered them to God in union with the merits of Jesus Christ for the same intention.

The abodes of the souls differ according to each one's state, yet they all struck me as being round like globes. I can compare them only to those places that I call gardens and in which I see certain graces preserved like fruits. So too are these sojourns of the souls like gardens, storehouses, worlds full of disagreeable things, privations, torments, miseries, anguish, etc., and some are much smaller than others. When I arrive I can clearly distinguish their round form and perhaps a ray of light falling upon some point, or twilight on the horizon. Some are a little better than others, but in none can the blue sky be seen—all are more or less dark and obscure. In some, the souls are near one another and in great agony; some are deeper down, others higher and clearer.

The places in which souls are separately confined are also of various forms—for instance, some are shaped like ovens. They who were united on earth are together in purgatory only when they have need of the same degree of purification. In many places the light is colored—that is, fiery or of a dull red. There are other abodes in which evil spirits persecute, frighten, and torment the souls, and these are the most horrible. One would take them for hell, did not the inexpressibly touching patience of the souls proclaim the contrary. Words cannot describe their consolation and joy when one among them is delivered. There are also places for penitential works—as those in which I once saw them raising and storming ramparts, the women on the islands cultivating the fruits that were taken away on rafts, etc. These souls are in a less suffering state; they can do something for others worse off than themselves. It may be symbolical, but it is symbolical of truth.

The vegetation is scanty and stunted, the fruits the same; yet they afford relief to those still more needy. Kings and princes are often thrown in with those whom they once oppressed and whom they now serve in humble suffering. I have seen in purgatory Protestants who were pious in their ignorance; they are very desolate, for no prayers are offered for them. I saw souls passing from a lower to a higher grade to fill up the vacancies left by some who had finished their purgation. Some can go around giving and receiving consolation. It is a great grace to be able to appear and beg help and prayers. I have also seen the places in which some souls canonized on earth were purified; their sanctity had not reached its perfection in their lifetime.

Journey on Behalf of Souls

I WENT to many priests and churches and ordered masses and devotions for the souls. I was at Rome in St. Peter's, near noble ecclesiastics—cardinals, I think—who had to say seven masses for certain souls. I know not why they had omitted doing so. While they were being said, I saw the neglected souls, dark and sad, gathered around the altar; they exclaimed, as if hungry: "We have not been fed for so long, so long!" I think it was Foundation masses that had been neglected. The confiscation of Foundations for masses for the dead is, as I see, unspeakable cruelty and a theft committed against the poorest of the poor.

On my route I saw few if any of the living, but I met souls, angels, and saints, and I saw many of the effects of prayer. During these days, I have had to drag to the confessional and to church many people who otherwise would never have gone.

Anne Catherine spent the whole day in prayer for the souls and recited for them the Office of the Dead. The wounds in her breast and side bled so copiously that her garments were saturated. When the pilgrim visited her in the evening he found her in ecstatic prayer. About half an hour after, her confessor entered the room. Anne Catherine suddenly left her bed, walked with a sure, firm step to the astonished Father, and, prostrating at his feet, attempted to kiss them. Father Limberg drew back in confusion but at last yielded to her desires; then kneeling, she begged his blessing for herself and the souls with her. She remained thus in prayer several moments, again asked a blessing for the souls, and rising, returned quickly to her bed. Her forehead was bathed in perspiration but her countenance glowed with joy. She was in ecstasy. The next day, when the pilgrim related to her the scene of the preceding evening, she could scarcely credit what she heard, although she distinctly remembered that some souls—former penitents of Father Limberg—had begged her to kiss his feet and ask him for his benediction. Of this, Anne Catherine said:

It was very painful to me that he showed so much reluctance and did not rightly understand me; besides, as he did not give the blessing with firm faith, I still had something to do last night for the souls.

Return to Purgatory

LAST night I had much to do in purgatory. I went northward and, as it seemed, around the pole of the globe. I saw the icebergs above me; and yet, purgatory does not appear to be at the center, for I can see the moon. In going around among the prisons I tried to make an opening, that a little light might enter. The outside looks like a shining black wall in the form of a crescent; inside are innumerable chambers and passages, high and low, ascending and descending. Near the entrance it is not so bad, for there the souls are free to move around; but further on they are more strictly imprisoned. Here lies one stretched as it were in a hole, a ditch; there several are together in different positions, higher and lower; sometimes one is seen seated on high as if on a rock. The further we penetrate, the more frightful it becomes, for demons there exercise their power. It is a temporary hell in which souls are tormented by horrible specters and hideous forms that wander around, persecuting and terrifying their victims.

I see also in purgatory a place of devotion, a sort of church in which the souls at times receive consolation. They turn their eyes wistfully toward it as we do to our churches. The souls are not helped directly from heaven. They receive relief only from earth from the living, who can discharge their debts by prayers, good works, acts of mortification and self-renunciation; but above all by the holy sacrifice of the mass offered to the Judge.

Leaving this place, I went northward over the ice to where the earth's circumference decreases,[1] and I saw purgatory as one sees the sun or moon very low on the horizon. Then we passed over a cylinder, a street, a ring [she could not find the right word] and came to another part of purgatory semicircular in shape. Some distance to the left is the mill.[2] To the right are works and entrenchments along which the souls must run, as I have seen before.

---

[1] I saw the earth in darkness, and more like an egg than a globe. Toward the north the descent is the steepest; it seems longest toward the east. The perpendicular descent is always toward the north.

[2] See pp. 84, 95–96, for more on this mill.

I never see any visitor in purgatory, excepting my guide; but away off on the earth I behold here and there anchorites, religious, and poor devout people, praying, doing penance, and laboring for the dear souls. This part of purgatory belongs to the Catholic Church. The sects are separated here as on earth, and they suffer much more, since they have no members praying for them and no holy sacrifice. The souls of males may be distinguished from those of females only on close examination. One sees figures, some darker, some brighter, the features drawn with pain, but at the same time full of patience. The sight of them is inexpressibly touching. Nothing is more consoling than their gentle endurance, their joy at the deliverance of their fellow-sufferers, their sympathy in one another's pain and for all newcomers. I have seen children there, too.

Most of the souls are expiating their levity, their so-called small sins, their neglect of trifling acts of condescension, of kindness, and of little self-victories. The connection of the souls with earth is something very sensitive inasmuch as they experience great relief from even an ardent desire formed by the living to soothe and lighten their pains. O how charitable is he, how much good does he not do, who constantly overcomes self for them, who longs ever to help them!

I have been in a region before purgatory, in the ice country near the mill in which princes, kings, and rulers have to grind, as formerly they made men and horses do. They have to grind ice and all sorts of choice food and precious objects that women bring to the mill, and that when ground are thrown to the dogs. Their former servants are now their task-masters.

Anne Catherine spoke of the road by which she went to purgatory, and the countries through which she passed. She seems to have traveled through Asia toward the north pole, passing through the ancient land of Jamshid into another, in which rises a lofty mountain full of monkeys large and small. When it is too cold for them on one side of the mountain they scamper to the other. She afterwards came to a land whose inhabitants are clothed in skins:

They are a long-haired race who live miserably and are drawn by dogs whose instincts are so sharp that they may be entrusted with whole sledges of merchandise, which they convey in safety to their destination without a driver. There are both whites and blacks here, but the latter are not natives. The inhabitants hunt small, long-bodied animals for the sake of their fur. These animals have long ears and short legs and are not so pretty as those at the foot of the mountain of the prophets. They are found still further north. There is here a region of marshes and deserts, which is a little warmer, as if the morning sun sometimes shone upon it. I saw some of the animals I have just mentioned running around, and here and there little people with flat noses. The vegetation is scanty.

Anne Catherine went on to describe the country, but not as inhabited—all was dark and foggy in the black distance. Passing over the metal or brass street or ring—as she called it[1]—she reached purgatory, under which is hell, deep down toward the center of the earth:

On such journeys the moon appears to me very large and full of cavities and volcanoes; but all on it is stony, like coral trees. It both attracts and discharges quantities of vapor, as if absorbing fluids, to pour them forth again. I never saw people like ourselves on the moon, or in any of the stars, of which many are like dead, burnt-out bodies. I saw souls and spirits in them, but no beings like men.

Behind this, all was dark and gray, but Anne Catherine knew not what this might signify. Neither could she clearly make out whether the city she saw was ideal, or real, though she thought the former more likely, as there was some marvelous sepulchral aspect to it. And yet at the same time she described this region as laid out with many different roads bearing some relation to human beings. In one way or another she always depicted this region as inclining downward along a gutter, perhaps into some deep declivity at the pole:

From those people living in the extreme parts I came to the pole over [great fields of] ice, whereas on the other side [of the pole], where there was more warmth, the ice melted and dripped by day, only to freeze again at night. The animals hunted by the people to the south would flee to this region, seeking out a warm defile, a valley or mountain-ridge that stretched toward the west,

---

[1] The German word used here could also be rendered as "gutter" or "drain."

coming in the evening to diminutive, flat-nosed men who make use of them, using their furs also as clothing. These people live north of us.[1]

After crossing this valley—which was perhaps several miles wide—I came to the metallic ring or gutter, which is quite narrow (by comparison). Far off to the west lay the mill, to the right the city and its environs, and falling away steeply before me purgatory, under which, in the depths—as it seemed—lay hell, again opposite me in the center of the earth. Animals could not reach the eastern side, and on the far side of the pole was a wasteland of ice where no human beings have ever been. In this region I often saw a great, fiery sky, and other times a most complete darkness.[2]

Some Other Lessons

I KNOW not where I have been nor why I had the following vision: I was taken into a beautiful mansion in which a lady showed me exquisite pagan statuary belonging to her husband. We descended, passing through doorways so low that we were obliged almost to creep through them. The statues grew uglier and uglier as we descended, becoming at last quite horrible. Then came a gentleman who took me through galleries of the most lovely pictures, each more beautiful than the last. I often thought: "Ah! If the pilgrim could only see this!" The longer we stood gazing at them, the more exquisite their loveliness became. At last we left the place, and I had another vision:

I saw a Protestant with his Catholic wife going through room after room filled with works of art. He pointed out the vaulted halls with their treasures of paintings and curiosities, in which he took the greatest delight. I heard the wife say that he practiced idolatry toward all these things, that he should rather think upon God and the Church. The husband replied that it was his opinion that God loves every honest man—religion being but a second-

---

[1] Here the word Greenland stands in the notes, followed by a question mark.

[2] Perhaps the northern lights.

ary consideration. The wife replied that it is not so, adding that when near him she felt her faith weakened, but that one lesson of her youth (here she named it) she had ever carefully practiced.

Then I saw her take him into a vault in which his ancestors were entombed. The hollow but powerful voice of one of them now sounded from a tomb containing but mould and dust, and for a long time addressed the husband in broken words. It was in the gentleman's power, he said, to make good what he himself had neglected in life—he had the means, nothing prevented him. Then he spoke of the domain he had forcibly wrested from its rightful owner, of his falling off from the Church, of the numbers who followed his example, and of the misery and confusion it had entailed. Balls, amusements, the fine arts were not the things for his descendants; his people would be given over to the wolves, which would tear them to pieces and fatten on their substance. Therefore, he should hearken to his commands, restore the true faith, and give back to the Church what belonged to her. If he delayed this work of restitution he would lose all his wealth and nothing would remain to him but the dust of the tomb.

During this long discourse, in which the whole family history was set forth, the gentleman swooned repeatedly, and more than once tried to make his escape; but his wife held him tenderly in her arms, encouraging him to remain and hear all. I have forgotten what followed and I know not what fruit the exhortation produced. The father of the gentleman, who I think already had two children, was still alive, but imbecile. This son was soon to take entire charge of the family estate. He was fondly attached to his wife, who had great influence over him. I had this vision in the morning when I was perfectly awake.

Souls of Fanatics

I HAVE been to purgatory, where I saw several members of Mme. Krüdener's sect,[1] some of the late martyrs. They were not in the purgatory of Catholics but in places like ditches below or

---

[1] Baroness Barbara Juliane von Krüdener (1764–1824), Baltic German religious mystic and author.

around it, some at the bottom, others nearer the top. They had been led into error by ignorance. They could speak to the poor Catholic souls, whom they earnestly implored to warn their friends on earth of their errors—that thereby they might return to the Church. But the souls replied that they could do nothing, that only the living can pray and work and have masses said.

Anne Catherine seemed to be charged with their deliverance, for she enjoined upon all to whom she gave alms to hear holy mass, and she also procured masses to be said.

I was told how the devil had urged on these people to those frightful murders and crucifixions. He rendered them insensible to pain. I saw that many of them are eternally lost. I learned also that a still more subtle sect is about to be formed (that of Hennhoefer). I saw that some of the demons whom Christ chained on his descent into hell have been let loose, and that this sect was raised up by them. I saw that some are let loose every second generation.

Heaven and Hell

Angelic Hierarchies • Heavenly Bodies

AT *the time of the feast of the Guardian Angels, 1820, Anne Catherine received the following far-reaching visions:*

I saw a church on earth and in it many whom I knew. Above were several other churches, higher and higher, like different storeys of a tower, filled with the angelic choirs; and higher still was the Blessed Virgin surrounded by the highest order, before the throne of the Most Holy Trinity.

Here above, heaven upon heaven was filled with the purest of angels, and throughout reigned indescribable order and activity. But below in the earthly Church all was drowsy and negligent to a degree. And this was the more remarkable as it was the feast of the Angels, who bear up to God with incredible swiftness every word pronounced carelessly and distractedly by the priest in the holy mass, and who repair all defects in the service offered to God.

At the same time I saw the guardian angels discharging their duties with surprising activity, chasing evil spirits from men, suggesting good thoughts, and presenting before them inspiring imaginations. They long for God's commands, and the prayers of their clients render them still more zealous. I have seen that every person receives at birth two spirits—one good, the other evil. The good one is heavenly by nature and belongs to the lowest hierarchy; the evil one is not a devil, not yet in torments, though deprived of the vision of God.

I always see in a certain circle around the earth nine bodies or spheres, separated one from another, like far-off stars. They are inhabited by spirits of different natures, from whom descend beams of light, every ray falling upon some determinate point on the earth with which I have always thought they must have some communication.

These nine worlds form three sections, above each of which I saw a great angel enthroned: the first holds a scepter, the second, a rod, the third a sword. They wear crowns and long robes, and their breast is decorated with many ribands. In these spheres dwell the bad spirits who at each man's birth are associated to him by an intimate relation which I clearly understand, which excites my wonder, but which I cannot now explain. They are not lovely and transparent like the angels. They shine it is true, but by an external, unsteady light, as if by reflection. They are either slothful, indolent, fanciful, melancholy, or passionate; violent, obstinate, stubborn, or frivolous, etc.—as though they are personifications of the different passions. They appear in colors, and among them I have remarked the same tints I see among men in their sufferings and interior struggles, and in the aureolas of the martyrs, whose passions purified by torments have been changed into colors of triumph.

These spirits have something sharp, violent, and penetrating in their countenance. They attach themselves with extraordinary tenacity to the human soul—as insects to certain odors and plants—rousing in them all kinds of thoughts and desires. They are full of stings, of rays, of seductive charms. They themselves produce no act, no sin, but they withdraw man from the divine influence, lay him open to the world, intoxicate him with self, bind him, attach him to the earth in many ways. If he yields, he plunges into darkness, the devil draws near and marks him with his seal—some act, some sin, akin to a birth—and thereby is his separation from God effected.

I have clearly seen that mortification and fasting weaken the influence of these spirits and facilitate that of the angels, while holy communion is the most effectual means of resisting them. I have seen that certain inclinations and aversions, certain involuntary antipathies—and especially the disgust we have for certain things, such as insects, reptiles, vermin, etc.—have a mysterious signification, since these creatures are images of those sins and passions to which, through their connection with these spirits, we are the most exposed. I was told that when one feels disgust for such things, he should recall his sins and evil propensities symbolized by them.

I have seen such spirits presenting to people in church all sorts of toys and trinkets, filling their heads with all sorts of thoughts and desires, while their angels are busy recalling them to better things. I cannot relate all these endlessly manifold pictures. The great ones of the earth are attended by the most powerful both of the good and bad spirits. I have often seen a man receive a higher and more powerful guardian when called to great things. I have seen the angels that protect the fruits of the earth spreading something over the trees and plants and over cities and countries. I have seen angels hovering over them, guarding and defending them, and sometimes abandoning them.

I cannot say what myriads of bad spirits I have seen—had they bodies, the air would be darkened. Wherever they have most influence, I always see mist and darkness.

Often have I seen how someone receives another guardian angel when some new protection may be called for—just so, have I myself had on more than one occasion a different guide.

As Anne Catherine finished the relation of the above, she stammered, her fingers twitched, and she fell silent, remaining thus for perhaps four minutes. It was as though she were beholding something most grave. Then she exclaimed with a sigh:

It is from so great a distance that they come! Those cruel, obstinate, violent spirits there descending, come from an immense distance!

Then, coming to herself again, she said: I was carried up to a great height and from the most distant of the nine spheres I saw a multitude of those violent, obstinate spirits descending toward a country to which strife and war are approaching. They come to the great ones of this world, making approach to them almost impossible. But I saw too a whole army of angelic spirits sent down to earth by the Blessed Virgin; they were led by a great angel burning with zeal and bearing a flaming sword. They will fight against the perverse spirits.

Such things as these Anne Catherine beheld all through the night, after which she said: There are, also, souls neither in heaven, purgatory, nor hell, but wandering the earth in trouble and anguish, aiming at something they are bound to perform. They haunt deserted places, ruins, tombs, and the scenes of their past misdeeds. They are specters. The variety to be perceived among the spirits is astounding, as is the order that obtains among them.

On another occasion, she said: I have often understood, in my childhood and later, that three whole choirs of angelic spirits—higher than the archangels—fell, but all were not cast into hell. Some, experiencing a sort of repentance, escaped for a time. They are the planetary spirits that come upon earth to tempt men. At the last day they will be judged and condemned. I have always seen that the devils can never leave hell. I have seen too that many of the damned go not directly to hell but suffer in lonely places on earth.

If men make progress in the spiritual life they receive guardian angels of a higher order, such as kings and princes have. The four-winged angels, the Elohim, who distribute God's graces, are Raphiel, Etophiel, Salathiel, and Emmanuel.

There is much greater order even among the bad spirits and demons than there is on earth. Whenever an angel withdraws, a devil steps instantly into his place and begins his own work. Great order reigns also among the planetary spirits, who are fallen spirits, but not devils. They are very, very different from devils. They go to and fro between the earth and the nine spheres. In one of these spheres they are sad and melancholy; in another impetuous and violent; in a third light and giddy; in a fourth stingy, parsimonious, miserly, and so forth. They exert an influence over the whole earth, over every man from his birth, and they form certain orders and associations.

In the planets I saw forms resembling plants and trees—but light and unsubstantial, like mushrooms. There are, also, waters on them, some clear as crystal, others muddy and poisonous. And it seemed to me that each planet contains a metal. The spirits make use of fruits adapted to their own nature. Some are an occasion of good, inasmuch as man himself directs their influence to good. Not all the heavenly bodies are inhabited; some are only gardens or storehouses for certain fruits and influences. I see places in which are souls who, although not Christian, yet led good lives on earth. They are now in uncertainty, feeling that some day or other their lot will change; they are without joy or pain. Like the others, they feed upon certain fruits.

The moon is chilly and rocky, full of high mountains, deep cavities, and valleys. She both attracts and repels the earth. Her waters are constantly rising and falling, drawing up masses of vapor from the earth, which like great clouds fill up the hollow places; again they appear to overflow and gravitate so powerfully upon the earth that men become melancholy. I see in her many human figures flying from light into darkness as if hiding their shame, as if their conscience were in a bad state. This I see more frequently in the center of the moon. In other parts are fields and thickets in which animals roam. I never saw any worship offered to God on the moon. The soil is yellow and stony; the vegetation like pith, fungi, or mushrooms. The moon exerts a wonderful influence over the earth and all nature. Men regard her so wistfully because one naturally turns to what belongs to him. I often see descending from her huge clouds like masses of poison that generally hang over the sea; but the good spirits, the angels, scatter them and render them harmless. Certain low districts on the earth are cursed on account of sin there committed, and over them I see falling poison, darkness, fog. The noblest races live in the most highly favored regions.

The souls that I see hiding in darkness seem to be without suffering or joy, as if imprisoned till the day of judgment. The moon's light is dull, of a bluish white, and the farther from the moon, the brighter it becomes. Comets are full of baneful influences; they are like birds of passage. Were there not between them and the earth so great tempests and other influences, exercised by the spirits, they might easily do the latter much harm. They are the abodes of the passionate spirits. Their tail—that is, their influence—follows as smoke from fire.

The milky way is formed of watery globules like crystals. It seems as if the good spirits bathe therein. They plunge in and pour forth all kinds of dew and blessings like a baptism. The sun follows an oval path. It is a beneficent body peopled by holy spirits. It has no heat in itself; light and heat are generated only around it. It is white and lovely and full of beautiful colors.

Many of the heavenly bodies are still uninhabited. They are beautiful regions awaiting a future population, gardens and storehouses of certain fruits. One can understand it only by representing to one's self a state perfectly well-regulated, a city, or a great, wonderful household in which nothing is wanting. Of all these bodies none has the grandeur or the internal force of the earth. The others possess certain special properties but the earth comprises them all. The sin of Eve made us fall, but we can now become conquerors, for the poorest saint has a higher rank than the highest angel.

Anne Catherine related these things with the simplicity of a child describing its garden. She continued:

When a little girl, I used to kneel out in the fields at night in the snow and look up joyously at the beautiful stars. I said to God: "Thou art my true Father, and Thou hast such lovely things in Thy house—now, then, show them to me!" And He took me by the hand and showed me everything—it all seemed perfectly natural. Full of joy I gazed at everything. I cared for nothing else.

Hell

A SHORT time later *Anne Catherine related further details regarding hell, as follows:*

As I was once very much disgusted and discouraged on account of the miseries around me and my own personal pains and troubles, I sighed: "O that God would grant me even one single day of peace, for I live as if in hell!"—and then came a severe reprimand from my guide: "That you may no more compare your state to hell, I shall show you hell," and he led me toward the north by the side on which the earth makes a steep declivity. First we mounted high in the air. I felt that the mountain of the prophets was on my right to the east, above which still further eastward I saw paradise. I was carried northward over steep paths of ice until we reached a horrible region. I felt that we had gone all round the earth, to the steep descents on the north. The way down to hell was wild, dark, and icebound. When I reached the abode of terror, I felt as if I had come to a lower world. I saw a disc, a section of a sphere; and when I think of what I there beheld, I tremble in every limb. I saw everything in confusion: here a fire, there smoke, everywhere pitchy darkness—a land of unending torments.

Archangel Michael
and the Heavenly Spheres

SOME *time later, Anne Catherine related the following, leading up to a grand vision, beginning with the Archangel Michael:*

I went up steep heights to an aerial garden. I saw on the north-eastern horizon, rising like a sun, the figure of a man with a long, pale face, his head covered with a pointed cap. He was strapped with ribands and had a shield on his breast whose inscription, however, I have forgotten. He bore a sword laced with many-colored ribands. He rose slowly and floated gently over the earth. He waved his sword from right to left and cast the ribands, which interlaced like nets, over some sleeping cities. Upon Russia, Italy, and Spain he scattered pustules and boils, laid a red noose around Berlin, and from there came on to us. The sword was naked. Blood-red streamers like the intestines of animals floated from the hilt, and blood dripped over our land. The figure flew in a zig-zag course.

Off in the southeast rises an angel. In one hand he bears a naked sword, in the other a scabbard full of blood which he pours out on the countries over which he flies. He comes here too and pours blood over the cathedral-place in Münster.

I had many wonderful visions of the feasts and apparitions of the Archangel Michael. I was in many parts of the world, and I saw his church in France on a rock in the sea. I saw him as the patron of that country. I saw how he helped the pious King Louis to gain a victory. On a command from the Mother of God, Louis had invoked Michael and placed his picture on his standard. He also founded an Order of Chevaliers in his honor. I saw Michael take the tabernacle from his church and carry it away, and I also saw an apparition of him in Constantinople and many other places, all of which I cannot now recall. I saw the miracle of the church on Mount Gargano. A great feast was being celebrated. It was attended by a great concourse of pilgrims, their robes tucked up and knobs on their staves. The angel served at the altar with the others.

Here Anne Catherine recounted the miracle of Mount Gargano pretty much as related elsewhere,[1] *adding that the site of the church had been designated by a figure traced on the rock with a chalice in his hand. She continues:*

Then I went with the Archangel Michael to Rome, where there is a church commemorative of one of his apparitions. I think it was built under Pope Boniface and upon a revelation from the Mother of God. I followed him everywhere as he floated above me, grand and majestic, holding a sword and girt round with cords. A dispute was going on in his church. Numbers were engaged in it, most of them Catholics, though not of much account; the rest were Protestant sectarians. It seemed as if they were arguing some point of divine worship. But the angel

---

[1] The Sanctuary of Monte Sant'Angelo sul Gargano, sometimes called simply Monte Gargano, is a Catholic sanctuary on Mount Gargano, Italy, in the province of Foggia, northern Apulia. It is the oldest shrine in Western Europe dedicated to the Archangel Michael and has been an important pilgrimage site since the early Middle Ages. There are three sections to the legend, recording three apparitions by Michael: the first and third sections appear to be part of the same narrative, while the second is possibly the account of a battle half a century later. According to the first and last parts of the legend, around the year 490 the Archangel Michael appeared several times to the bishop of Sipontum near a cave in the mountains, instructing that the cave be dedicated to Christian worship and promising protection of the nearby town of Sipontum from pagan invaders. These apparitions are also the first appearances of Saint Michael in western Europe. The second section of the text describes Michael's intercession on behalf of the Sipontans and the Beneventans against invading pagan Neapolitans. On the eve of the battle, Michael appears with flaming sword atop the mountain; the Sipontans and Beneventans are victorious. In commemoration of this victory, the church of Sipontum instituted a special feast on May 8 honoring the archangel, which then spread throughout the Catholic Church during the ninth century.

Monte Sant'Angelo was a popular pilgrimage site on the way to Jerusalem; pilgrims traveled from as far as the British Isles to visit the "Celestial Basilica." Among the pilgrims who visited the Saint Michael Archangel Sanctuary were many popes (Gelasius I, Leo IX, Urban II, Alexander III, Gregory X, Celestine V, John XXIII as Cardinal, John Paul II), saints (Bridget of Sweden, Bernard of Clairvaux, Thomas Aquinas); and emperors, kings, and princes (Louis II of Italy, Otto III, Henry II, Matilda of Tuscany, Charles I of Naples, Ferdinand II of Aragon). Francis of Assisi also visited the sanctuary, but, feeling unworthy to enter the grotto, stopped in prayer and meditation at the entrance, kissed a stone, and carved on it the sign of the cross in the form "T" (tau).

descended and scattered the crowd with his sword, leaving only about forty persons, who went on with the service very simply.

When all was over, Michael took up the tabernacle with the most holy sacrament and flew away. My guide ordered me to follow. I did so, flying just below the archangel toward the east, until we reached the Ganges, when we turned more to the north. On one side lay the mountain of the prophets, and there our road began to descend, becoming colder, darker, wilder, until we arrived at a vast plain of ice. I was seized with terror in this solitude; but some souls appeared to encourage me, among them my mother, Antrienchen, old Soentgen, and others.

We came to an immense mill through which we had to pass, and here the souls of my friends left me. The ice kept constantly cracking, the water foamed, and again I was seized with fear, but my guide gave me his hand and reassured me.

The water that turned the mill ran under the ice, and it was warm. The mill was full of great lords and rulers of all nations and periods who were condemned to grind without intermission toads, serpents, and other disgusting and venomous reptiles, as well as gold, silver, and all kinds of costly objects which, when thus deprived of their baneful properties, fell into the water and were borne away to shore. The lords took turns and worked like servants. They had constantly to sweep the horrid things under the millstone; otherwise they would have been much annoyed. The mill appeared to me to be a place of penance for such princes as had involved the affairs of their own and of other states, and had introduced institutions whose pernicious consequences are still felt. Their souls cannot attain beatitude while such consequences exist. These consequences now come to them under the form of hideous reptiles whose destruction will prevent their propagation. The warm water in which all was ground flowed back into the world, carrying with it nothing hurtful.

As we passed through, one of the souls approached us and quickly swept the reptiles under the millstone, that we might not tread on them. The soul spoke to me, explained the nature of the place, and expressed his own and his companions' satisfaction at our coming that way, as our footsteps loosened a little of the enormous mass of ice; for, until the whole disappeared, would they have to grind. We left them, crossing the ice-sea through a deep furrow (it had such cracks here and there) and then for a time ascended an iceberg, glad to leave behind us a tolerably long track for the poor grinders.

As we mounted, I beheld the Archangel Michael floating above me. The sky became clearer and of a more beautiful blue, and I saw the sun and the other heavenly bodies as I had seen them before in a vision. We went around the whole earth and through all the celestial worlds—in which I saw innumerable gardens with their fruits and signification. I hope some time to be allowed to enter, for I want to get medicines and recipes to cure pious sick people. I saw the choirs of the blessed, and sometimes—here and there—a saint standing in his sphere with his own distinctive insignia.

Still soaring upward, we arrived at a world of unspeakably wonderful magnificence. It was shaped like a dome, like an azure disc, surrounded by a ring of light above which were nine other rings, on every one of which rested a throne. These circles were full of angels. From the thrones arose many-colored arches filled with fruits, precious stones, and costly gifts of God, which met in a dome surmounted by three angelic thrones. The middle one was the Archangel Michael's. Thither he flew and placed the tabernacle on top of the dome. Each of the three angels, Michael, Gabriel, and Raphael, stood severally over a part of the dome formed by three of the nine angelic choirs, and four great, luminous angels, veiled with their wings, moved constantly around them. They are the Elohim: Raphael, Etophiel, Emmanuel, and Salathiel—the administrators and distributors of God's superabundant graces, which they receive from the three archangels and scatter throughout the Church, to the four points of the compass. Gabriel and Raphael were in long, white robes like a priest's. Michael wore a helmet with a crest of rays, and his body seemed encased in armor and girt with cords, his robe descending to the knees like a fringed apron. In one hand he held a long staff surmounted by a cross under which floated the standard of the lamb; in the other was a flaming sword. His feet also were laced.

Above the dome lay a still higher world in which I saw the Most Blessed Trinity represented by three figures: the father, an old

man like a high priest, presenting to his son on his right the orb of
the world; the son, who held a cross in one hand; and to the left of
the father stood a luminous winged figure. Around them sat the
twenty-four ancients in a circle. The cherubim and seraphim,
with many other spirits, stood around the throne of God hymning
incessant praise.

In the center above Michael stood Mary surrounded by innumerable circles of luminous souls, angels, and virgins. The grace
of Jesus flows through Mary to the three archangels, each of
whom radiates three kinds of gifts upon three of the nine lower
choirs. These in their turn, pour them forth upon all nature and
the whole human race.

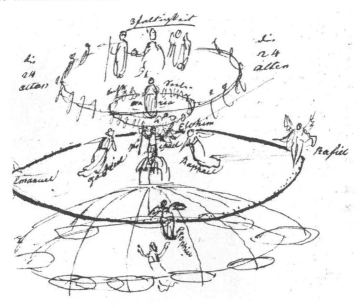

As the tabernacle reposed there, I saw it—by the influx of grace
descending upon it from Mary and the cooperation of the whole
heavenly court—increase in size until it became first a Church and
then a great Shining City that slowly sank to the earth. I know not
how it was, but I saw multitudes of living beings, first only their
heads and then the whole figure, as if the earth on which they
stood were drawing near to me, and at last they were suddenly
landed in the New Jerusalem, the New City that had descended
upon the Old Jerusalem, and that had now come upon earth. And

here the vision ended. I plunged again into the darkness and directed my way homeward.

I had then a picture of an immense battle. The whole plain was a mass of dense smoke and the bushes were full of soldiers who kept up an incessant fire. The place lay low, and there were great cities in the distance. When all seemed lost, the Archangel Michael, at the invocation of one of the leaders, swept down with a legion of angels and the victory was instantly gained.

Anne Catherine knew not the time of this battle, although she said it would happen in Italy not far from Rome, where many ancient things would be destroyed and many holy things—unknown till then—would come to light.

Further on the Trinity

THE feast of Candlemas was represented to me in a great picture, but one very difficult to describe, although I recollect much of what I saw. I saw a feast being celebrated in the Church, transparent and floating above the earth, as I always am shown the Catholic Church when I am to contemplate it—not as some particular local church, but as the Universal Church itself.

I saw this Church filled with choirs of angels surrounding the Most Holy Trinity. Since, however, I saw the Second Person of that Trinity being presented and redeemed in the Temple—incarnate in the form of the infant Jesus and yet present in the Trinity—it seemed to me, as it did a short time ago, that the child Jesus was sitting near me and comforting me at the same time that I saw a vision of the Holy Trinity.

I saw the appearance of the Word become flesh, the infant Jesus, at my side, connected with the vision of the Trinity as it were by a path of light. I could not say: "He is not there, since he is with me." Nor could I say: "He is not with me, since he is there." And yet in the instant when I had a vivid sensation of the child Jesus being near me, the representation of the Most Holy Trinity was shown to me, but in a different form from that in which I see it when it is a picture of the Godhead alone.

I saw an altar appear in the center of the Church—not an altar like those in our churches today, but just an altar. On this altar stood a little tree of the same kind as the tree of knowledge in the garden of Eden, with broad hanging leaves. Then I saw the Blessed Virgin rise before the altar with the infant Jesus in her arms as if she had come up out of the earth; and I saw the tree on the altar bow before her and then wither away.

Then I saw a great angel in priest's vestments, with only a ring round his head, approach Mary. She gave him the child, whom he placed on the altar, and in the same moment I saw the child thus offered up pass into the picture of the Holy Trinity, which I now saw once more in its usual form. I saw too that the angel gave the Mother of God a little bright globe surmounted by the figure of a child in swaddling-bands, and that Mary floated with this gift towards the altar. I saw crowds of poor people coming to her from all sides bearing lights: she handed all these lights to the child on the globe, into whom they passed. And I saw a light and a radiance being thrown by these lights on Mary and the child, illuminating everything. Mary had a flowing mantle that spread over the whole earth.

The picture was then transformed into a festal ceremony. I think that the withering of the tree of knowledge at Mary's appearance, and the passing of the child on the altar into the Holy Trinity signified the reunion of humankind with God. That is why I saw all the scattered individual lights handed to the Mother of God and given by her to the child Jesus: for he was the light enlightening all humankind, in whom alone all the scattered lights became one light to enlighten the whole world, symbolized by the globe, the orb of a king. The lights presented to the Blessed Virgin signified the blessing of the candles at today's feast.

Habitations of the Heavenly Jerusalem

Little Caspar and the Children's Heaven

ON *January 8, 1820, Dean Overberg had sent to Anne Catherine by Father Niesing a reliquary in the shape of a tower, which the reverend gentleman carried under his arm from Münster to Dülmen. Anne Catherine knew nothing of the precious present destined for her, and yet she beheld Father Niesing journeying with a white flame under his arm. She said*:

I was surprised that it did not burn him, and I could scarcely restrain a laugh at seeing him so perfectly unconscious of the many-colored flames like the rainbow that he was carrying with him. At first I saw only the colored light, but as he drew near I saw the vase also. He carried it past my lodgings and all through the town. I could not understand it, and it made me sad when I thought he was going to carry it away by the other gate. The relics it contained attracted my attention. I felt that there were some very ancient ones and some of a more recent period which at the time of the Anabaptists had been removed from their shrines.

The next day Father Niesing delivered the reliquary to Anne Catherine. She received it with expressions of joy and gratitude and, on January 12th, related the following vision respecting one of the relics it contained:

I saw the soul of a youth approaching me under a luminous form and in a robe something like that of my guide. A white aureola surrounded him and he told me that he had gained heaven by self-denial and victories over his own nature. It had even been a help to him to refrain from gathering roses, which he very much loved.

Then through a further alteration of my consciousness I was immersed in another vision. I beheld this soul as a boy of thirteen, playing with his companions in a beautiful, large pleasure garden. He wore a plaited hat with a tail, a tight yellow jacket open in front, the sleeves trimmed around the wrist. His small-clothes and stockings were all in one and laced tightly up the side with another color; he wore knee-buckles and shoes strapped with ribands.

The garden hedges were neatly trimmed, and scattered round were many rustic ornaments and summerhouses, square outside and round within. There were also orchards, and at work in them men clothed very much in the way I used to dress up the shepherds for our Christmas crib in the convent.

The garden belonged to distinguished people of the neighboring city—which was of some importance in the region—and was open to the public. The boys dashed gaily along gathering red and white roses from the numerous rose hedges; but the spirit youth of whom I speak overcame his desire to do the same, whereupon his companions teased him by holding their great bouquets under his nose.

Here the blessed spirit said to me: "I was prepared for this little victory over self by one much greater. I had a playmate, a beautiful little girl—one of our neighbors—whom I dearly loved with an innocent affection. My pious parents often took me to hear a sermon, and once the preacher warned his congregation against such intimacies. And so I did violence to my feelings, shunned the company of the little girl, and from this victory gained strength to renounce the roses."

As he spoke, I saw the little maiden, delicate and blooming as a rose, walking in the city. I also saw the handsome house of the youth's parents situated in a large business square, in which was a fountain enclosed by a beautiful iron railing artistically wrought in life-size figures. From the center of the basin arose a figure from which spouted the water. At the four corners of the square were little buildings like sentry stalls. The city lay in a fertile region bounded on one side by a ditch and on the other by a tolerably large river. I cannot say exactly where it was, but it looked like a German city. It had about seven churches, but no remarkable steeple. The roofs of the houses were slanting, the fronts square with covered archways.

The youth's father was a rich cloth and wine merchant. Before his house stood wagons laden with merchandise. I entered and saw the father, the mother, and several children—a pious Chris-

tian household. The father, a tall, stout man, was elegantly dressed and wore a leathern purse at his side. The mother, a strong, stately lady above middle height, was dressed in red and brown with a rich, though odd-looking head-dress. Her hair was rolled above her forehead and fastened by a silver clasp; on the back of her head was a pointed cap of broad lace from which hung wide ribands. The youth was the eldest of the children.

The picture changed and I saw the youth sent to study in a solitary convent about twelve leagues from the city on a mountain covered with vineyards. He was very industrious and so full of confidence in the Mother of God that, when he found something too difficult in his books, he turned earnestly to his picture of Mary. "Thou didst teach thy Son," he would say, "thou art my mother also. O then, teach me too!"—and Mary used to appear and help him out of his difficulty. He was full of simplicity and confidence. His piety won for him the esteem of all who knew him, but his great humility would not allow him to enter the priesthood.

After three years in the convent, the last of which was passed on a sickbed, he died and was buried. He was only in his twenty-third year.

Among his acquaintances was a man of about thirty years who often fell into sin from his unbridled passions. He had great confidence in the deceased, and several years after—having come to pray at his grave—the youth appeared to him, exhorted him to good, and told him to look on his corpse for a certain mark which he gave him as a sign that he had really appeared to him. The mark was on his finger in the form of a ring he had received at his betrothal to Jesus and Mary. The friend reported what had happened, the body was disinterred, the mark found, and the finger taken off to be preserved as a relic. The youth has never been canonized. He reminded me very much of St. Aloysius Gonzaga in his ways.

The youth took me to a place like the heavenly Jerusalem, for it was all shining and transparent. We went to a great circular place surrounded by beautiful, sparkling palaces. In the center stood a large table covered with dishes perfectly indescribable. From four of the palaces stretched arches of flowers that united above the table in a magnificent crown around which sparkled the names of Jesus and Mary. It was not a production of art, it was all alive and growing, each part producing fruit according to its kind, the arches formed of most varied flowers, fruits, and shining figures. I knew the signification of each and every one, not only symbolically but as a substance, an essence that penetrated and enlightened the mind like sunbeams—but I cannot express it in words. On one side, a little beyond the palaces, stood two octagonal churches: one was Mary's, the other the Christ child's.

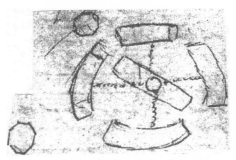

As I approached, there floated from all parts of the shining palaces—even through the walls—innumerable souls of deceased children who came to bid me welcome. They appeared at first in the usual spiritual form, but afterward were shown me as they were during life. I recognized several of my playmates long since dead. Among them was little Caspar, Diericke's little brother, a frolicsome, though not a bad child, who had died in his eleventh year after a long and very painful illness. He showed me all around and explained everything. I wondered to see naughty little Caspar now so fine and beautiful. I expressed my surprise at being there, when he said: "Yes, your feet have not brought you here; it was your good life!"—and this gave me great joy.

As I did not recognize him right away, he said: "Don't you remember how I sharpened your knife once? I overcame myself in that, and it turned out to my own good. Your mother had given you something to cut, but your knife was too dull; you cried, for you were afraid your mother would scold. I was looking on, and my first thought was: Now, let's see what her mother will do to her! But my second thought was: I'll sharpen the poor little thing's knife. I did it. I helped you, and all for the good of my own soul.

"Do you remember the day when the children were playing so naughtily? You said it was a wicked game, they must not play it, and then you went and sat down by the ditch and cried. I went to you and asked why you would not play with us. You answered that someone had led you away by the arm. I thought it over and resolved not to play such games any more, and that too was for my own good.

"And do you remember the day we all went together to gather fallen apples? You said we ought not to do it, but I replied that if we did not take them others would. Then you said we must never give any one a subject for scandal, and you would not touch them. I remarked that also and drew a lesson from it.

"One day I threw a bone at you, but something drew you suddenly aside from the stroke, and that went to my heart."

And so little Caspar went on recalling all sorts of incidents by which I saw that we receive for every victory over self, for every good action, a special reward, a certain kind of food that we eat in this sense—*that we have the full perception of it.* It shines through us. But it is inexpressible! We did not sit down at the table, but floated from one end to the other, tasting a particular enjoyment for every act of self-renunciation. A voice was heard proclaiming: "Only those can comprehend this nourishment who partake of it."

The food consisted for the most part of marvelous flowers, fruits, sparkling stones, figures, and herbs of quite another—a more spiritual—substance than those here below. They were served in glittering, transparent dishes of indescribable beauty, and furnished wonderful strength to those who—by such or such an act of renunciation performed on earth—were brought into a certain relation with one or another of them. The table was covered with little crystal, pear-shaped glasses, like those in which I used to receive health-giving beverages, out of which we drank. The glasses look like this: ⸽. One of the first dishes was marvelously prepared myrrh. On a golden plate stood a small covered cup on which was a knob surmounted by a delicate little crucifix, like this:

Around the rim of the plate were violet-blue letters that I could not make out, but I will understand them after a while. From the plate grew the most lovely bunches of myrrh, yellow and green, in the form of pyramids, reaching to the top of the cup. There were tiny, crisp leaves with blossoms like carnations of uncommon beauty, above which was a red bud surrounded by the most exquisite violet-blue flowers.

The bitterness of the myrrh was changed for the spirit into a wonderful aromatic and strengthening sweetness. I shared in this dish because of the bitterness of heart I had silently borne all my life. For the fallen apples that I would not touch I now received a whole branch of apples glittering with light, and I had a dish also for the quantities of dry bread I had distributed to the poor. It looked like sparkling colored crystals shaped like loaves of bread. The plate likewise was of crystal. For shunning the improper game I received a white robe. Little Caspar explained everything to me as we went around the table.

I saw intended for me a little stone on a plate I had once received in the convent, and I was told that before my death I should receive a white robe and a stone on which would be inscribed a name which only I could read. At the end of the table the love of one's neighbor received its reward—white robes, white fruits, great white roses, and all kinds of wonderful dishes and objects of dazzling whiteness. I cannot describe them.

Then little Caspar said: "Now, you must see here what we have in the shape of cribs, for you always loved to play with them," and we all went to the churches, first into that of the Mother of God, in which the sweetest singing was constantly going on. In it was an altar upon which all the scenes from Mary's life were inces-

105

santly succeeding one another, and all around, row above row, were crowds of worshippers. We had to pass through this church to reach the little crib that was in the other church, the church of the Christ child. In it also was an altar upon which was a representation of his birth and successive scenes of his life up to the institution of the blessed sacrament, as I always see them in vision.

Here Anne Catherine interrupted her narrative to exhort the pilgrim to labor more ardently at his salvation, to do what he can today, not to put off till tomorrow, for life is so short and judgment rigorous! Then she continued as told below.

The Garden of a Higher Heaven

FROM the church I mounted to a higher region, to a garden full of magnificent fruits, richly ornamented tables, and cases of elegant gifts. On all sides I saw souls floating who, by their studies and writings, had been useful to others. They were dispersed throughout the garden singly and in groups, and they paused at the different tables to receive their respective rewards.

In the center of the garden arose a semicircular structure in tiers. It was laden with the most exquisite objects, and from the front and sides extended arms holding books.

The garden opened by a beautiful gate onto a road along which came a superb procession. All the souls crowded over to that side of the garden and ranged in two rows to welcome the newcomers—a troop of souls escorting the lately deceased Count von Stolberg. They advanced in regular order with banners and garlands. Four bore upon their shoulders (but without weight) a litter of state in which the count half-reclined. They who went to

106

meet the procession also had flowers and crowns. Stolberg wore a crown formed principally of white roses, sparkling gems, and stars; it rested not on his head but hovered just over it. The souls all appeared at first under similar forms, like those I saw lower down in the children's heaven; but afterward each assumed the garb that distinguished him on earth. I saw that they were only such as had by their labors and teaching led others to salvation.

Stolberg descended from the litter, which then disappeared, and advanced toward the gifts prepared for him. I saw an angel standing behind the semicircular tiers, to whom the surrounding spirits gave books one after another. After he had erased something from them or written something in them, he laid them on two stands at his side. Then he gave to the spirits writings, great and small, which they passed on from one to another. On one side I saw an extraordinary number of little pamphlets circulated by Stolberg. It seemed to be a continuation in heaven of the earthly labors of those souls. Then Stolberg received a large, transparent plate in the center of which stood a beautiful golden chalice. Around it were grapes, little loaves, precious stones, and tiny crystal flasks. The chalice was not stationary, as upon the plate of myrrh. The souls drank from it, as also from the flasks, and they partook of the other things also, for Stolberg passed them around. In their communication I often saw the souls giving their hand to one another. Then all went up on high to give thanks.

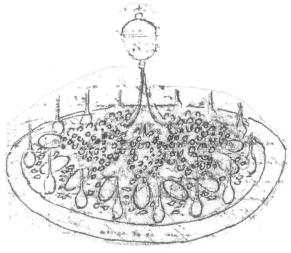

There was the throne of the Holy Trinity; and the Holy Virgin Mary stood in a shimmering archway somewhat lower down, through which she led many to her Son.

This next part of the vision is for me beyond description, all the more so as I am so afflicted in my head just now. I can remember nothing more of the great vision of this night, except that afterward my guide told me I must go to Rome to excite the pope to greater ardor in prayer, and he explained to me all that I should have to do.

SINCE yesterday evening I have been absorbed in a prayer-vision. I was in this vision all last night, and I am still in it. I have passed through all the choirs of the saints, and of the angels, and have begged for their prayers and succor. Even now am I in this state, even now among the angels.[1]

I was taken by my guide up an immensely high staircase and I saw people in prayer coming from all directions—drawn, as it were, by threads. I was on the top of the staircase, but still about five steps below a great, dazzlingly bright city, or rather a world. An immense blue curtain, so great as to span heaven and earth, was drawn aside to allow me to gaze into the magnificent scene. Rows of palaces and flower gardens ran toward the center, where all was so brilliant that one could not look upon it. Wherever I turned my eyes I beheld hierarchies of saints and angels, whose intercession I implored.

The virgins and martyrs were the first to present their petitions before the throne of God, and they were followed by the other choirs. The Holy Trinity appeared to draw near to them like the sun breaking through the clouds. The angelic choirs were composed of small, delicate forms swimming in light. The cherubim and seraphim were winged spirits, their wings formed of sparkling rays. They were in ceaseless motion, and as though ruffled and bowed. Other choirs of angels I saw, and guardian angels.

---

[1] The following morning Anne Catherine reported that she had been ill throughout the night and uninterruptedly engaged in this vision. Unfortunately, of this immense vision she could only retain what follows. CB

Among the holy virgins I saw souls who had lived in the married state—St. Anne and others of early times, St. Cunegundes and other chaste spouses, but not Magdalene. There were no birds or animals in the gardens. When I looked down from the steps on which I stood all was gray to right and left—it was blue only behind the curtain.

I saw—as though islands—cities, fields, and gardens; earthly regions that appeared in proportion as my soul wandered toward them. I saw all sorts of people praying, their prayers mounting like pennants, like written scrolls, or inscribed slips of paper, to the hearts of the blessed, from whose countenance they shot in dazzling rays to the throne of God. I saw some of these scrolls turning black and falling down again to earth, and some unfinished ones taken up and offered by others. It was like an exchange among men and among the saints and angels. There was great movement, especially among the latter, as they bore aid to the needy and miserable: for instance, to ships in distress.

Yes, last night, though very sick, I was carried away by my guide. It was strange how curious I was to know what was behind the blue curtain!—I thought the mountain of the prophets lay to the left as I ascended.

Heavenly Jerusalem I

IN *early August of 1819, at a time when Anne Catherine had had disturbing visions of the forces of persecution arrayed against her, she had the following further vision regarding the heavenly Jerusalem:*
In this vision my guide led me by the hand like a child. He lifted me out of the window of my father's cottage, led me over the meadow, across the marsh, and through the grove. We went on a long, perilous journey over desert countries, till we reached a steep mountain up which he had to draw me after him. It was strange to think myself a child, although so old! When we gained the summit, he said: "See, if you had not been a child, I should never have been able to get you up here. Now, look back and see what dangers you have escaped, thanks to the providence of God!"

I did so and I saw the road behind us full of pictures of different kinds. They represented the various snares of sin, and I comprehended how wonderfully I had been preserved by the watchfulness of my angel. What on the way had appeared to me simply as difficulties I now saw under human forms as temptations to sin. I saw all kinds of troubles that, thanks to the goodness of God, I had escaped. I saw people blindfolded. This signified interior blindness. They walked safely on the edge of the abyss for a time, but at last they fell in. I saw many whose safety I had procured. The sight of these dangers filled me with alarm and I knew not how I had escaped.

When my angel had pointed all this out to me, he went on a few steps ahead and I at once became so weak and feeble that I began to stagger like a child not yet able to walk alone, to cry and lament like a little infant. Then my guide came back and gave me his hand with the words: "See, how weak you are when I do not lead you! See what need you have of a guide in order to pass over such dangers!"

Then we went to the opposite side of the mountain and descended, crossing a beautiful meadow full of red, white, and yellow flowers, so thickly crowded that I was in dread of crushing them. There were, too, some rows of apple trees in blossom and different other trees. Leaving the meadow, we came to a dark road with high hedges on either side. It was muddy and rough, but I passed over gaily, holding my guide's hand. I did not even touch the muddy path, I only skimmed above it. Then we came to another mountain pleasant to look upon, tolerably high, and covered with shining pebbles. From the top I cast a glance back upon the perilous road, and my guide said that the last road, so pleasant with its flowers and fruits, was typical of spiritual consolations and the manifold action of grace in the soul of man after resisting temptation.

My fear of walking on the flowers signified scruple and false conscience. A childlike spirit abandoned to God walks over all the flowers in the world without thinking whether it bruises them or not: and indeed, it does them no harm. I said to him that we must have been a whole year on the journey, it seemed to me so long. But he replied: "To make the journey you see, ten years would be needed!"

Then I turned to the other side to look at the road that lay before me. It was very short. At the end of it, only a little distance from where I stood, I saw the heavenly Jerusalem. The gloomy, perilous road of life lay behind me, and before me only a little way off was the magnificent City of God shining in the blue heavens.

The plain I still had to cross was narrow, and beyond it was a road from which, right and left, branched by-paths in different directions, but which finally returned to the main road. By following them the journey would be considerably lengthened. They did not seem so very dangerous, though one might easily stumble on them. I gazed with joy into the heavenly Jerusalem, which appeared much larger and nearer than it had ever done before.

Then my guide took me to a path that led down the mountain, and I felt that danger threatened. I saw the pilgrim in the distance. He seemed to be carrying something away, and I was eager to go to him. But my guide took me into a little cottage where the two religious, whom I know, prepared a bed and put me into it. I was again a little nun and I slept peaceably in uninterrupted contemplation of the heavenly Jerusalem until I awoke. On the journey, I gave my hand at several different times to people whom I met, and made them travel part of the way with me.

The heavenly Jerusalem I saw like a glittering, transparent, golden city in the blue sky, supported by no earthly foundations, with walls and gates through which I could see far, far beyond. The view was rather the instantaneous perception of a whole than of a succession of parts such as I have here been obliged to present. It had numerous streets, palaces, and squares, all peopled by human apparitions of different races, ranks, and hierarchies. I distinguished whole classes and bodies bound together by ties of mutual dependence. The more I gazed, the more glorious and magnificent did it become. The figures I saw were all colorless and shining, but they were distinguished from one another by the form of their raiment and by various other signs—scepters, crowns, garlands, croziers, crosses, instruments of martyrdom, etc. In the center arose a tree upon whose branches, as if on seats, appeared figures still more resplendent. This tree extended its branches like the fibers of a leaf, swelling out as it rose. The upper figures were more magnificent than those below; they were in an attitude of adoration. Highest of all were holy old men. Crowning the summit was a globe representing the world surmounted by a cross. The Mother of God was there, more splendid than usual. It is all inexpressible! During this vision I slept in the little cottage, until I again awoke in time.

Heavenly Jerusalem II

I SAW in the shining streets of the City of God brilliant palaces and gardens full of saints, praising God and watching over the Church. In the heavenly Jerusalem there is no Church, Christ himself *is* the Church. Mary's throne is above the City of God. Above her are Christ and the Most Holy Trinity, from whom falls upon Mary a shower of light that then spreads over all the Holy City. I saw St. Peter's Basilica below the City of God, and I exulted at the thought that, in spite of all humanity's indifference, it ever receives the true light from on high. I saw the roads leading to the heavenly Jerusalem, and pastors conducting therein perfect souls among their flocks; but these roads were not crowded.

I saw my own way to God's City and I beheld from it, as from the center of a vast circle, all whom I had ever helped. There I saw all the children and poor people for whom I had made clothes, and I was surprised and amused to see what varied forms I had given them. Then I saw all the scenes of my life in which I had been useful, if only to a single person, by counsel, example, assistance, prayer, or suffering; and I saw the fruit they had drawn from it under the symbol of gardens planted for them which they had either cared for or neglected. I saw every one upon whom I had ever made an impression and what effect it produced.

The fact of Anne Catherine's retaining the liveliest remembrance of those actions most dear to her in her natural state is quite characteristic of her, so simple and yet so heroic. Her labors for the sick and the poor ever constituted her greatest delight. Day and night, awake or in vision, in the midst of her sufferings, she was constantly occupied in works of this kind, and great was her delight when she finished some pieces of clothing for her needy clients. We shall give the pilgrim's remarks on this subject below, just as they fell from his own pen over a span of days:

"I found her mending some coarse woollen stockings to be given away. I thought it all a waste of time and I said so to her, whereupon she gave me a beautiful instruction on the way to perform charity.

"She was unusually gay this morning, working away at little caps and binders, made out of all kinds of scraps, for poor women and children at Christmas. She was enchanted with her success, laughed and seemed perfectly radiant. Her countenance shone with the purity of her soul; she even looked a little mischievous as if about to introduce someone who had lain concealed. She says she is never so happy as when working for little children. This joyousness was, however, accompanied by a peculiar sensation—she was, as it were, absent and beholding an infinity of things against her will. She recollected herself repeatedly, glancing around her little room as if to assure herself that she was really there; but soon it all disappeared again and she was once more surrounded by strange scenes.

"She was very bright again today, making clothes for poor infants. Nothing pleases her more than to receive some cast-off garments and old scraps for this purpose. Her money has also been again miraculously multiplied. For two days she knew not what to do, having only four thalers left. She recommended the affair to God when, all at once, she found ten in small change. She thinks their being in small change signifies that she should make use of them right away. She is surprised at the quantity of work she has finished. Her scraps and old pieces are dearer to her than the most costly treasures, though she is so rapt in contemplation during her work that she sees the scissors moving as if in a dream, and she often thinks she is cutting up the wrong thing."

Anne Catherine then described the following vision:

Last night I saw a woman of this place who is near her accouchement. She confided to a friend her destitute condition, not having clothes in which to wrap the child. I thought: "Ah! if she would only come to me!" Her friend said to her: "I shall see if I can get you something." And today she came to tell me of the poor creature's distress. I was so glad to be able to provide for her wants.

Brentano: When I entered she was talking to her little niece about poor children; she was quite bright, although suffering a good deal. She said to the child:

Last night I saw a child in a new jacket, but it had only one sleeve." "Yes," replied the child, "it was little Gertrude. You gave her some stuff for a jacket, but there was not enough for both sleeves; she told me so in school today."

Tears sprang to Anne Catherine's eyes and she told me that she always felt such consolation in speaking to the innocent child that she could hardly restrain herself; she was sometimes obliged to send her away that she might not witness her emotion. She put herself to much trouble, she has everything in perfect order. She said:

I have nearly all my gifts ready for midwinter, then I shall have to begin again. I am not ashamed to beg for the poor. Little Lidwina used to do it. I have seen her in her room on the ground-floor; it was about twice as large as mine, the miserable walls of clay, all was very poor. On the right of the door stood her bed around which hung a black woollen cloth like a curtain. Opposite the bed were two little square windows with round panes opening upon a court, and against the wall between the windows stood a kind of little altar with a cross and ornaments. Good Lidwina [St. Lidwina of Schiedham] lay patiently in the dark corner with no feather bed, only a heavy, black quilt. She wore a black mantle which covered her all over, even her hands, and she looked very sick, her face full of fiery red marks. I saw her little niece by her, a remarkably good and amiable child, about as large as my niece. She waited on her so compassionately! Lidwina sent her to beg some meat for the poor and she brought back a shoulder of pork and some peas; then I saw her in the corner to the left of the door, where the fireplace was, cooking both in a great pot or kettle. Then I had another picture, Lidwina looking for her heavenly Spouse whom she saw coming. I saw him too. He was mine also. But a man who had hidden himself between the door and her bed distracted her, and she was so worried that she began to weep. I had to laugh, for the same thing often happened to me too. I saw that her lips were greatly swollen.

When I felt the cold last night, I thought of the freezing poor, and then I saw my Spouse, who said: "Thou hast not the right kind of confidence in me. Have I ever let thee freeze? Why dost thou not give thy extra beds to the poor? If thou hast need of them again, I shall give them back to thee." I was ashamed of myself and I resolved, in spite of Gertrude, to give away the beds not in use.

That very evening she did so, saying: If my relations want to visit me, they may sleep on straw, or stay at home. She cried out in ecstasy:

There I see all the children for whom I have ever made anything! They are so merry, they have all the things, they all shine— my little boy is there, too. Come here, dear little one, sit there (and she pointed to a seat). O how I thirst for my Savior! It is a burning thirst, but it is sweet—the other thirst is disgusting. O what thirst Mary must have had for her child! Still, she had him only nine months under her heart, and I can receive him so often in holy communion! Such food is upon earth, and yet many die of hunger and thirst!

The land in which this blessing is given to man is just as desolate and poor as the rest of the world! But the blessed let nothing go to loss. Wherever a church once existed, it still exists. O how many churches I see around Bethlehem and in the whole world, floating in the air above the places on which they formerly stood! Feasts are still celebrated in them. There is the church in which Mary's conception was so magnificently celebrated. Mary's spotlessness consists in this, that she had in her no sin, no passion; her sacred body never endured sickness. She possessed however no grace without her own co-operation, excepting that by which she conceived the Lord Jesus.

Soul Worlds

Soul Worlds I

I WAS as though in an open field gazing up at a boundless starry heaven where I beheld manifold constellations seemingly distinct yet each comprising a community. The sun and moon I saw as far higher and deeper in heaven—and infinitely nobler—than the other stars, which I seemed to see receiving from the highest ones glorious rays in a manner both ordered and free.

I saw this highest glory quite distinctly, but with the feeling that there were still far loftier heights, such as those in which I customarily see the Holy Trinity surrounded by the most varied hierarchies of powers and virtues, angels and saints. And from the center of this glory rays streamed down upon the other lustrous bodies—which had each their rank and order. The highest glory I shall name the throne, and those below the throne I shall call seats of grace.[1] Around the throne I saw hierarchies and powers; around the seats of grace I saw images of castles, buildings, gardens, waters, bushes, and other such things. And among all these I perceived life—whether that of men, I know not for certain.

Each seat of grace received rays both from the throne and from its more immediate surroundings. But these surroundings did not furnish light to the seats of grace. On the contrary, the seats of grace reflected *into* their surroundings light they had first themselves *received*. Not every seat of grace received its light—or rather, took it—without intermediary from the throne, but some among them took their light only from other seats of grace—and such as these were darker, indeed some of them were wholly dark. For these latter it was as if a cloud, or body of shadows, obscured

---

[1] *Gnadenstühle.*

116

the light. All this is to say that the throne shed its rays without stint and equally in all directions, but not all received the light.

On the earth, however, where I stood looking all around me, I could make out here and there individuals turned prayerfully toward heaven. And upon these I saw fall rays from the throne—rays that remained with them. Others I saw, book in hand, praying for a ray of light, and—having received it—marking out a circle of blessing with their hands, conveying the light received further into their surroundings. But very few received rays in this way, and those few were widely dispersed.

Great shadow-masses appeared, as though separating or isolating their small company. And I saw how the many confined within these shadow-masses cast their eyes down upon the earth, stampeding dully in a mass, imagining themselves accomplishing all sorts of things but in fact achieving nothing more than to squander what time and opportunity they may have had still to receive the light.

I was greatly saddened to see how few upon the earth receive and further disseminate light. This is because such a small number offer up with inner supplication their own pure soul vessels[1] to the emanation of the light of the All-Highest on His throne.

I said that the communication and reception of these rays of light was orderly—that is, conforming to rule and pattern[2]—because they streamed out ceaselessly in regular forms. But there is an element of freedom as well, for those that did not receive or did not accept the light rays *could* have done so had they but submitted their particular dark nature to the universal law of love. Let me put this another way: The throne is the source of the stream of grace, and the seats of grace are its many springs, which—having been filled to overflowing from the great stream of grace—let that grace flow further into the surrounding gardens. In turn, these surrounding gardens, in addition to this dispensation from the springs of the seats of grace, *also* receive

---

[1] The German term used here is simply *Gefässe*, or "vessels," but clearly it is the soul-spiritual "body" or "receptacle"—howsoever conceived—that is being described thus pictorially. Perhaps "chalices" would serve also, given this word's many related connotations of the same kind.

[2] The German original here is *gesetzliche Formen* (lawful, or ordered, shapes).

grace *directly* from the rain and dew. Or yet again: the throne was God; the seats of grace the churches; and the surroundings the communities in the natural world.

Then I awoke and was again here below.

Soul Worlds II

I WAS as though standing in an open field, gazing up into a starry heaven. What I saw, however, was the throne of God, the dwelling-places of the saints, and the dwelling-places also of many souls in an intermediate condition. Finally, I beheld all around me the condition or state of the manifold forms of divine worship upon the earth, as well as the relationship of the soul-communities[1] [associated with those diverse forms of worship], not only to God but among themselves as well, and even more particularly to their own form of worship. Then, at a great height disappearing into the infinite depths of heaven, I beheld the Holy Trinity surrounded by worshipping choirs of angels, powers and virtues.

From the throne of God shone down manifold rays of light upon glories or light-centers surrounded by choirs of saints, and thence further down upon another circle or round of light-centers centered also around the throne of God. One might think of this arrangement best in the form of a cupola at the center of which is the throne of God surrounded by the hierarchies of angels. From this center light rays forth to countless light-vessels representing in turn midpoints surrounded by choirs of saints. These saints are in turn arrayed—according to varying qualities and values—in yet lower rounds or rings, descending in this way further and further toward the earth along the line established by the center of the cupola.

For the purposes of this representation, I shall call the original source of the light the Godhead. The heavenly hierarchies are then secondary springs of light[2] filled from above by the great source of the Godhead. Furthermore, just as the light originating from the original source flows down through the hierarchies of

---

[1] *Seelenvölker.*

[2] *Lichtbrunne,* hereafter abbreviated as springs.

angels, mights, and virtues—and thence, as various powers and species of light, into the lower or secondary fonts and springs—so do these latter in their turn radiate light downward, through the hierarchies that surround each one of them, in the most varied forms and types.

All these outpourings of light are both structured and free. They are *structured* through their part in the order and form of the whole of Creation, as well as through the eternal, divine righteousness of God. And they are *free* through the love according to which they are offered, and through the love by which they may be received. For any being that does not establish its center in itself or in some other created thing, but instead seeks its midpoint in the great source of all—having divested itself of its own limiting nature—can become a vessel receptive to the rays from the original source, whether directly therefrom or mediated through the secondary fonts or springs. Those whose love is inner and true become themselves vessels of light that may thenceforth illuminate with this selfsame light those in their own surroundings, so that in time they also may develop into vessels of light.

The writing on the drawing is as follows:
place of purification (l); paradise and Abraham's bosom (r).

Again, all these outpourings of light from the source, although determined and ordered, are at the same time free, for love alone sends them forth, and by love alone can they be received. For only such a person receives [love] who can give [love].

Further down below the heavenly cupola of the Godhead and

the holy hierarchies I saw off to the right still more centers of light. These I shall call light receptors.[1] In a circle around each receptor I saw all manner of shrubs, gardens, buildings, and waters. The particular constellation of these things varied according to the nature of each receptor. These places were like dwellings, and at each I saw many souls at work—at some dwellings more souls, at others fewer. All the receptors received their light either from the original source alone, or mediated through the higher, secondary springs of light—or from both sources—and dispersed it further to their surrounding gardens.

Opposite these receptors, to the left of the original source, I saw perhaps four times as many other centers of light that I shall call light absorbers,[2] because although each of these points of light did receive at least a thin ray into their center, that would then be to a greater or lesser degree obscured in mist or shadow.

Around each of these absorbers were dwellings, but they were more or less darkened; and in such shadowy places I saw many souls gone astray. They received no rays of light from either the source or the springs of light.

Then I saw a very large absorber, and floating or fluttering around it many beautiful, exceptional beings gazing down uninterruptedly around me upon the earth, and these beings then received light from a type of light-vessel scattered upon the earth itself.

Over the whole face of the earth I saw the many different collectivities of those who worship the divine. These collectivities took the form of choirs gathered around their customary places of worship, whose shape I saw.[3] I shall call these places of worship light vessels.[4] I saw also in the region around some such vessels

---

[1] *Lichtbehälter,* hereafter abbreviated as receptors.

[2] *Lichtverschlüsse,* hereafter abbreviated as absorbers.

[3] The German word here is *Kirchen* (churches), but it seems better, in this more general context of the different forms of divine worship over the whole earth—that is, presumably, not only different confessions of Christianity, or even only the three Abrahamic traditions, but all religions—to use the expression "places of worship," which could include mosques, synagogues, stupas, etc.

[4] *Lichtgefässe,* hereafter abbreviated as vessels.

further points of light that were like separate, smaller communities or sects, and these I shall call light chalices.[1] And further, from these latter I saw separated out individual human beings bearing light, and then to a greater or lesser degree further distributing this light to their surroundings. Such human beings I shall call candles.[2]

The brightest, most radiant of all the vessels was the Catholic Church, together with its many chalices and candles, for here only did I perceive the light body of the Very Light Itself in God's infinite and omnipresent Becoming-Man, and in God's Atonement in the most holy sacrament, descending from the original source of light through the ordination of the priests.

From this vessel of the Catholic Church I saw beams of light stream toward the obscure absorbers, whose surrounding souls gazed down toward the earth because, owing to their sins, they could receive no light from their closed center of light. In truth, these absorbers may have been purgatory itself. The places of worship or vessels of one and the same light of faith upon the earth I saw ripped apart, and their spreading of light interrupted by shadow-masses and darkened vessels.

In many places I saw how the vessel of the Catholic Church shone brightly over all, although in its individual members the community of believers was hardly illumined. The vessels of the Catholic Church receive their light first directly from the original source of the Godhead, and thereafter also, here and there, from outpourings mediated through the springs of the saints.

In addition to what I have so far described, I saw also a living relationship and reception of light on the part of vessels of the Catholic Church from the receptors to the right, which received, and then dispersed further, light from the original source and the springs. And it was as though each vessel upon the earth stood in some relation to one of the receptors to the right of heaven, which occupied a small space and lay nearby the springs. It may be that this was the region of paradise and the abode of spirits and souls that—being in a peaceful, intermediate condition lacking any ele-

---

[1] *Lichtbecher,* hereafter abbreviated as chalices.
[2] *Lichter.*

ment of torment—were still able to exert an influence upon souls yet living.

Among the vessels upon the earth I recognized the places of worship of all peoples. One among them, however, was quite lacking in light. This place of worship was inside, without an altar, and empty, its people here and there on the ground in the vicinity, on bended knees. There was one who stood in the midst of them, seeming to pray over and to bless them all. I saw them as deficient in light, and yet some among them—inwardly raising their prayers on high—did receive without intermediation rays of light from the Godhead. The attire of these people had something of the culture of the three kings about it.[1]

I saw two other groups that had much of the Catholic Church about them also. The more numerous of the two—also the least refined—clung with off-putting stubbornness to their opinions, holding themselves to be the more ancient and authentic. This group was further from the Catholic Church, yet nevertheless enjoyed more rays shining upon it than the less numerous group. This latter, which belonged in some way together with the first, was however less severe, more refined, closer to the Catholic Church—but had nevertheless fallen into a more darkened state.[2]

I saw the people around the dark, empty places of worship, and houses surmounted by something like weather vanes, to be quite lacking in light as compared to their respective light-centers; nevertheless, here and there I saw beams of light falling from the Godhead upon some of these people as they prayed. However I did not see these latter as standing in any relation with the springs of the saints. Neither did they provide light to the darkened absorbers or engage in any visible exchange of light with the receptors. I saw as well, drawn from among those of this latter

---

[1] This passage may refer to Muslim worship.

[2] This passage may refer, first, to Eastern Orthodox Christianity, and secondly, to one of the confessions combining Catholic and Orthodox elements. Or it could even refer to Anglicanism. No further remarks were recorded that might have helped further clarify these points. Here as elsewhere in these visions—received nearly two centuries ago in a small country village—due consideration must be made for an inevitable parochialism in matters such as these.

place of worship, a circle that was stricter and more pious, as well as very desirous of finding a connection with the Church, but which nevertheless remained still without light.

I saw individual priests of the Catholic Church disseminating rays of light in a circle around them—illuminating it thereby—through a blessing from their hands. I saw others at prayer who received rays of light but did not pass them further on. I saw numerous small communities of Catholics gathered near their vessel, which glowed brilliant from light poured into it from the original source and the springs. It was quite otherwise with some great cities I saw which, though replete with lavish ceremonies, were illuminated only here and there through one or another of its community members.

As I beheld this whole drama—in all its reciprocal relationships—of the receiving and passing-on of light, I became very anxious that the soul-community[1] living in the vicinity of the darkened absorber located to the left would receive no rays from above, but instead seek their light from earth only. And I thought to myself: "Ah, if only they could come into a right relationship, through all the vessels and chalices and candles upon the earth, with the receptors to the right; if only they could do this and come thereby into connection with the springs of the saints and the original source of the Godhead!"

The vessels upon the earth were in communication with each other through light bearers who moved back and forth among them. But not all the vessels were in such communication—some being hindered by shadows and dark marks or stains. Together with these shadows were many human beings gazing fixedly upon the earth, engaged solely in dragging things about here and there, squandering time.

I saw also new communities of light springing up among uncivilized peoples. One or two teachers were among them, around whom gathered men, women, and children who listened to them with eager attention, hastening to them like lambs [to a shepherd], receiving many rays of light from on high. I saw among these people other teachers as well, some shining far more radi-

[1] *Seelenvolk.*

antly, and through their marvelous powers broadcasting light far and wide.

After receiving this vision I awoke and found myself here in bed.

Dark Worlds
(A Great Vision Related to Driving Out Demons)

LAST night I had a great and wonderful vision about Jesus driving out demons, which I saw near Bethany; but it is difficult to present everything in proper order. One image always led into another, so that I am sure neither of the beginning point, nor of the arrangement throughout. I do know that I saw a black vapor rising out of the mouth of the one possessed, in which I discerned three knots, or clusters, connected together with dark cords of steam. I was not able to understand what I was seeing, but as I mulled it over the following images came to me.

At a glance I beheld again the Lord moving his foot over the one possessed, who was lying on the ground, and from whose mouth I saw emanating connected clouds of dark vapor. I saw all this as though it hung before me in the air. Then the image of the possessed vanished from my sight, and as I looked at what remained of the dark, connecting cords I passed over more and more into further details of the vision, which waxed ultimately into a whole world.

It was, to put it as clearly as I am able, as though one saw first a moving shadow, then recognized it as a human shadow, then as a human form in which could be distinguished all the limbs; the insides could be seen also, that is, heart, brain, and all the rest. Then appeared the functions of these various parts—their actions, feelings, and thoughts; and through these latter one passed further into both the body and the soul of the one who had been perceived at first as no more than a passing shadow. It was possible then to perceive also his comportment with others. But I cannot explain how all this could possibly happen.

I saw the three knots or clusters in different shades of darkness. Then different compartments or segments appeared within them. Before my eyes they became like different gardens laid out in beds wherein I beheld all manner of evil things. In one such garden, for example, there appeared the strangest, most dreadful tools of martyrdom, as well as all manner of weeds and poisonous plants and animals. In the center of each of these three garden-complexes was a pool or spring—in each case teeming with frogs, snakes, and other horrible, disgusting things—whence the garden beds were irrigated. The three gardens differed one from another, yet everything in each was inwardly connected and related to the others in a way that brought forth nothing but evil, abomination, pain, sin, night, and blindness. The more I decried something individual in any of these three gardens, the more I myself entered into the space itself that they occupied, so that I could not mark its boundaries with any exactitude.

I saw finally within the three domains diminutive figures, and then human beings, as though forming a connected realm, all life and bustle. The gardens were now distinct circles of such busy activity.

When the image was at this stage of formation, the circles, the knots or clusters, were no longer suspended in the air; rather was everything now like a world.

I also saw illuminated circles and garden-complexes opposed to the tenebrous ones, interrupting them—but I did not see this individually, except in cases where I beheld people passing from the bright circles into the dark ones.

In beholding the circles as worlds—replete with human beings and deeds—I saw that what in the beginning were springs filled with terrible animals were now become as churches of darkness.

In the lowest, darkest circle I saw underway a truly gruesome service to the devil. All was dark and frightful. In place of an altar stood something like a hillock, and behind it a pit in which a conflagration of great split logs was kept burning, its flames flickering dull red and the smoke thereof descending into the earth. The entire service, each and every prayer thereof, went as though downward. I saw then a sanctuary, a sacrifice; but scorn, horror, perversion, disgust, and sacrilegious deeds were all admixed therein. The entire ceremony was a celebration of the devil. I cannot express the horror of it. Everything was scorn, hideousness, filth, terror. Around this center I saw people at work at great kettles cooking herbs (whose names I recognized as those before which I had shuddered when I came upon them as a child) together with other horrible ingredients. I saw them anointing themselves with this brew as they lay there—and then again elsewhere, when they came together with others similarly benumbed, indulging every species of lechery.

I saw threads go forth from their souls, reaching out to other places, and from thence returning. I saw how through this means they knew and saw each other, but all in an abominable confusion. It was as though black birds established these reciprocal connections through the medium of the threads or spirit canals I have described. I saw also how they introduced all kinds of suffering and illness to human beings, inflicting on them astonishing filth and muck, hair and needles and suchlike, which was mixed into their ointments.

From among these souls I discerned inhabitants of many different places (unfortunately, from our time and place as well), but especially many Jews from foreign regions. In its entirety, the throng was not so great. Everything took place in deepest secrecy, and they brought forth nothing but nonsense, horror, and evil—nothing of benefit even to themselves. I saw in the environs of this church an entire life of abominable deeds and unnatural works, murder, fornication, and abnormality. These things were, one might say, the "good works" of these servants of the devil. I saw also how these depraved ones—who knew not even that they were such—had fallen into the devil's church.

In this circle I could make out conditions and relationships of all sorts that are usually not considered permissible in life. I mean especially the case of benumbed ones who would rub themselves with ointments and fall into telepathic visioning, as also those (many of whom were magnetized) falling into the most hateful sins with others. In this latter case I saw something most horrible taking place between them and the one magnetizing them—I saw black clouds moving back and forth between them. I have never once witnessed someone magnetized, into whom there was not introduced at the very least a fine, corporeal impurity. I also always see that it is evil spirits who make possible this sort of visionary connection. I saw how some from the realm of light (which I saw above), through participation and an only seemingly cultured interest in this magical art of healing, themselves fell into the dark realm. Yes, I saw such persons themselves magnetized, and—seduced through a deceptive success—dragged down from the realm of light. They seemed disposed to combine or mix this merely apparent healing in darkness, this reflection of night, with the true healing of light and the vision of the blessed. I saw quite excellent individuals among them, who however had no inkling that they were engaged in the realm of the church of abomination.

In the other circle and its surroundings was another church, something secret—more like a collection of brotherhoods. There was no obvious devil's service here; neither did I see satan himself, or some horrid congregation of willful sluts working evil. But there was a whir of activity bringing into play all sorts of secret arts and nature mysteries to do with making gold, and walking with little sticks on which they carved a comb used to hit the ground, and other things difficult to explain. There was much about rings with inscribed letters, amulets, festive parties, card tricks, fevered discussions—all accompanied the while with miraculous healings, the throwing of blood-soaked cloths from wounds into running water, and children's fairs. I saw a thousand wondrous scenes seemingly to do with bodily healing and temporal human pleasures, but in all these things I understood there to be hidden some service to the devil; a will to be healed, yes, but without first making amends for the sin giving rise to the illness or death in question; that is, a seeking succor—not from Jesus and his Church—but from fallen nature. All these sorts of healings appeared to me as superficial and corrupting. This was shown me through images, for example as a hole overlaid with paper so that it might not be noticed. This church was surrounded by magnetic persons also, indeed by more than the darker church, though these people appeared not in so sinful a state. But still, everything was like a preparatory school for the most malicious evil.

I saw this world populated with the most varied sorts of people, whose comportment toward its center was as that of laity to priests. Whereas in the world below I beheld the horrible devil's service surrounded by whoring, murder, unnatural vices, poison fabrication, and the production of disgraceful pictures and writings, in this present world I beheld people in love and those pining for such, the idolatry of nature and creatures, blind adoration of parents, love letters, worldly music, dancing, locks of hair, rings, and love portraits. In the previous world I had seen an admixture of poison, a rendering infertile, whereas the present world consisted largely of superstitious means to kindle love.

The third and highest realm was, again, different from the others, and yet the same—the difference being but a matter of degree. Here also was a church at the center, but in this case not made up entirely of Freemasonry and such things. This domain was replete with charity, but of a kind that lacked Jesus entirely. Likewise did it offer an enlightenment wanting in light. This region consisted of nothing but science, luxurious living, comfort, etc. Those inhabiting this third world did not believe in the other two worlds and thought they were working against them, whereas in truth they opposed only religion and let other worlds grow, and even themselves grew on their soil.

All three worlds were connected with one another through triply-intertwined channels, and through many other separate connectors and rays. They all three labored with great trouble and effort, yet whatever they brought forth was nothing but confusion, night, affliction, and despair. All their so-called healing was but a covering over, or sometimes, even more harmfully, a transference of evil. In this last circle, and in the one previous, I most commonly saw ensnared the learned, especially physicians and pharmacists.

I cannot any longer recall exactly the order of the images, for they had come to represent a whole world teeming with activity. I no longer saw the world of light separated from the darker circle, but rather, everything was jumbled together, and I entered into this confusion wherein I beheld certain of my friends and acquaintances tumbling towards the dark circles, from which I struggled to hold them back.

I no longer recall clearly my state at the time. It was as though I was in a cavity with my sister, in a purgatorial fire. I had little Marie Katherine by the hand and was holding her back. My father and mother were there with me also. Then the child Jesus brought me something, though I don't remember what. I hid it from my sister, but my parents said I should not do so. Then I raised up the child Jesus, waving with him to my erring friends, who then hastened to me. Wesener[1] tumbled [toward the darkness] also. The pilgrim often ran around this realm of night speculating dangerously. They all came to me, even Bernard,[2] who had run far away.

Just how the images drew to a close I no longer recall, except that it was a kind of harvest picture—a reaping, winnowing, burning of tares, gathering in of the wheat—and I ran along with my friends toward the illuminated side of the field.[3]

---

[1] Anne Catherine's physician.

[2] Anne Catherine's brother.

[3] It was impossible to write down this vision entirely in Anne Catherine's words, as she often repeated herself and spoke confusedly. Moreover, nothing has been added here, although she said a great deal more [that was lost]. The order in which the images have been related, she herself provided subsequently when the notes of her communications were read back to her. In each of the circles described, Anne Catherine beheld an entire plant and animal world related to it physically, morally, and mystically—and in all three worlds she observed various species of abuse. She saw in relation to sins, and their opposing virtues, the importance of animals and their applications, both real and symbolic. She saw the nature of the fallen world in service to the devil as it exists outside the Church of Jesus Christ: it works *directly* as a true abomination; it works *indirectly* in fallen nature; and in our reason, *it worships itself*, hoping thereby to provide its own deliverance, etc. CB

From Chapter Ten of Revelations

I SAW many wonderful things regarding John. I no longer recall how I came to this, in what connection the vision came forth. I am so tired: can you understand me then? It is for me as though my speech rings hollow, coming from a great distance; as if I am sinking deeper and deeper (nonetheless, to the pilgrim her voice was as distinct as ever).

I beheld John upon a desert island. I had never before seen him in such a wild place. He wore a long robe with a belt or girdle upon which were many letters. He was reposing against a tree, supporting his head upon his right arm. His gaze was turned in the direction of the sea, but raised up toward heaven. He was not far from the sea. Then I saw heaven open before him. It was as though I were looking through his very eyes.

I beheld a great and wonderful city, like the heavenly Jerusalem. The surroundings I did not see. I was looking directly into the middle of the city. I can no longer recall more of that particular moment. Then I beheld a lamb and a book with seals, and then many other cities or midpoints, and around these in turn hierarchies of angels. Yet further, beyond these things, I beheld four most wonderful creatures: an angel, an eagle, an ox, and a lion. All had wings. These seemed to be stationary. But in the middle of the city I perceived movement. This was a scene from the *Revelations* of John, but I do not myself know that book. I was once told however that there is an angel that flies through heaven pouring forth bulls. But I know nothing of that.[1]

I saw lying beside John a rolled-up leaf or folio, and in his hand a bent stem like a tube—the sort of writing implement I always saw from that time, quite unlike the quills of our day. A wondrous angel then descended out of heaven as though from a stream of

---

[1] In truth, Anne Catherine knew nothing of *Revelations* and had never read it. CB

light, and there was a rushing sound of the kind I always hear when the Holy Spirit comes at Pentecost. John looked around him, as though he heard himself being called. He seemed to want to write, but did not, and then raised himself into a sitting position.

I saw now that the angel was of tremendous size. It was surrounded as though by rainbows, its countenance like the sun, its body in a cloud, and its legs like fiery pillars. The right foot stood upon the land and the left upon the sea. In its hands the angel held a book. John rose up, went to the angel, and swallowed the book. Then he wept and bent over as though in great pain.

This is all I can now recall of what I saw, for I was awoken at that point by someone who came to bring me communion. But I do remember that the angel was so large that it was like a holy Christophorus. I could not understand what I had seen, neither do I know how I came to receive the vision, for I have never read anything about such things.

I do recall more, but only dimly. I was told something about time. It was to the effect that what I had beheld pertained to our own time, which however I cannot understand.

While Anne Catherine was relating these things, the pilgrim sought out a small copy of the New Testament and located scenes corresponding to the visions in the tenth chapter of Revelations. *Anne Catherine had by then fallen asleep, however, so he placed the book beside her on the bed, laying the tip of her right hand upon the page where Chapter Ten commenced, hoping that in this way she might come to see in vision more of what it contains. Her hand then moved to the exact place where she had left off, and then further, as though she were reading. He could not move his pencil fast enough to record all she then related, even by using abbreviations whenever he could, for she had so much to say:*

The words "Now is the time that John swallows the book" signifies that all these mysteries—all these treasures and good things—are veiled, hidden, no longer recognized. That John suffered so in his body signifies that a time of great tribulation and trouble is coming on account of the fact that the treasures of wisdom have been swallowed, concealed, and characterized falsely. But see! All will come again! See how it all flows down again from heaven as though in streams of crystal-clear water. It is all returning, and most clearly signified. Look how one sits here, and another there.

At this juncture Anne Catherine looked around her twice and —like one who notices from a height certain objects and speaks with someone whom she believes can see the same things she does, mentioned the following individuals upon whom the crystal-clear streams of the waters of life were pouring down:

I saw one here, another there, quite close by; and yet another not so far from the last. Two in the city with so many ruined buildings (Rome), among them a priest. Four more upon a distant island, one of them a priest also. Three in the high mountains (Switzerland), including a priest, and there in the great city by many waters, another—making twelve in all. (She counted these figures out twice in a most recollected way, quite exactly).[1]

These twelve are not old, scarcely more than forty. One of them, a priest, seems to me quite young. The streams of the water of life are coming down upon them. They receive it, though they hardly know how—for it is given to them as though in flashes of lightning. Something like a stream of water flows down upon them from the mountain of the prophets, and along the full length of those streams is something written. It is as though each receives a page from the Book of Life that John swallowed. And should one of the twelve discharge the mission assigned on their page, another page is provided them. Each labors at the same great work, but from different sides, though they know not of each other. But all they represent must again be joined, so that what has lain hidden may come again to light, and all things be renewed. At that time a new pope will come, and all will sprout and bloom anew. But before this there will be tribulation and misery, war and destitution. That is the great pain of the body, for all that is good has been swallowed up and lies hidden in the entrails.

Brentano: Are there women among these prophets?

Yes, there are women who see these things, which the prophets can then make use of from time to time.

Brentano: Have you a role in this?

When the time comes, I must read my five pages in the book.

Brentano: What book is that?

[1] See also "Apocalypse, Tribulation, Twelve New Apostles."

This book here (*Revelations,* upon which her hand was resting).
Brentano: Are all the prophets Catholic?
Yes, all of them.

At this point the pilgrim hoped to refer to certain scenes from the ensuing chapters of Revelations, *but Anne Catherine said:*

Those are the five pages that I may not yet read.

And therewith she shut the book. The pilgrim then counted the pages and noted that in this particular edition, quite circumstantially, precisely five pages followed the ending of the tenth chapter.

When asked again about the animal creatures she had seen, Anne Catherine responded (rather opaquely):

These are the different types. They must swallow and consume all that is superfluous. (Something incomprehensible followed.) The waters that poured down upon the prophets did not spring from the great cataract behind the mountain of Elijah, which takes its source from the great flood, and whence ever-purifying waters flow down and cleanse the earth. It is of this water that the Lord spoke at the well [of the Samaritan Woman]. This water can never be halted in its course, but flows ever on.

At this point she emerged from the vision.

Further on the Above Vision

IN *considering more closely what Anne Catherine conveyed in her vision of the pictures John beheld in heaven, the following fragments—which, fortunately, were not lost—are noteworthy.*

Philadelphia

AS *the pilgrim turned the pages of* Revelations *(because he also did not know it very well, and so was not clear just where to find the section relevant to the foregoing vision), he happened to speak out the name "Philadelphia," whereupon Anne Catherine, awaking, said:*

Philadelphia? It seems to me that I know of it. It must not be so very far from here, for I have been there.

He said then that the Philadelphia familiar to most is the city of that name in America, which is of course quite distant. This Anne Catherine took in good spirits, laughing to herself and remarking how far she must have gone astray, then, upon her wonderful spirit-journey. However it came to light later that in her vision she had indeed heard the name Philadelphia, regarding which she recalled that there were good people there, Catholic people, that it was the city nearest the heavenly Jerusalem, and that it seemed to her it had greatly deteriorated but was now coming again to full bloom. It seemed to her that she had been present there in her vision, and as though the city was nearby (she had seemingly taken it more as an image of the Church and of the greater Catholic community). Regarding the other communities of which Revelations *speaks she knew nothing, not even their names.*

The Locale of the Vision

I SAW the vision as though through John, and yet I saw within it also John himself. I beheld [the images of] the vision above in the heavens, as though I were lying on my back looking up at a ceiling. The four living creatures were stationed at the four corners, and in their midst was the heavenly Jerusalem, around which were many other cities and gardens, or abodes, surrounded in turn by great hierarchies of blessed spirits. Always I was looking from below, upward and inward.

If I am thought of as lying on my back, the image of the winged angel would be directly above my right side, and over my left that of the eagle. Above my feet to the right the winged ox, and to the left the winged lion. These four creatures seemed higher and further away from heaven than how things usually appear to me. And they were in ceaseless movement.

I recall that the angel—which reached upward with one arm and downward with the other—had six wings: two at the shoulders; under these another pair at the hips opening downward; and between these two more, each extended to one side, like this:

The angel's mighty legs were extended and separated. Unlike most angels, this one was not wearing a long robe—but was more like a bare, radiant human shadow. The eagle had several heads, I don't recall how many—only that with one head the eagle looked toward the heavenly City, with others toward various divine abodes, with yet another toward the earth, and finally with one head looked straight upward. The ox and the calf [it seems she would have meant lion] had many wings. All four creatures were equal in their extraordinary size.[1]

When I was at the midpoint—so that the heavenly City stood directly above me—and I looked into it, I could make out no encompassing boundaries or walls. It was as though I were myself within the City. But when I turned my gaze to the side I again saw that which was not the heavenly City itself; that is, to describe it in human terms, I could see what lay without. Nevertheless all would be again gathered within.

Chapters Four and Five

ANNE *Catherine saw in vision also the scenes John depicts in the fourth and fifth chapters of* Revelations. *Of these she was able to recall the following*:

The figure in the center, seated upon the throne, was like the most majestic of the ancients. He was clothed as though in a white mantle. His hair fell in locks upon his shoulders. He was as one, but also as three, in a manner I cannot express. This one-in-three was made clear to me by a wondrous streaming in and out and among them that I was shown.

His countenance seemed in some way human, yet I cannot distinctly call to mind the eyes, for I was so irradiated by three torrents of light shining upon me through them that it seemed as though those light-streams were nothing other than his eyes, or his power of sight. To put it in words, I would have to say that there was upon his brow a triangle, like the eye of God as one

---

[1] Anne Catherine did not recall having seen "many eyes" [as is written in *Revelations*] but said nonetheless that they could see all things.

sometimes sees it depicted, and through this triangle shone forth unending streams of light. There was another such triangular source of streaming light on his breast, and another in the region of the stomach.

Upon the shoulders shone another figure of some kind, and I had the sense that this was something very special. From all the triangular centers, as also from other points on his body, emanated currents of light that began in a point and then broadened out, thus: ◄══

In the left hand was a scepter, and in the right a large book. This book was not a scroll, but like a great missal. The book was held spine outward. The pages were replete with figures of all kinds, around and between which were printed letters—as also on the back. Wrapped around the book—front, sides, and back— were shining ribbons hung on one side with gleaming hearts serving as fasteners, like this:

The numerous rays and streams I saw emanating from this fig- ure seemed to me like all manner of influences and powers. I can- not accurately say that I heard something, but there was something like voices and flashes of lightning. I cannot describe it. I saw arrayed upon seats all around the throne many old men in white, with crowns upon their heads. I know not how many.

Then I saw an angel, and the angel called something out. I was so sad, for I could see that the book had been closed shut, and I said: "O God, now nobody can open the book, whether upon the earth or in heaven, so that none can know what stands written therein. That is grievous indeed." Then I saw that John in great sorrow weeping.

Then all of a sudden I heard something sound forth from the circle of the ancients. I beheld one of them, who made motions as though speaking—but whether I heard actual words, or received them inwardly, I cannot say. I heard in this way something like

"Jesus alone can resolve this," whereupon a lamb suddenly appeared at the center of the scene. It seemed sick.[1]

It was as though the lamb left the throne and approached ever closer, with the intention to take hold of the book from his right side. Earlier I had seen all the ancients lay their crowns before the throne, and prostrate before it.

As the lamb took hold of the book I perceived much movement in the scene before me: for the four living creatures approached, and along with them the ancients with their harps and incense burners, who then fell before the living creatures praying and celebrating. I saw also all the hierarchies moving around the individual cities, and myriads of angels approaching, bearing palms. It was as though all heaven and earth were in movement and singing praises. But below all this I saw the cities of the earth, and they were all repulsive, bleak, and dim. Thus far had I seen, when the angel came and John looked around him.

More Fragments Pertaining to the Vision

THE four living creatures, or animals, were all of equal size. They were composite beings, like the angel with the book. Their legs also were like shafts or pillars. Their feet were all the same, as was the arrangement of their wings also. Only the heads and breasts distinguished the three formed as animals. Within them all was also unceasing movement, as within the innumerable hierarchies in my visions—but the movement was preeminently symmetrical and measured, ordered or orchestrated throughout like the most diverse voices of a choir. The legs, or pillars, stood fast while the wings beat ever so gently. The individual feathers of the wings whispered like aspen leaves, always in unison—sometimes falling still, then again fluttering faster and faster, in harmony with the degree of adoration or illumination emanating from the throne of God. They would sway like the treetops, or the waving grain and flowers of the field, according to the strength of the wind passing by.

---

[1] Anne Catherine did not at this time see the horns and eyes, as John describes.

The wedges or bolts of light streaming from the three triangles—on the brow, breast, and abdomen of the ancient upon the throne—formed ordered interlacings on all sides, maintaining their articulation and never tangling despite their intricacy. The triangles emanated light upon all, and each received from it something unique to them. On the shoulders was something heavy like a shimmering stone that seemed made up of round and pointed gemstones.

As the angel that spoke the words "Who is worthy to open this book?" stepped forward, he did so ceremonially as though charged to do so. This angel was not winged, and wore a long robe.

The lamb, which bore upon its head like a crown many small, curved white horns, appeared at the midmost triangle—that upon the breast.[1] Immediately all the effusions of light were set in motion. They formed themselves into the shape of a cross at the place whence emerged the lamb, which gently approached the right hand of the ancient upon the throne and took the book. In the left hand he held a scepter like that drawn here:

At the lower end was a knob, with something hanging from it (something Anne Catherine could not further describe). Above

---

[1] The triangle on the brow seemed to be in harmony with the breastplate that, according to Eusebius, John bore, and with the Urim and Thummim. CB

In Eusebius's *Ecclesiastical History* we read of "John that rested on the bosom of our Lord, who was a priest that bore the sacerdotal plate." This priestly plate is that which Aaron and his lineal successors bore, and is the breastplate referred to in the following text from the same source: "And Aaron shall bare the names of the children of Israel in the breastplate of judgment upon his heart, when he goeth unto the holy place, for a memorial before the Lord continually. And thou shalt put in the breastplate of judgment the Urim and the Thummim; and they shall be upon Aaron's heart."

that, at the grip, the shaft grew thinner but then broadened out again higher up. At the upper end was a cross, and above that something like a small umbrella.

The lamb with the book was venerated by the ancients and the hierarchies of all the surrounding cities. However the four living creatures did not quit their stations or prostrate themselves, but bowed only.

Before the throne I saw seven shining figures in human form. They were surrounded with flames, as when I see souls burning. And some distance to the front was a shimmering surface, gleaming like quicksilver. It was in the form of a ship, but not itself confined in a vessel. The throne was surrounded on all sides with a rainbow, in which I discerned many different colors and gradations of light amid a unison of ceaseless movement.

Supplementary Explanation

ON *another night Anne Catherine received further on the significance of the four animals. It was quite straightforward, but she was unable to recall it. After dinner, when she had fallen asleep, the pilgrim took from his pocket a New Testament, upon which she suddenly said:*

Look, the pictures are coming again!

Brentano: Of the four animals?

No, others, it is in the present, the locust, they are like men. I can say no more about it. I am familiar with some of them. They have crowns, because they rule; they have yellow hair, and are still most flattering. I am not yet allowed to say it. There is an animal also. I know what it is, but may not yet tell more about it. It drags a tail behind; I know it, but must not tell. In the five pages (that I have not read yet) I will tell all. For the present, it appears only briefly.

The pilgrim then lay her hand upon the fourth chapter, but she spoke instead of the ninth, of which she had known nothing.

Vision Fragment

I HAD another vision from the revelations to John, of which I cannot recall very much. I beheld John lying [upon the ground on the island of] Patmos, and saw how an animal with four heads appeared to him from out of the ocean.

And something else I beheld, from out of our own time. It was a time of neither war nor peace—a time of great misery. Many wished that the crown would fall from one of the heads of the beast. This animal was deeply shocking to me, and he seemed to be receding ever further into the distance—though I cannot be quite certain on this point. It seemed to me that he bore a particular name, like the angel names in *Revelations*—at least that is how he seemed to be called.

Revelations

ON *December 27th, the feast of St. John the Evangelist, as Anne Catherine beheld St. Peter's Basilica shining like the sun, its rays streaming over all the world, she said:*

I was told that this referred to St. John's *Revelations*. Various individuals would be enlightened by it and they would impart their knowledge to the whole world. I had a very distinct vision, but I cannot relate it.

During the octave she had constant visions of the Church, of which, however, she could relate but little. Nor could she give a clear idea of the connection existing between them and the prophet mountain, but we may infer from the pilgrim's notes that they formed a cycle of visions singularly grand:

I saw St. Peter's. A great crowd of men were trying to pull it down, while others constantly built it up again. Lines connected these men one with another and with others throughout the whole world. I was amazed at their perfect understanding. The demolishers, mostly apostates and members of the different sects, broke off whole pieces and worked according to rules and instructions. They wore white aprons bound with blue riband. In them were pockets, and they had trowels stuck in their belts. The costumes of the others were various.

There were among the demolishers distinguished men wearing uniforms and crosses. They did not work themselves, but they marked out on the wall with a trowel where and how it should be torn down. To my horror, I saw among them Catholic priests. Whenever the workmen did not know how to go on, they went to a certain one in their party. He had a large book that seemed to contain the whole plan of the building and the way to destroy it. They marked out exactly with a trowel the parts to be attacked, and they soon came down. They worked quietly and confidently, but slyly, furtively, and warily.

I saw the pope praying, surrounded by false friends who often did the very opposite to what he had ordered, and I saw a little dark fellow (a lay person) laboring actively against the Church. While it was thus being pulled down on one side, it was rebuilt on the other, but not very zealously. I saw many of the clergy whom I knew. The vicar-general gives me great joy. He went to and fro, coolly giving orders for the repairing of the injured parts. I saw my confessor dragging a huge stone by a roundabout way. I saw others carelessly saying their breviary and, now and then, bringing a little stone under their cloak or giving it to another as something very rare. They seemed to have neither confidence, earnestness, nor method. They hardly knew what was going on. It was lamentable!

Soon the whole front of the Church was down; the sanctuary alone stood. I was very much troubled, and I kept thinking: "Where is the man with the red mantle and white banner whom I used to see standing on the Church to protect it?"[1] Then I saw a most majestic lady floating over the great square before the Church. Her wide mantle fell over her arms as she arose gently on high, until she stood upon the cupola and spread it over all the Church like golden rays. The destroyers were taking a short repose, and when they returned they could in no way approach the space covered by the mantle.

On the opposite side the repairs progressed with incredible activity. There came men, old, crippled, long-forgotten, followed by vigorous young people, men, women, children, ecclesiastic and lay, and the edifice was soon restored.

Then I saw a new pope coming in procession, younger and far sterner looking than his predecessor. He was received with pomp. He appeared about to consecrate the Church, but then I heard a

[1] The Archangel Michael.

voice proclaiming it unnecessary, as the blessed sacrament had not been disturbed. The same voice said that they should solemnly celebrate a double feast, a universal jubilee and the restoration of the Church.

The pope, before the feast began, instructed his officers to drive out from the assembled faithful a crowd of the clergy both high and low, and I saw them going out, scolding and grumbling. Then the pope took into his service others, ecclesiastic and lay. Now commenced the grand solemnity in St. Peter's. The men in white aprons worked on when they thought themselves unobserved, silently, cunningly, though rather timidly.

Some days later: Again I saw St. Peter's, with its lofty cupola on whose top stood Michael shining with light. He wore a blood-red robe, a great banner in his hand. A desperate struggle was going on below: green and blue combatants against white, and over the latter—who seemed to be worsted—appeared a fiery red sword. None knew why they fought. The Church was all red like the angel, and I was told that it would be bathed in blood.

The longer the combat lasted, the paler grew the color of the Church, the more transparent it became. Then the angel descended and approached the white troops. I saw him several times in front of them. Their courage was wonderfully aroused, they knew not why or how, and the angel struck right and left among the enemy, who fled in all directions. Then the fiery sword over the victorious whites disappeared. During the engagement, the enemy's troops kept constantly deserting to the other side; once they went in great numbers.

Numbers of saints hovered in the air over the combatants, pointing out what was to be done, making signs with the hand, all different, but impelled by one spirit. When the angel had descended, I beheld above him a great shining cross in the heavens. On it hung the Savior, from whose wounds shot brilliant rays over the whole earth. Those glorious wounds were red like resplendent doorways, their center golden-yellow like the sun. He wore no crown of thorns, but from all the wounds of his head streamed rays. Those from his hands, feet, and side were fine as hair and shone with rainbow colors; sometimes they all united and fell upon villages, cities, and houses throughout the world. I saw them here and there, far and near, falling upon the dying, and the soul entering by the colored rays into the Savior's wounds. The rays from the side spread over the Church like a mighty current, lighting up every part of it, and I saw that the greater number of souls enter into the Lord by these glittering streams.

I saw also a shining red heart floating in the air. From one side flowed a current of white light to the wound of the sacred side, and from the other a second current fell upon the Church in many regions; its rays attracted numerous souls who, by the heart and the current of light, entered into the side of Jesus. I was told that this was the heart of Mary.

Besides these rays, I saw from all the wounds about thirty ladders let down to the earth, some of which however did not reach it. They were not all alike, but narrow and broad, with large and small rounds, some standing alone, others together. Their color corresponded to the purification of the soul—first dark, then clearer, then gray, and at last brighter and brighter. I saw souls painfully climbing up. Some mounted quickly as if helped from above, others pressed forward eagerly but slipped back upon the lower rounds, while others fell back entirely into the darkness. Their eager and painful efforts were quite pitiful. It seemed as if they who mounted easily, as if helped by others, were in closer communication with the Church. I saw too many souls of those that fell on the battlefield taking the path leading into the body of the Lord.

Behind the cross, far back in the sky, I saw multitudes of pictures representing the preparation begun ages ago for the work of redemption. But I cannot describe it. It looked like the stations of the way of divine grace from the creation to the redemption.

I did not always stand in the same place. I moved around among the rays; I saw all. Ah, I saw inexpressible, indescribable things! It seemed to me that the prophet mountain drew near the cross while at the same time it remained in its own position, and I had a view of it as in the first vision. Higher up and back of it were gardens full of shining animals and plants. I felt that it was paradise.

When the combat on earth was over, the Church and the angel became bright and shining, and the latter disappeared. The cross also vanished, and in its place stood a tall, resplendent lady extending over it her mantle of golden rays. There was a reconciliation going on inside, and acts of humility were being made. I saw bishops and pastors approaching one another and exchanging books. The various sects recognized the Church by her miraculous victory, and by the pure light of revelation they had seen beaming upon her. This light sprang from the spray of the fountain gushing from the prophet mountain. When I saw this reunion I felt that the kingdom of God was near. I perceived a new splendor, a higher life in all nature, and a holy emotion in all humankind, as at the time of the Savior's birth. I felt so sensibly the approach of the kingdom of God that I was forced to run to meet it uttering cries of joy.[1]

Then I had a vision of Mary in her ancestors. I saw their whole stock, but no flower on it so noble as she. I saw her come into this world. How, I cannot express, but in the same way as I always see the approach of the kingdom of God, with which alone I can compare it. I saw it hastened by the desires of many humble, loving, faithful Christians. I saw on the earth many little luminous flocks of lambs with their shepherds, the servants of him who, like a lamb, gave his blood for us all.

Among men reigned boundless love of God. I saw shepherds whom I knew, who were near me, but who little dreamed of all this, and I felt an intense desire to arouse them from their sleep. I rejoiced like a child that the Church is my mother, and I had a vision of my childhood when our schoolmaster used to say to us: "Whoever has not the Church for his mother looks not upon God as his Father!" Again I was a child, thinking as then: "The Church is stone. How then can it be thy mother! Yet it is true, it is thy mother!" And so I thought that I went into my Mother whenever I entered the Church, and I cried out in my vision: "Yes, she is indeed thy mother!"

Now I suddenly saw the Church as a beautiful, majestic lady, and I complained to her that she allowed herself to be neglected and ill-treated by her servants. I begged her to give me her Son. She put the child Jesus into my arms and I talked to him a long time. Then I had the sweet assurance that Mary is the Church;

---

[1] This she really did in her vision, praying in a loud voice.

the Church, our mother; God, our Father; and Jesus, our Brother—and I was glad that when a child I had gone into the stone mother, into the Church, and that through God's grace I had thought: "I am going into my holy mother!"

Then I saw a great feast in St. Peter's which, after the victorious battle, shone like the sun. I saw numerous processions entering it. I saw a new pope, earnest and energetic. I saw before the feast began a great many bad bishops and pastors expelled by him. I saw the holy apostles taking a leading part in the celebration. I saw the petition: "Lord, thy kingdom come," being verified. It seemed as if I saw the heavenly gardens coming down from above, uniting with pure places on earth and bathing all in original light. The enemies that had fled from the combat were not pursued; they dispersed of their own accord."

These visions upon the Church were soon absorbed in one great contemplation of the heavenly Jerusalem.

The Octangular Church

I SAW a wonderful and almost indescribable vision of a feast. I saw a church that looked like a slender, delicate, octangular fruit, the roots of whose stem touched the earth over a bubbling fountain. The stem was not high—one could just see between the church and the earth. The entrance was over the spring, which bubbled and bubbled, casting out something white like earth or sand and rendering all around green and fruitful. There were no roots over the spring in front of the church. The center of the interior was like the capsule in an apple, the cells formed of many delicate white threads. In these cells were little organs like the kernels of an apple. Through an opening in the floor one could look straight down into the bubbling spring. I saw some kernels that looked withered and decayed falling into it. But while I gazed the fruit seemed to be developing more and more into a church, and the capsule at last appeared something like a piece of machinery, like a loose artificial nosegay in the center of it.

And now I saw the Blessed Virgin and Elizabeth standing on that nosegay and looking again like two tabernacles—the one the tabernacle of a saint, the other that of the Most Holy. The two blessed women turned toward each other and offered mutual felicitations. Then there issued from them two figures, Jesus and John. John, the larger of the two, lay coiled on the earth, his head in his lap; but Jesus was like a tiny child formed of light, just as I so often see him in the blessed sacrament. Upright and hovering, he moved toward John and passed over him like a white vapor as he lay there with his face upon the earth. The reflection from the snowy vapor glanced through the opening in the floor down into the spring, and by it was swallowed up. Then Jesus raised the little John and embraced him, after which each returned to the womb of his mother—who meantime had been singing the *Magnificat*.

I saw also during that singing Joseph and Zechariah issuing from the walls on opposite sides of the church and followed by an ever-increasing flow of people, while the whole building continued unfolding, as it were, taking more and more the appearance of a church and the occasion that of a sacred festival. Vines with luxuriant foliage were growing around the church, and they became so dense that they had to be trimmed.

The church now rested on the earth. In it was an altar, and through an opening over the bubbling spring arose a baptismal font. Many people entered by the door, and there was at last a grand and perfect festival. All that took place therein, both in form and in action, was a silent growth. I cannot relate all; words fail me.

On John's feast I had another vision of a festival. The octangular church was transparent, as if formed of crystal or jets of water. In the center was a wellspring above which arose a little tower. I saw John standing by it and baptizing. The vision changed. Out of the spring grew a flower stalk, around which arose eight pillars supporting a pyramidal crown. Upon the crown stood the grandparents of Anne, Elizabeth, and Joseph; a little distant from the main stem were Mary and Joseph with the parents of the latter and those of Zechariah. Upon the central stem stood John. A voice seemed to proceed from him, and I saw nations and kings entering the church and receiving the blessed eucharist from the hands of a bishop. I heard John saying that their happiness was greater than his.

Three Attacks

ON *one occasion Brentano found Anne Catherine enduring a martyrdom. "It would be vain," he writes, "to attempt a description of her sufferings. To understand it even slightly, one would have to watch the various phases of her inexplicable state." The cause of her pains none could divine. Her life glided by in this daily struggle without sympathy or support. She never appeared to lose the remembrance of her thorny crown; even when the rest of her person became rigid, she retained command over her head, supporting it in such a way that the thorns might not penetrate too deeply. Sometimes her whole body was slashed and torn with whips, her hands were tied, she was bound with cords; the torture she endured forced the cold sweat from every pore, and yet she related all without a sign of impatience. Suddenly she extended her arms in the form of a cross with an effort so violent that one would have thought the distended nerves were about to snap. She lowered them again, her head gradually sank upon her breast as if she were dead, her limbs were motionless, she lay like a corpse. "I am with the poor souls," she murmured, and on returning to consciousness, she related the following, though with an effort:*

I have had three violent attacks, and I have suffered everything just as my Lord did in his passion. When I was about to yield, when I groaned in agony, I beheld the same suffering undergone by him. Thus I went through the whole passion as I see it on Good Friday. I was scourged, crowned with thorns, dragged with ropes, I fell, I was nailed to the cross, I saw the Lord descend into hell, and I too went to purgatory. I saw many detained therein; some I knew, others I knew not. I saw souls saved who had been buried in darkness and forgetfulness, and this afforded me consolation.

The second attack I endured for all that were not in a state to bear patiently what falls to their lot, and for the dying who were unable to receive the blessed sacrament. I saw many whom I helped.

The third attack was for the Church. I had a vision of a church with a high, elaborate tower, in a great city on a mighty river.[1] The

---

[1] These details point to Vienna, the Austrian capital.

patron of the church is Stephen, by whom I saw another saint who was martyred after him. Around the church I saw many very distinguished people, among them some strangers with aprons and trowels who appeared about to pull down the church with the beautiful tower and slate roof. People from all parts were gathered there, among them priests and even religious, and I was so distressed that I called to my Lord for assistance. Xavier with the cross in his hand had once been all powerful, the enemy ought not to be allowed to triumph now! Then I saw five men going into the church, three in heavy antique vestments like priests, and two very young ecclesiastics who seemed to be in holy orders. I thought these two received holy communion, and that they were destined to infuse new life into the Church.

Suddenly a flame burst from the tower, spread over the roof, and threatened to consume the whole Church. I thought of the great river flowing by the city—could they not extinguish the flames with its waters? The fire injured many who aided in the destruction of the Church and drove them away, but the edifice itself remained standing, by which I understood that the Church would be saved only after a great storm. The fire, so frightful to behold, indicated in the first place a great danger; in the second, renewed splendor after the tempest. The Church's destruction is already begun by means of infidel schools.

I saw a great storm rising in the north and sweeping in a half-circle to the city with the high tower, and then off to the west. I saw combats and streaks of blood far and wide in the heavens over many places, and endless woes and misery threatening the Church, the Protestants everywhere laying snares to entrap her. The servants of the Church are so slothful. They use not the power they possess in the priesthood! I shed bitter tears at the sight.

Anne Catherine wept while recounting this vision, imploring almighty God to deliver her from such spectacles. She mourned also over the flocks without shepherds, and counseled prayer, penance, and humility to avert a portion of the impending danger.

Church Triumphant and Church Militant

I HAVE seen as usual the feast of Pentecost, and many pictures of the communication of the Holy Spirit throughout the whole world, also the Twelve New Apostles and their connection with the Church. I saw from several parishes—which received the Holy Spirit—a spiritual church formed, symbolical of the infusion of new life into the Church Militant,[1] and I saw also numerous individuals receiving the Holy Spirit.[2]

I had a great vision in which I beheld accounts settled between the Church Triumphant and the Church Militant. The former was not a building, but an assembly of the blessed. The Most Holy Trinity appeared above them as the living fountain of all, with Jesus on the right and Mary just below, the choirs of saints and martyrs on the left. Around Jesus were the instruments of his passion and pictures of his life. The latter related especially to the mysteries of God's mercy and the history of redemption, whose feasts are commemorated in the Church Militant. I saw our Lord's temporal and redeeming life as the source of all the graces that flow upon us, inasmuch as the Church Militant, mystically celebrating its mysteries, gratefully appropriates them and renews them among her children by the holy sacrifice and the divine eucharist. I saw the never-failing, outflowing streams of the Most Holy Trinity and the passion of Christ, and their influence over all creation.

---

[1] In Catholic theology, the *Church Militant* consists of those on earth who struggle as soldiers of Christ against sin, against the devil, "against principalities, against powers, against the world-rulers of this darkness, against the spiritual hosts of wickedness in the heavenly places" (Eph. 6:12); the *Church Penitent* (or *Church Suffering*) consists of those presently in purgatory; and the *Church Triumphant* consists of those who have the beatific vision, and are in heaven.

[2] "In recent times the Church did not have people able to receive this light. Neither could the most profound among the Protestants do so, for they were not from the Church. But they will all stand testimony to the Church, and many will be humiliated and others become proud. Yes, many of the more profound Protestants were enlightened by this—though they did not turn immediately to the Church, but will first turn to their people, hoping to convert them. Even now is this process astir, sending forth shoots, and will in due course reach its fulfillment after the great storm in the Church."

I saw all the feasts of our Lord's life to the descent of the Holy Spirit. I learned that on this day when her cycle recommences, the Church receives the Holy Spirit in her pure and well prepared members in proportion to each one's desire. Whoever wishes lovingly and zealously to repair whatever might be an obstacle to the general reception of the Holy Spirit will endure sufferings for Jesus and, uniting them to his merits, offer them for this intention. Everyone can draw down upon himself the effusions of the Holy Spirit in such measure as his love and self-offering participate in the sacrifice of Jesus. I saw the effusion of the Holy Spirit over the works of the apostles, disciples, martyrs, and saints. Suffering gladly for Jesus, they suffered in Jesus and in his body, the Church, becoming thereby living channels of the grace flowing from his passion—yes, they suffered in Jesus and Jesus suffered in them, and from him sprang the good they rendered to the Church.

I saw the multitudes converted by the martyrs. The martyrs were like canals dug out by pains; they bore to thousands of hearts the living blood of redemption. The martyrs, teachers, intercessors, penitents appeared in the Church Triumphant as the substance of all graces profitable to the Church Militant, which are renewed or of which she takes possession on the feasts of her saints. I saw in these visions their sufferings of short duration; but their temporal effects—because they proceeded from the eternal mercy of God and the merits of Jesus Christ—I saw working on perpetually for good in the Church, kept alive by her feasts, lively faith, prayer, devotion, and good works. I saw the immense treasures of the Church and the little profit some of her members derive from them. It is like a luxuriant garden above a desert waste. The former sends down thousands and thousands of fertilizing influences, which the latter rejects; it remains a waste and the rich treasures are prodigally squandered.

I saw the Church Militant, the faithful, the flock of Christ in its temporal state upon earth, dark, and desolate; and the rich distribution of graces from on high received carelessly, slothfully, impiously. I saw the feasts celebrated with such apathy and levity that the graces flowing from them fell to the ground, the Church's treasures were turned into sources of condemnation. I saw all this in a general way and in a variety of pictures. Such negligence must be expiated by suffering; otherwise the Church Militant, unable to settle accounts with the Church Triumphant, would fall still lower.

I saw the Blessed Virgin putting everything in order. This was the end of the task I had begun with her in the nuptial house on St. Catherine's day, that tiresome gathering of fruits and herbs, bleaching of sacristy linen, and cleaning of church ornaments. It is hard to describe, for nature—man himself—has fallen so low, is in so constrained a position, man's senses are as it were so tightly bound, that the visions in which I really act, which I understand, which never surprise me at the time, appear to me—when returned to consciousness—as strange as they do to others. I had for instance to press honey from thistles with my bare hands and carry it to the Blessed Virgin to pay off the balance of the Church debt. She boils and refines it, and mixes it with the food of those who are in need of it. This signifies that during the ecclesiastical year the faithful have neglected or squandered grace, the right use of which would have changed into multiplied blessings, into sweet strengthening food for which many poor souls are languishing.

The Lord supplied all that was necessary from the Church Triumphant. The Church Militant must now render an account, must pay capital and compound interest too. In this account, the honey had been omitted—God's grace appears in the natural world under the form of honey—and it should have been represented. In the flowering season it might easily have been gathered—a little care bestowed on the hives was all that was needed. But now it can be procured only with suffering and fatigue, for the flowers have disappeared and thistles alone are to be found. The merciful Jesus accepts the pains and sufferings of some as an expiatory sacrifice for the omissions of others, and with blood-stained hands had the honey to be extracted from the thistles. The Blessed Virgin, the Mother of the Church, cooks and applies it where the gifts of grace, which it typifies, have been wanting during the year.

Thus was my martyrdom accomplished during those days and nights by manifold labors in vision. The two churches were ever before me and, as her debt was paid off, I saw the lower one issuing from its obscurity.

I saw the members of the Church Militant, as I had seen those of the Church Triumphant. I saw about one hundred thousand great in faith and simple in their actions. I saw six persons, three men and three women, working with me in the Church in the same manner as I do. The stigmatisee of Cagliari, Rosa Maria Serra, and a female laden with great bodily infirmities; the Franciscan of the Tyrol, whom I have often seen united in intention with me, and a young ecclesiastic in a house with other priests in a mountainous country. He grieves bitterly over the state of the Church, and through God's grace endures extraordinary pains. He prays earnestly every evening to be allowed to expiate all the failings of the Church that day. The sixth of my fellow-laborers is a married man of high rank. He has a wicked, perverse wife, and a large household of children and servants. He resides in a great city full of Catholics, Protestants, Jansenists, and Free-thinkers. His house is perfectly regulated. He is very charitable to the poor and bears most nobly with his bad wife. There is a separate street for Jews in that city, closed at either end by gates. Immense traffic is carried on in it.

My labors were mostly in the nuptial house and garden. The visions in which I drew milk from all my members and which weakened me so, referred to my frequent effusions of blood on those days.

When I had finished my work I saw by the Savior two large tablets on which were recorded all neglects and their expiation. All my labors were shown me in figures. and I saw whatever was lost. On one side were beautiful crowns, ornaments, and flowers; on the other, faded garlands, garments slovenly made or only half-finished, and scraps of fruits and vegetables. On one side a pile of the most magnificent of God's gifts, on the other a heap of rubbish and potsherds. I was overcome by sorrow. I prostrated on the ground and wept bitterly for two whole hours. I felt that my heart would break.

Then I saw the Blessed Virgin extend her mantle over the Church, and a crowd of the poor, the sick, and the lame raise it in some way until it floated in the air clear and shining, where it met and united with the Church Triumphant. Jesus and the apostles appeared in the upper choir and distributed the holy eucharist as a renewal of strength, and numerous souls, among them kings and princes, went from Abraham's bosom into the Church. I saw, above all, many a soul, thought to be among the saints, still in Abraham's bosom, not yet in possession of the vision of God, and I saw others going to heaven after one or two days' purification. I saw purgatory in this vision as the Church Suffering, a vast, somber cave in which souls were paying off their debt. There was a dull glare in it, like candlelight, and a kind of altar. An angel comes several times a year to administer something strengthening to the poor sufferers, but when he retires everything church-like disappears with him. Although the poor souls cannot help themselves, yet they intercede for the Church.

When I have visions of the Church as a whole, I always see to the northwest a deep, black abyss into which no ray of light enters, and I feel that that is hell. Afterward I saw a great feast in the Church and multitudes uniting in it. I saw several churches, or rather meeting-houses, surmounted by weather-cocks, the congregations—disunited from the Church—running here and there like beggars hurrying to places where bread is distributed, having no connection with either the Church Triumphant or the Church Suffering. They were not in a regularly founded, living Church, one with the Church Militant, Suffering, and Triumphant, nor did they receive the body of the Lord, but only bread. They who were in error through no fault of their own and who piously and ardently longed for the body of Jesus Christ were spiritually consoled, but not by their communion. They who habitually communicated without this ardent love received nothing; but a child of the Church receives an immense increase of strength.

Other Places

The Spring at Matarea

IN Matarea, where the inhabitants had to quench their thirst with the muddy water of the Nile, a fountain sprang up as before in answer to Mary's prayers at the time of the flight into Egypt. At first they suffered great want and were obliged to live on fruit and bad water. It was long since they had had any good water, and Joseph was making ready to take his water-skins on the donkey to fetch water from the balsam spring in the desert, when in answer to her prayer an angel appeared to the Blessed Virgin and told her to look for a spring behind their house. I saw her go beyond the enclosure around their dwelling to an open space on a lower level surrounded by broken-down embankments. A very big old tree stood here. The Blessed Virgin had a stick in her hand with a little shovel at the end of it, such as people in that country often carried on their journeys. She thrust this into the ground near the tree and thereupon a beautiful clear stream of water gushed forth. She ran joyfully to call Joseph, who on digging out the spring discovered that it had been lined with masonry below, but had dried up and was choked with rubbish. Joseph repaired and cleaned it, and surrounded it with beautiful new stonework. Near this spring, on the side from which Mary had approached it, was a big stone, just like an altar, and indeed I think it had once been an altar, but I forget in what connection. Here the Blessed Virgin used to dry Jesus's clothes and wrappings in the sun after washing them. This spring remained unknown and was used only by the holy family until Jesus was big enough to do various little commissions, such as fetching water for his mother. I once saw that he brought other children to the spring and made a cup with a leaf for them to drink from. The children told this to their parents, so others came to the spring, but as a rule it was used only by the Jews. I saw Jesus fetching water for his mother for the first time.

Mary was in her room kneeling in prayer, and Jesus crept out to the spring with a skin and fetched water; that was the first time. Mary was inexpressibly touched when she saw him coming back, and begged him not to do it again, in case he were to fall into the water. Jesus said that he would be very careful and that he wanted to fetch water for her whenever she needed it. The child Jesus performed all kinds of services for his parents with great attention and thoughtfulness. Thus I saw him, when Joseph was working near his home, running to fetch some tool that had been left behind. He paid attention to everything. I am sure that the joy he gave his parents must have outweighed all their sufferings.

I also saw Jesus going sometimes to the Jewish settlement about a mile from Matarea to fetch bread in return for his mother's work. The many loathsome beasts to be found in this country did him no harm; on the contrary, they were very friendly with him. I have seen him playing with snakes. The first time he went alone to the Jewish settlement (I am not sure whether it was in his fifth or seventh year) he was wearing a new brown dress with yellow flowers around its edge which the Blessed Virgin had made and embroidered for him. He knelt down to pray on the way, and I saw two angels appearing to him and announcing the death of Herod the Great. Jesus said nothing of this to his parents, why I do not know, whether from humility or because the angel had forbidden him to, or because he knew that the time had not yet come for them to leave Egypt.

Once I saw him going to the settlement with other Jewish children, and when he returned home I saw him weeping bitterly over the degraded state of the Jews living there.

The spring that appeared at Matarea in answer to the Blessed Virgin's prayers was not a new one, but an old one, which gushed forth afresh. It had been choked, but was still lined with masonry. I saw that Job had been in Egypt long before Abraham and had dwelt on this spot also.[1] It was he who found the spring, and he made sacrifices on the great stone lying there.

---

[1] The Book of Job gives no clue to the ancestry, offspring. or homeland of Job, and (as Anne Catherine remarks elsewhere) it is difficult to recognize the true history of Job from it. Job is only mentioned elsewhere in the Old

When Abraham was in Egypt, he also had his tents beside this spring, and I saw him teaching the people here.[1] He lived in the country several years with Sarah and a number of his sons and daughters whose mothers had remained behind in Chaldea. His brother Lot was also here with his family, but I do not remember what place of residence was assigned to him. Abraham went to Egypt by God's command, firstly because of a famine in the land of Canaan and secondly to fetch a family treasure that had found its way to Egypt through a niece of Sarah's mother. This niece was of the race of the shepherd-people belonging to Job's tribe who had been rulers of part of Egypt. She had gone there to be serving maid to the reigning family and had then married an Egyptian. She was also the foundress of a tribe, but I have forgotten its name. Hagar, the mother of Ishmael, was a descendant of hers and was thus of Sarah's family.[2] The woman had carried off this family treasure, just as Rachel had carried off Laban's household gods, and had sold it in Egypt for a great sum. In this way it had come into the possession of the king and the priests.

Testament as a just man, together with Noah and Daniel (Ezekiel 14:14, 16:20). Rabbinic lore has, however, many accounts of the circumstances of Job's family; some texts place Job as a contemporary of Abraham, while others place him earlier or later. There are several accounts of his visit to Egypt. The list of such Rabbinic texts is too great to insert here, but a general account of them will be found in the *Jewish Encyclopedia*, art. Job, p. 193b.

[1] Flavius Josephus (lib. I, *Antiquitat. Jud.*, c.8) and others state that Abraham instructed the Egyptians in arithmetic and astrology. CB

Abraham in Egypt: Gen. 12:13. That Lot was with him is shown by 13:1. He pretended that his wife was his sister a second time (20:2), after which the explanation referred to is given (20:12). That Abraham taught the Egyptians is an old Jewish tradition, preserved in Josephus, *Ant.*, I, viii, 2, and there are many Rabbinic stories about his sojourn in Egypt, especially in the Midrash (e.g., *Genesis Rabba*, XLI and XLIV).

[2] Anne Catherine says elsewhere of Hagar: "She was of Sarah's family, and when Sarah herself was barren she gave Abraham Hagar for his wife and said she would build from her and have descendants through her. She looked upon herself as one with all the women of her tribe, as if it were a female tree with many blossoms. Hagar was a vessel, or flower, of her tribe, and she hoped for a fruit of her tribe from her. At that time the whole tribe was as one tree and each of its blossoms formed part of it." CB

Gen. 16:1 simply states that Hagar was an Egyptian.

I have seen many things about the spring at Matarea right down to our own times, and remember this much: already at the time of the holy family it was used by lepers as a healing well. Much later, a small Christian church was built on the site of Mary's dwelling. Near the high altar of this church one descended into the cave where the holy family lived until Joseph had arranged their dwelling. I saw the spring with human habitations round it, and I saw it being used for various forms of skin eruptions. I also saw people bathing in it to cure themselves of evil-smelling perspirations. That was when the Muslims were there. I saw, too, that the Turks always kept a light burning in the church over Mary's dwelling. They feared some misfortune if they forgot to light it. In later times I saw the spring isolated and at some distance from any houses. There was no longer a city there, and wild fruit trees grew about it.

The Pool of Bethesda

I ALSO saw that the pool of Bethesda with its five ambulatories and five entrances was related to the five journeys of Jesus and the five wounds. I saw many things about this pool, and I am sorry that I can speak of no specific time and only in small pictures. I once saw that the Temple was smaller and that animals were slaughtered underneath a wood shed,[1] and that the pool did not yet exist. I saw a hill quite distant from the Temple, and in times of danger people dug a pit there and buried many holy receptacles, lamps, and two-handled fire pans, placing the holy fire from the altar in the middle. On top of the pit were laid all sorts of beams, and I saw that the beam from which the trunk of the holy cross was made was also laid over it. On top of this hiding place earth was filled so that nothing would be noticed.

The tree whose trunk was laid there and afterwards used for the cross stood previously at the brook Kedron about three hours from Jerusalem. The tree had small jagged leaves and yellowish fruit like figs. On a particular occasion it had bent down over the

---

[1] "Holzschoppen" is a mystery; if the word should be "schuppen," then "wood shed" makes more sense; yet the syntax ("underneath") is unclear.

brook, and, continuing to blossom and bear fruit, served as a foot-bridge over it. After the pool of Bethesda was cleaned up, it continued to be used for many things.

A long time afterwards I saw Nehemiah coming from the Babylonian captivity and saw the place where the fire had been hidden cleaned away, and in that same place they found a sweetish black mash and also removed from it all kinds of receptacles. Nehemiah had the offertory wood coated with the mash, and when the wood dried it burst into flames.

I also saw that five lambs were always separated from the herd, and the two purest ones washed by the priests from a basin. But once I also saw that the water and blood penetrated into the earth and disappeared, and that they dug and found five canals through which it had flowed, and then discovered that the black morass in the hole where the fire had been became clear and full of reddish water, and there the pool became enclosed, filling up completely and having an underground outlet. Afterwards a basin was placed over the discovered canals, which were under level, but not covered ground, and it was through a pump that water entered in and was able to flow off again through the canals into the pool. As I dimly recall, the canals remained from the time of Melchizedek when he built there.

Melchizedek took possession of many parts of Palestine by marking them off. He measured off the site for the pool of Bethesda, and long before Jerusalem existed he laid a stone where the Temple was to stand. I saw him planting in the bed of the Jordan the twelve precious stones upon which the priests stood with the Ark of the Covenant at the departure of the children of Israel. He planted them like seeds, and they increased in size. I always saw Melchizedek alone, save when he had to busy himself with the uniting, separating, or guiding of nations and families.

When it was so ordained, the lambs were slaughtered on a table made from the covering of the wash fountain, which was taken off. It was when the blood of the offertory lambs flowed into the pool that those who were sick hurried particularly to its waters, for it was then that it was in motion and the angel came down.

Everything was later arranged in a more artful and splendid way, and the pool with five ambulatories and entrances was reno-

159

vated according to God's will. The Temple, too, was widened
and all of these spaces drawn into it. When Mary lived near the
Temple, the status of everything was much more splendid, for
these things that I saw today were before Solomon's time.

Baptism proper came into use only after Pentecost. Jesus never
baptized. The Mother of God was baptized alone at the pool of
Bethesda by John after Pentecost. Before the ceremony he celebrated holy mass, that is, he consecrated and recited some prayers
as they were accustomed to do at that time.

ON Wednesday, September 7, AD 29, Jesus passed the whole day
in most confidential conversation with Eliud, who asked him various questions about his mission. Jesus explained all to the old
man, telling him that he was the messiah, speaking of the lineage
of his human genealogy and the Mystery of the Ark of the Covenant. I learned then that that Mystery had, before the deluge,
been taken into the ark of Noah, that it had descended from generation to generation, disappearing from time to time, but ever
again coming to light. Jesus said that Mary at her birth had
become the Ark of the Covenant of the Mystery. Then Eliud who,
during the discourse, frequently produced various rolls of writing
and pointed out different passages of the prophets which Jesus
explained to him, asked why he, Jesus, had not come sooner upon
earth. Jesus answered that he could have been born only of a
woman who had been conceived in the same way that, were it not
for the fall, all humankind would have been conceived; and that,
since the first parents, no married couple had been so pure both in
themselves and in their ancestors as were Anne and Joachim.
Then Jesus unfolded the past generations to Eliud, and pointed
out to him the obstacles that had delayed redemption.

I learned from this conference many details concerning the
Ark of the Covenant. Whenever it was in any danger, or whenever there was fear of its falling into enemies' hands, the Mystery
was removed by the priests; yet still was it, the Ark, so holy that
its profaners were punished and forced to restore it. I saw that the
family to whom Moses entrusted the special guardianship of the
Ark existed until Herod's time. At the Babylonian captivity, Jere-

miah hid the Ark and other sacred things on Mount Sinai. They were never afterward found, but the Mystery had been removed. A second Ark was at a later period constructed on the first model, but it did not contain the sacred objects that had been preserved in the first. Aaron's rod, and also a portion of the Mystery were in the keeping of the Essenes on Horeb. The sacrament of the Blessing was however—but I know not by what priest— again replaced in the Ark. In the pit, *which was afterward the pool of Bethesda*, the sacred fire had been preserved. I saw in pictures very many things, which Jesus explained to Eliud, and I heard part of the words, but I cannot recall all.

About ten months later, on Monday, July 10, AD 30, Jesus gave instruction to the people who came to be baptized. Following the instruction, four of the disciples baptized them at a reservoir that served as a baptismal font. The baptismal font was that into which the water from the arm of the Jordan flowed. The basin here, as in other places, was surrounded by a canal so broad as to afford a passage for two, and from it five conduits connected with the basin. These conduits could be opened or closed at pleasure, and at the side of each ran a path over the little canal. In the center of the basin rose a stake which, by a crosspiece that reached to the bank, could be made to open and close the basin.

This reservoir with its five canals had not been especially constructed for the baptism. The number five was a frequent recurrence in Palestine, and the five aqueducts leading to the pool of Bethesda, to John's fountain in the desert, to the baptismal well of Jesus, bore reference no doubt to the five sacred wounds, or to some other mystery of religion.

Just shy of half a year later, on Wednesday, January 3, AD 31, during the feast in Machaerus and the beheading of the Baptist, Jesus was in Thanat-Shiloh. There he heard from those that had returned from Jerusalem of the catastrophe that had just occurred in the Holy City. A crowd of laborers lately engaged on a great building near the mount upon which stood the Temple, along with eighteen master workmen sent thither by Herod, had been buried under the falling walls. Jesus expressed compassion for the innocent sufferers but said that the sin of the master workmen was not greater than that of the Pharisees, the Sadducees, and all those that labored against the kingdom of God. These latter would likewise be one day buried under their own treacherous structures. The aqueduct that had cost the lives of so many was probably a quarter of an hour in length. It was intended to conduct the water flowing from the pool of Bethesda up to the mount on which the Temple stood, thus to wash down from the court to the lower ravine the blood of the slaughtered animals. Higher up on the mountain was the pool of Bethesda, which discharged the waters received from its source, the Gihon. Three vaulted aqueducts ran far in under the Temple Mount, and long arcades extended northward across the valley and up to the mount. Nearby stood a high tower in which, by means of wheel-work machinery, water was raised in great leathern vessels from the reservoir far below. The work had long been in progress.

On the occasion of his last discourse in the Temple, on Monday, March 30, AD 33, Jesus spoke of baptism and the other sacraments. He said he would send to them the Holy Spirit who, by his baptism, would make them all children of redemption. They should after his death baptize at the pool of Bethesda all that would come and ask for it. If a great number presented themselves, they should lay their hands upon their shoulders, two by two, and baptize them there under the stream of the pump, or jet. As formerly the angel, so now would the Holy Spirit come upon the baptized as soon as his blood should have been shed, and even before they themselves had received the Holy Spirit.

On Holy Thursday, April 2, AD 33, a short time after Judas had received the price of his treason, a Pharisee had gone down and dispatched seven slaves to procure the wood and get Christ's cross ready at once in case he should be judged, for next day, on account of the Passover feast, there would be no time to attend to it. They brought the wood from a distance of about three-quarters of an hour, where it lay near a long, high wall with a quantity of other wood belonging to the Temple, and dragged it to a square behind the tribunal of Caiaphas. The trunk of the cross belonged to a tree that once grew in the valley of Jehosaphat near the brook Kidron. Having fallen across the stream, it had long served as a bridge. When Nehemiah hid the sacred fire and the holy vessels in the pool of Bethesda, with other pieces of wood it had been used as a covering; later on it was again removed and thrown on the side of another wood pile.[1]

On the following day, Good Friday, when the executioners insulted and mocked Jesus after his first fall under the cross, one of them said: "Woman, what dost thou want here? If thou hadst reared him better, he would not now be in our hands." I perceived however that some of the soldiers were touched. They obliged the Blessed Virgin to retire, but not one of them laid a finger on her. John and the women led her away, and she sank, like one paralyzed in the knees by pain, on one of the cornerstones that supported the wall near the gateway. Her back was turned toward the procession, and her hands came in contact with the obliquely projecting stone upon which she sank. It was a green veined stone. Where Mary's knees touched it, shallow hollow places were left, and where her hands rested, the impression remained. They were not very distinct impressions, but such as might be made by a stroke upon a surface like dough, for the stone was very hard. I saw that, under Bishop James the Less, it was removed into the first Catholic church, the church near the pool of Bethesda.

The place of execution, which was on the level top of the

---

[1] In James Tissot's monumental multi-volume work on the life of Christ (all 350 of whose primary illustrations are reproduced in the three-volume series *The Visions of Anne Catherine Emmerich*), he writes: "We have thus far refrained from relating certain legends about the wood of which the cross was made . . . such as the following story, according to which the Queen of Sheba, when she went into the palace of Solomon—which was called the house of the forest of Lebanon—noticed a beam in it and predicted that that beam would be used in the execution of a man who would cause the ruin of all Israel. Solomon, continues this strange legend, anxious to guard against the fulfillment of the sinister prophecy, had the beam buried in the very spot where the troubled pool, or pool of Bethesda, spoken of by John, was afterward situated. At the time of the passion of our Lord, this beam is said to have been discovered, dug up, and used to form the cross of the Savior. Here is another story of a similar kind: Seth, third son of Adam, having obtained entrance to the terrestrial paradise, from which his parents had been expelled, obtained from the angel who guarded the Tree of Life three of its seeds, which he planted on the grave of his father. From these three seeds grew three small stems, which, being joined together, formed the beam just alluded to as having been used by Solomon and hidden by him."

mount, was circular, and of a size that could be enclosed in the cemetery of our own parish church. It was like a tolerably large riding ground, and was surrounded by a low wall of earth, through which five pathways were cut. Five paths, or entrances, of this kind seemed to be peculiar to this country in the laying out of different places; for instance, bathing places, baptismal pools, and the pool of Bethesda. Many of the cities also were built with five gates. This arrangement is found in all designs belonging to the olden times, and also in those of more modern date built in the spirit of pious imitation. As with all other things in the holy land, it breathed a deeply prophetic signification, which on this day received its realization in the opening of those five ways to salvation, the five sacred wounds of Jesus.

On the day of Pentecost, May 24, AD 33, before departing for the pool of Bethesda to consecrate the water and administer baptism, the apostles received on their knees the benediction of the Blessed Virgin. Before Jesus's ascension, this ceremony was performed standing. On the following days I saw this blessing given whenever the apostles left the house, and also on their return. The Blessed Virgin wore on such occasions, and generally when she appeared among the apostles in her post of dignity, a large white mantle, a creamy white veil, and a scarf of sky-blue stuff that hung from her head down both sides to the ground. It was ornamented with embroidery, and was held firmly on the head by a white silken crown.

Baptism at the pool of Bethesda had been arranged by Jesus himself for this day's feast, and the disciples had in consequence made all kinds of preparations at the pool, as well as in the old synagogue that they had appropriated for their own use. The walls of the synagogue were hung with tapestry, and from the building down to the pool a covered tentway was erected. The apostles and disciples went in solemn procession, two by two, from the house of the Last Supper to the pool. Some of the disciples carried a leathern bottle of holy water and an asperges. The five apostles upon whom Peter had imposed hands separated, each taking one of the five entrances to the pool, and addressed the people with great enthusiasm. Peter stepped upon the teacher's chair that had been prepared for him in the third circle of the pool, counting from the outside one. This terrace was the broadest. The hearers filled all the terraces of the pool. When the apostles spoke, the multitude hearkened in amazement, for everyone listened to what sounded to him his own language. It was owing to this astonishment of the people that Peter lifted up his voice, as is recorded in the Acts of the Apostles. As many presented themselves for baptism, Peter, assisted by John and James the Less, solemnly blessed the water. The holy water, which they had brought in a leathern bottle from the house of the Last Supper, Peter sprinkled in fine streams far over the pool with an asperges. The preparations for baptism and the baptism itself occupied the whole day.

The neophytes approached Peter's chair in bands and by turns, the other apostles preaching and baptizing at the entrances. The Blessed Virgin and the holy women were busy in the synagogue near the pool distributing the white garments to the neophytes. The sleeves of these garments were bound over the hands with black bands, which were taken off after baptism and laid together in a pile. The neophytes leaned upon a railing. The water was scooped up in a basin and then with the hand poured three times over the head. It flowed again through a channel into the pool below. One basin held enough water for about ten couples. Every two baptized gave place to two neophytes upon whom they laid their hands as sponsors.

Those baptized here today were they that had received John's baptism only. The holy women too were baptized. Three thousand people were added to the community today. That evening the apostles and disciples returned to the house of the Last Supper, where they took a repast and distributed blessed bread.

On the following days also, preaching and baptizing went on at the pool. Before the apostles and disciples went down for these duties, they received the blessing of the Blessed Virgin.

The Church at the Pool of Bethesda

THE pool of Bethesda lay in a ravine of the valley that separated Mount Zion from the Temple and the rest of that quarter of the city, and which declined eastward into the valley of Jehosaphat. It seemed to have been constructed in such a way as to cut off the view of the Temple on the west, for on one side one could not see all around, as could be done on the others. The way to it was indeed broad enough, but the walls were partly overturned and the road was full of grass and sedge. Just at that point it ran down into a ravine that became greener in proportion to its depth. From the pool could be seen off to the southwest an angle of the holy of holies.

The sheep pool lay to the north of the Temple near the cattle market, and was entirely enclosed by a wall. From the house of the Last Supper, which stood on the eastern height of Mount Zion, the way led to the pool of Bethesda first to the east around the height of Zion, then wound in a half-circle to the north, then turned to the west, and lastly eastward again down into a curve. The whole of this quarter of Zion as far as the pool and across down into the valley of Jehosaphat, presented an appearance of desolation. In the dilapidated buildings were formed dwellings for the poor, on the slopes grew groves of juniper trees, and the hollows were covered with high grass and reeds. The Jews shunned this locality, so the new converts now began to settle in it.

The pool of Bethesda was oval in form and surrounded by five terraces, like an amphitheater. Five flights of steps led down to the pool from these terraces to the little trough-like skiffs in which the sick who were seeking a cure were laid when waiting to be sprinkled by the bubbling waters. There was also in the pool a copper pump that arose to nearly the height of a man above the surface of the water and was about as large around as a churn. A little wooden bridge with a railing led to it. I saw by the bridge a tube and piston, which were connected with the pump. When the piston was forced down, a valve was opened and a stream of water squirted out of the pump. By changes made in the opening, the stream could be increased or diminished and made to flow in different directions. The top of the pump could be closed also, and from side jets the streams could be made to spurt all around, like water from a watering pot. I often saw the sick in the skiffs rowing up to the pump to receive the streams over them. The entrance to the pool was usually closed. It was opened for the sick only. This pump was out of use, and on the feast of Pentecost was not yet repaired, but a few days later I saw it restored. The terrace walls contained little vaulted halls in which were stone benches hollowed out in the form of a trough. They were for the accommodation of the sick. They could from all sides look down upon the pool to see whether the waters were being stirred or not. The lowest terrace, the one nearest the pool, was provided with little parapets, or bars. The bottom of the pool was covered with shining white sand, through which three springs bubbled up and sometimes jetted above the surface of the water. The blood of the animals offered in sacrifice flowed through pipes under the altar in the Temple down into the pool.

With its surroundings and the old buildings in its vicinity, the pool covered a very large area. Before reaching it, one had to pass a wall through which there were only three openings. To the east of the pool, the valley made a steep descent, but westward, back of the pool, it was less deep and was spanned by a little bridge. The north side too was steep and overgrown, and on the northeast was a road conducting to the Temple. But it was now gone to ruin and altogether impracticable. Little footpaths, however, led into the city, so that one did not have to go by the public gates. Jesus had often made use of these paths.

The whole pool had hitherto been out of use, for it as well as its surroundings had been allowed to fall to decay. Like many old sanctuaries of our own day it was quite neglected. Only some poor people with lively faith still held it in veneration and visited it. After the healing of the paralytic by Jesus, the pool was again more frequented, though all the more hateful to the Pharisees. The outer walls were in some places quite in ruins, and many parts of the terraces were in a dilapidated condition. But now all was repaired. The fallen walls were partly replaced by movable screens, and from the pool to the synagogue was raised a covered tent-way.

AS Jesus stepped out [of the baptismal well] I saw above him a great pathway of light leading up to heaven, in which was also a voice; and in this [pathway of light] I saw something like a circle opening itself, which was even brighter within, while outwardly raying forth brilliant light of rainbow colors. In its midst I beheld a being with outspread wings. It did not have exactly the form of a dove, neither was it altogether human in shape. It was winged, though, and manifested both uncommon strength and grace. It was far larger than any dove. Now, the being that lowered itself to the pool of Bethesda to stir its waters was much more human; it was an angel. However, the being that [later] appeared above those baptized in this same pool of Bethesda at Pentecost was the *same* I beheld at the baptism of the Lord in the Jordan. I beheld this same figure *also* at the outpouring of the Holy Spirit upon the disciples. Indeed, never did I see Jesus himself baptize, and it seems to me that baptism first became a sacrament after the feast of Pentecost, when I saw the Holy Spirit thus descend upon those whom the disciples baptized at the pool of Bethesda.

The Holy Sepulcher

I HAVE often wondered how it happens that the entrance to the holy sepulcher, as we know it today, is quite other than what it was earlier. When the chapel was raised above it, the former entrance must have been walled up, and many sacred relics have been preserved therein. At present the sepulcher in not as spacious as it was formerly, as it is lined throughout with white marble. The cave formerly positioned before the sepulcher is no longer there, though I believe indications of it still exist below ground. At the time of the burial of Christ Jesus the sepulcher was more brightly lit, for light passed through the doors, whereas at present its interior is entirely dark. It seems to me also that the two great doors still exist somewhere—though I know not where—and are in use in somewhat altered form in the Church of the Holy Sepulcher in Jerusalem.

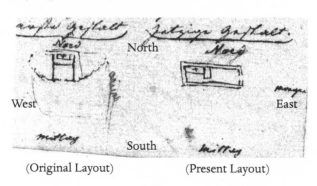

(Original Layout)   (Present Layout)

The Layout of the Praetorium

FROM *Anne Catherine's many references on the subject, it was possible to put together a drawing of the praetorium and its environs, the only remaining uncertainty being the location of the citadel Antonia, which was not described with sufficient exactitude to position it on the drawing with confidence—other than to say that it lay toward the northwestern corner of the Temple. She said:*

The distance between the place of scourging to Pilate's arch was approximately that from here to Borken's gate [in Anne Catherine's locale]. The distance from the sheep gate to the arch at the entrance to the market was about that from here to the entry to the Lüdinghauser [another local reference].

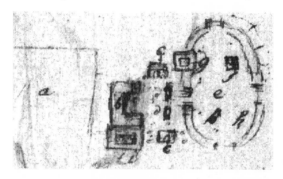

(*a*) The northwest corner of Temple Mount, or perhaps the citadel Antonia, because that is where Anne Catherine always said it lay. Most likely Pilate's house and the forum lay at its feet.

(*b*) Pilate's castle, along with its forecourt or plaza, which was closed off to the west and east with... [text missing]

(*c*) Two arched gates.

(*d*) Stone benches on which sat the Pharisees while they leveled their accusations against Jesus. Columns were set here also.

(*e*) A marketplace, or the forum, bordered the north side of the forecourt of Pilate's palace. Its western side offered a prospect over the northwest corner of Temple mount. Anne Catherine said also that from there one could see Mount Zion. This plaza was surrounded with arched halls for the use of merchants, and these halls were in several places interrupted by larger arches serving as gateways to the forum as a whole. This portion of the grounds lay somewhat higher than the surrounding streets, so it was reached in places by steps, and in others by upward-sloping lanes. The outer perimeter of merchant halls was itself bordered on the outside by dwellings.

(*f*) The Lithostratos, Gabbatha, the so-called pavement of Justice, the place in the forum where a scaffold with stairs leading to it had been mortared in place, the place where Pilate held court publicly, as also in the case of the Savior.

(*g*) The guardhouse, with its inner court where Jesus was crowned and mocked, and beneath which were the prison cells where Barabbas and the two thieves were held.

(*h*) The whipping pillars. A number of such pillars stood around the market, some intended for scourging, others used simply as hitching posts for livestock for sale.

(*i*) Herod's judgment hall, with its inner court where the massacre of the innocents took place, the whole contiguous with Pilate's palace. Its entrance was situated on the eastern side, but there was another entry Pilate could use from within his own quarters. Pilate's palace was somewhat elevated, so that it offered an overview of the market. To reach the terrace where Pilate made his appearance it was necessary to ascend a considerable number of marble stairs. To the rear of Pilate's palace were still higher terraces with gardens and a pleasure house. These gardens communicated with the residence of Caia Procula, Pilate's wife. Then came a culvert that surrounded this side of Temple Mount, as well as residences for those who served in the Temple.

ON this side of the city, four streets ran from east to west. Three opened onto the market, the fourth ran to the city gate leading to Beth-zur. Lazarus's Jerusalem property, or castle, lay not so far distant from this gate.

The first street led out through the sheep gate. Upon entering through this gate, the sheep pool was immediately to the right, positioned so close by the wall that it lay under its very arches, and its eastern outlet lay outside the wall itself, emptying into a drainage pool or morass. The sheep pool was surrounded with all sorts of contrivances, for this is where the lambs intended for use in the Temple were washed before being driven to the Temple.

The house or manor of Anne, Mary's mother, lay along the next street. This was her family's domicile when they came to the Temple, also where they ordered and housed livestock intended for sacrificial use. It was in this same house that the wedding of Joseph and Mary was celebrated.

Way of the Cross in Ephesus

DURING the evening I followed behind two women as they walked Mary's way of the cross. They make this devotion both mornings and evenings, and I trail behind them as quietly as ever I can. At each of the twelve stations, which Mary measured out, John had stone monuments set up. Originally, simple rough stones had been employed to this purpose, but by degrees the whole route was later improved and more beautifully arranged. John gave orders for regular monuments to be set up.

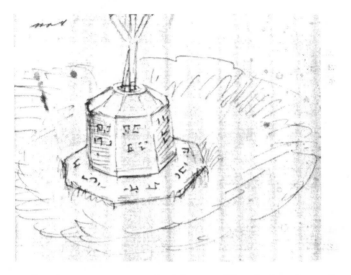

I saw also the cave representing the sepulcher being cleared out and made more suitable for prayer. The memorial stones lay in hollows of greater or less depth, which were covered with grass and flowers and surrounded by a hedge. They were at this time of polished white marble. The thickness of the underlying surface could not be seen on account of the grass.

The faithful, when performing this devotion, carried a cross about a foot in length with a support which they placed in the little hollow on the upper surface of the stone while they were meditating, either kneeling or prostrate on their face. The path that ran in a hollow around the stone was wide enough for two persons to walk side by side. There were twelve such stones. When the devotion was ended, each was covered with a mat.

The sides and base of each stone bore similar inscriptions in Hebrew characters, but the hollow places in which they rested differed, some being larger, others smaller. The first station, or that of the Mount of Olives, was in a little valley. There was a small cave in it, in which several could kneel together. The Mount Calvary [or Golgotha] station was the only one not in a hollow. It was on a hill. For that of the holy sepulcher, one had to cross another hill on whose opposite side stood the memorial stone in a hollow. Thence one descended to the foot of the hill and into the tomb itself, in which later on Mary's remains rested. I think this tomb is still in existence under the surface of the earth, and that it will come to light someday.

An Island of the Philippines

LAST night I made a long journey—partly by land, partly by water—to an island of Japan. For a long time I sailed with both Christians and Jews, to the latter of whom I spoke of Jesus. I saw that they were touched by my words. It was rather similar to a case that happened lately here in Dülmen. I had to speak in vision to some persons whom I convinced and who after a few days came to me asking if they ought not to do such and such a thing. They could get no peace—it was the effect of my remonstrances.

The island on which I landed lay in the midst of others, large and small (I think it was one of the islands of the Philippines) in the open sea, and it is called P-ah-g-a-i."[1] [Anne Catherine pronounced each letter separately]. The shores are steep and rocky. It is dark and bleak all around. Ships seldom touch here. The island may be ten leagues in circumference; it contains a city, but there are no Christians on it. I saw the inhabitants adoring something like a lion that they carry in procession.

I went to an old sick woman belonging to a tribe, brownish and ill-favored but well-disposed, who dwell in caves around a high mountain. They build sheds before these caves, lighter or heavier according to the season. It was daylight when I arrived. The woman lay on a bed of very white moss, a sort of shaggy skin

---

[1] Most likely the island now called Pagasa.

around her shoulders and a covering over her. On first seeing me she appeared startled, but soon gained confidence. I told her all about the little Christ child and urged her to make a crib, where- upon she recalled some confused traditions of her people's ances- tors. She was perfectly resigned to die. When I asked if she did not want to be cured, she did not show any anxiety that way but thought it was time for her now to go home, as she expressed it. I told her to invoke the infant Jesus with all her heart that she might get well. She obeyed most earnestly and promised to make as beautiful a crib as she could.

She had always sighed for the true religion. "All my life," she said, "I have longed for fair-skinned people (she herself was dark brown in hue) who could instruct me, and often in the fields I had so strong a feeling that they were behind me that I would look back to see them." She had a son and daughter whom she greatly lamented, as they were in slavery and she had no hope of ever seeing them again. Ah! if they did but know the true reli- gion! If her son would only return and announce it to his people! She had no other religion than that of making offerings of rice before a cross she always carried with her, and that she stuck in the ground for that purpose. She also lay upon three iron crosses placed side by side in her bed of moss. Her people form a kind of procession around the fields and burn rice in honor of the Sup- reme Being. They gather in the harvest three times a year.

I told her how I used to play with my little companions when a child, how we used to make a crib in the fields, say our prayers before it, and choose one of our number to preside as priest and keep order.

Her people weave most beautifully. They make lovely baskets and other things out of fine rushes, grasses, and willows, and she had woven a beautiful body for her cross. I taught her all that she should teach her people and all that they should do. I prayed with her and, though with difficulty, prevailed upon her to rise. She thought she could not, that she was still too ill, and that she must now go home. But when I repeated that the infant Jesus can refuse nothing to earnest prayer, she prayed and arose.

She wore a long cotton garment, a fur skin about her neck, and around her head a colored handkerchief that seemed to be padded with moss. After she arose it appeared as if she no longer saw me. She called her people together, told them that she had been cured by a person who had come to her from a star (I forget from what star or heaven), who had related to her the history of a newborn Savior whose feast occurred the next day, and who had instructed her how to pray to him, the infant Jesus. She also informed them of her promise to make a crib, for which she had received all necessary directions. The joy of these simple-hearted, innocent people was great on hearing the above; they believed all that she said, for they both loved and esteemed her.

I learned also that around the year 1100—or in that century at least—a Christian traveler had visited the island, found the pagans honoring for twenty days in the year a child in a crib, and reported this fact to Rome. He was not himself a priest.

Later, I was again with the woman on the island, and I saw the simple, beautiful crib she had made. The child was a doll in swathing bands, the features drawn in lines without relief, the body beautifully woven. It lay in a basket of lovely flowers and moss in the center of a garden and under a tent made of the best materials that could be produced. There was a figure dressed in finely plaited paper to represent the Blessed Virgin, but I thought the child rather large compared with the mother. Joseph, the three kings, and the shepherds were all dressed in paper. All around were long, hollow reeds stuck in the ground, furnished with oil and a wick; around the stem was a ring to force the oil up. The effect of these lights under the trees was very beautiful. These flambeaux were trimmed off with colored paper folded to represent roses, stars, garlands, etc.

The people own flocks of very agile animals which they keep penned up. They are not sheep or goats like ours; they have long hair and run very swiftly. The whole scene was wonderfully beautiful! Crowds of grown people and children came in procession with torches in their hands and bearing crowns and garlands; they knelt around the crib and offered all sorts of things as alms for the poor. The woman instructed them, explained all that had happened to her, all that had been told her of the birth of Christ, his childhood, doctrine, passion, and ascension. Her hearers were full of joy and eager to know more. The woman was very old, but still uncommonly active and vigorous. I saw the Blessed Virgin and the child Jesus assisting at this celebration, both clothed as they had been in the cave at Bethlehem. The infant wore a cap with a pointed fold on the forehead. The people did not see them.

I spoke again on the following day with the old woman and learned that two centuries before, on an island not far off, the inhabitants used to erect a tomb on the anniversary of St. Thomas's death and go on a pilgrimage to it for the space of twenty days—a timespan common in their festivals. They used to lay fine white bread on the tomb, which, the apostle appearing, blessed. It was then divided as a sacred thing. But something happened later on that deprived the people of this grace, and the apostle came no more. They think that he was offended. I cannot remember the reason for this, only that it seemed a simple thing, even somewhat amusing. Such is the tradition, such the belief of these people, handed down from parent to child.

As I listened to the old woman's earnest desires that her only son, who was at sea, might introduce into his country some ideas of Christianity, it was given me to glance at him. He was more than a common sailor, something like a pilot on the ship, which had a mixed crew. He had spoken in some place with so much earnestness of his people's longing after Christianity that two men resolved to visit them. I do not think they are priests, but they will report the case at Rome—perhaps they will ask for a priest.

There dwells in another, wild part of the island a darker race who are slaves. The people to whom my woman (whose name I have unfortunately forgotten) belongs wear long garments and pointed caps, larger or smaller. In their chambers they keep a small round pillow with a depression in its center. They are rich in rice and immense nut trees. The monkeys climb the rocks like men and leap around freely. The woman lives about two leagues from the sea.

Star-Themes, Gospels, Vignettes

Egyptian Star Wisdom

ASENATH experienced the profoundest of visions.[1] She was wholly immersed in the Egyptian's service to the stars. I never beheld her in any way involved with magic. She had an inner premonition of the Jewish religion. She wrote much, filling many pages. She wrote on a sort of paper fabricated from a water plant, and also sometimes worked hides. The books that she burned together with Joseph had been written on hides. Her writing was of a curious sort: the letters she formed were simple animal and bird shapes, but fashioned of their heads only.

The Egyptians at this time did not yet worship the Bull god, but instead various sorts of figures partly like swaddled infants and partly like serpents.

Some of these forms could be drawn out, or compressed. They bore all manner of singular objects in their hands. On their chests were shields or breastplates upon which wonderfully wrought representations of cities and water courses were inscribed. It was the Egyptians' custom to mount high buildings to gaze upon the stars, whose movements they studied in order to depict on such shields or breastplates where they should build their cities and dig their water courses. In just this way were both cities named Memphis built, as well as another that lay further off [she meant Thebes]. In one Memphis, on the Nile, lived the pharaoh. The other Memphis lies further to the north.

Anne Catherine then quickly described the lay of the land as represented on the following page. According to what she indicated, New Memphis is situated about seven hours north of Old Memphis (she

---

[1] See "Joseph and Asenath" in *Mysteries of the Old Testament*.

meant the city now called Cairo), which she believed to have been built in Joseph's time, as also a city called Babylon (not the great Babylon, but a smaller city of the same name within Egypt) that was put at the disposal of the Jews. She continued:

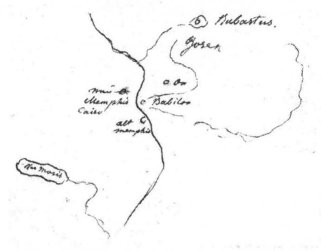

The Jews wandered between the cities of On and Bubastis, mostly to the east of the latter. The grave of Joseph is located in the midst of On, Bubastis, and Old Memphis. Between Old and New Memphis ran beautiful roadways as well as canals connecting dams along the route. Along the way, on a great block of stone, lay an immense figure—beautiful but also quite grave and as though sad—in the form of a woman forward and a dog behind.

Those who studied the stars prepared themselves first with fasting and purification. Some even donned sacks and coated themselves with ashes. Any sort of impurity was a disqualification for this study. When offerings were to be made, they would ascend to the first or second storey of the structure built for this purpose. Here was a small garden from which they would gaze at the stars by the light of the moon. In this way they would enter a state of rapture whereby they could make out clearly what lay within even the small orb of a star and thereafter depict what they saw upon the breastplates of statues or puppet-like figures. It was through visions of this kind that the locations for cities and waterways were determined.

*It was because Anne Catherine was chosen of God that she perceived
the truth in the images of the heavens and stars that came forward in
such raptures as these. She herself said:*

But I have witnessed others, some of them priests, who see
in such pictures only the most hideous of things, the most frightful of works—and are thereby drawn into wholly alien, demonic
worlds. In the hands of such as these, the communications of
Asenath are degraded into atrocities and idolatry of the worst sort.

The Star of the Three Kings and Jacob's Ladder

IN *a visionary state Anne Catherine reported that the three kings had
been able to reckon the advent of the star by making use of Jacob's ladder. They had knowledge of this ladder, and from the number of its
rungs, and their associated images, had been able to calculate when the
fulfillment of the Promise must come. They had seen the ladder among
the stars, and it had led them on. Upon this ladder—comprised of a
beam with three rows of sprigs or offshoots—they beheld many images,
some of which appeared later among the stars themselves. It was in this
way that they came to know what was to follow, and how long they
must wait. [Here the pilgrim notes: How? Perhaps in some way from the
numbers of intermediate sprigs?]*

*Anne Catherine saw upon the ladder the Virgin holding the balance,
and some distance below her, the Virgin with child. She saw Bethlehem
also, but in the form of a beautiful castle, or a house, in which much
blessing was gathered together and then distributed. In this castle she
beheld the Virgin with child surrounded with a great brilliance. She saw
several kings kneel before him. She saw the heavenly Jerusalem also, and
between the house or castle and the heavenly Jerusalem she saw a dark
road full of thorns, strife, and blood.*

*She held all this to be real and true. She believed that the kings had
been born in all magnificence, so that all bowed before them. It was for
this reason, she believed, that the people followed the kings, offering all
their gifts and setting upon the far journey. They believed the heavenly
Jerusalem to be Jesus's kingdom on earth, in which they desired their
part. They understood the dark path to represent an arduous journey
they must undertake under threat of war, whereas in truth what was*

meant was Jesus's way of sorrows. They sought Jesus in great hope and expectation, and so were astonished to discover how little these were met:

The kings were much troubled by the way Herod received them, and also by the many uncertainties they heard voiced. And when they came to Bethlehem—finding Jesus not in a beautiful castle but in an ancient underground vault instead—they fell prey to doubt. And yet still they held true to their beliefs and in the end perceived in the eyes of Jesus all they had foreseen in the stars.

At a lower point on the ladder, the kings (and I also) saw an artfully constructed tower with many doors. The Virgin with child had once sought refuge from a storm in one of its antechambers. I cannot recall just how this was, but the tower was like those I have seen upon the mountain of the prophets.

Apart from this I saw all sort of other pictures—kings with scepters and other figures offering branches.

The kings saw such pictures as these—and what followed from them—in the stars. During the final three nights before commencing their journey, they saw such images without cease. The noblest of them sent word then to the others. Then, after receiving the final signs, they set out.

All the lineages arising from these star-worshippers saw the birth-star, but only these three followed it. The star that went before them was not a comet, but a shimmering brilliance borne by angels. During the day, they followed the angels.

The Writing of the New Testament

YESTERDAY evening I found myself wondering why it was that so little of the life of Jesus was written down, and of that little, how seemingly disordered it is. Then I was shown in vision how the gospels came to be written. Unfortunately however I cannot well remember all that was shown me. But it was clear how little concern the apostles and disciples gave to writing things down, even though they were often entreated to do so by those whom they instructed regarding the life and miracles of Jesus. In vision I have seen individuals who made such earnest requests, but have forgotten their names.

I saw how any such writings undertaken were inevitably composed in conditions of continual upheaval and interruption, and that the disciples often had to resume their task after events necessitated that the writing be left off for a time—so that much went missing and had to be rewritten from the beginning. In this way, however, sometimes episodes missing from the earlier attempts were later restored.

I beheld how after their martyrdom the writings of the apostles and disciples were zealously sought after by the authorities and marked for destruction, so that much was burnt, and what survived often passed into other hands.

I saw how heretics drew much of their poison from, and underpinned many of their false doctrines upon, writings they did not understand—writings that, on account of their sheer volume and wide dispersal, could no longer be grasped as a whole. Not only this, but in many places only a few were up to the task of comprehending even what writings did pass into their hands—so that I saw all too well how heretics wrought so much damage. This I beheld in many images and examples.

I saw that the sheer volume of writings made it difficult to preserve them during the persecutions of the Christians, and how the first popes twice assembled a comprehensive collection of all writings in circulation at the time—and then, after having compared them all, struck from the gospels not only any passages contradicting other documents in the collection but also any that were repetitive, or even merely those they themselves could not understand. This is why what remains of the gospels sometimes evinces gaps or sudden shifts in sequence. However the itinerary between the beheading of John the Baptist and the following winter is given quite accurately in what has come down to us.

Then I saw how the gospel texts were further abbreviated, hearing often the words: "This is mere conjecture." Any passages regarded as suppositious were excised, so that only what was considered absolutely certain remained.

In connection with such interrogations I saw much cast into the fire, so that only what was regarded as orthodox content remained.

I saw a text by Andrew consigned thus to the flames after some passages he had written were first salvaged and preserved. I saw also how God permitted much that was true to be discarded either as superfluous or in some way as a danger to the world.

I saw many writings carefully preserved, protected [against the elements], and then sunk to the bottom of the sea with an anchor. Many writings are surely still extant in Rome also, secreted in a great underground vault. Others are preserved underground in a similar way, I believe, in Alexandria. I was told that in due course such writings will come again to light and facilitate a great period of conversions.

I understood that in many parts the Old Testament is far more complete because it was meant to represent the law, whereas the New Testament has more to do with human beings themselves, and their souls. I cannot fully express this. All that is written in the New Testament is true, but much else that is true was either not written at the time, or made inaccessible in other ways—or is being preserved until such time as God sees fit to reveal it.

A Christian who is simple-hearted, faithful, and true, can know all that is necessary, even without access to writings. Many have understood this, among them Stephen and Ignatius. John's *Revelations* is true as written, though he had many other visions that were not recorded—for example, regarding heaven and earth, and their reciprocal workings upon each other, especially the great drama of strife and triumph.

Regarding the Gospels

ON *one occasion Anne Catherine saw in vision how from the very earliest days the Church had itself abbreviated the gospels, often cutting out repetitious passages regarding events in the life of Christ and letting stand only what seemed necessary. However she was unable to say more at the time, owing to ill health. But she did recall enough to say that she felt quite certain John wrote his gospel last, deep in a forested region, and in the Hebrew language. She said:*

John wrote last of all, quite alone, and in his mother tongue.

She said that either it was either Pope Eugenius or Pope Gelasius who shortened Luke's gospel. She spoke also of other gospels that had been translated, though some passages not so well, and that in one of them the descent into hell and the appearance to Mary[1] was described. But she was unable at the time to further clarify these points.

The Chalice
Used at the Last Supper

THE chalice that the apostles brought from Veronica's house was wonderful and mysterious in its appearance. It had been kept a long time in the Temple among other precious objects of great antiquity, the use and origin of which had been forgotten. The same has been in some degree the case in the Christian Church, where many consecrated jewels have been forgotten and fallen into disuse with time. Ancient vases and jewels, buried beneath the Temple, had often been dug up, sold, or reset. Thus it was that, by God's permission, this holy vessel—which none had ever been able to melt down on account of its being made of some unknown material, and which had been found by the priests in the treasury of the Temple among other objects no longer made use of—had been sold to some antiquaries.

It was bought by Veronica, was several times made use of by Jesus in the celebration of festivals, and, from the day of the Last Supper, became the exclusive property of the Christian community. This vessel was not always the same as when used by Christ Jesus at his Last Supper, and perhaps it was upon that occasion that the various pieces that composed it were first put together. The great chalice stood upon a plate, out of which a species of tablet could also be drawn, and around it were six little glasses. The great chalice contained another smaller vase; above it there was a small plate, and then came a round cover. A spoon was inserted in the foot of the chalice, and could be easily drawn out for use. All these different vessels were covered with fine linen, and, if I am not mistaken, wrapped up in a case made of leather. The great chalice was composed of the cup and of the foot,

---

[1] Presumably referring to the appearance of the Risen Christ to Mary *prior to* Magdalene's encounter with the "gardener," as described elsewhere in Anne Catherine's visions.

which last must have been joined on to it at a later period, for it was of a different material. The cup was pear-shaped, massive, dark-colored, and highly polished, with gold ornaments and two small handles by which it could be lifted. The foot was of virgin gold, elaborately worked, ornamented with a serpent and a small bunch of grapes, and enriched with precious stones.

The chalice was left in the Church of Jerusalem in the hands of James the Less, and I see that it is still preserved in that town—it will reappear some day, in the same manner as before. Other churches took the little cups that surrounded it; one was taken to Antioch, another to Ephesus. They belonged to the patriarchs, who drank some mysterious beverage out of them when they received or gave a benediction, as I have seen many times.

The great chalice had formerly been in the possession of Abraham; Melchizedek brought it with him from the land of Semiramis to the land of Canaan when he was beginning to found some settlements on the spot where Jerusalem was afterwards built. He made use of it then for offering sacrifice, when he offered bread and wine in the presence of Abraham, and he left it in the possession of that holy patriarch. This same chalice had also been preserved in Noah's ark.

Apocalypse, Tribulation, and the Twelve New Apostles

THE *following vision, though chiefly upon the ravages made in the Church by the infidelity of Anne Catherine's own day, comprehends many other things and embraces seven periods of time. This was indicated to her, but her sufferings unfortunately prevented her from specifying these periods or saying which among the events would be realized in her own lifetime, or which would take place only after her demise:*

I saw the earth's surface covered with darkness and obscurity, all creation, trees and shrubs, plants and flowers, withering and dying. The waters seemed to have flowed back to their sources; brooks, fountains, rivers, and seas to have returned to the waters above the firmament around paradise. I wandered over the desolate earth. I saw the rivers like fine threads; the seas like black abysses with here and there a tiny stream; and, wallowing in the slime, lay huge animals struggling with death. I went so far that I could distinctly see the shore on which Clement was drowned.[1]

Humankind was in a sad state of confusion, and as the earth became more arid and desolate, the deeds of darkness increased. I saw in detail many abominations. I recognized Rome, and I beheld the oppression of the Church, as also her internal and external decadence. Then I saw immense troops marching from various quarters to a certain place near which was a great black spot like an enormous abyss, into which numbers of the troops seemed to fall, unnoticed by their companions.

Again I saw in the midst of these disasters the twelve new apostles laboring in different countries, unknown to one another, each receiving streams of living water from on high. They all did the same work. They knew not whence they received their tasks; but as soon as one was finished, another was ready for them. They were twelve in number, not one over forty years. Three were priests, and others aspired to that dignity. I have often met one of them; he is either known to me or he is near me. They were not dressed alike, but each according to the custom of his country and the fashion of his time. They received from God all the graces squandered by others; they did good everywhere; they were all Catholics.

Among the dark destroyers I saw false prophets and people who labored against the writings of the twelve new apostles. I

---

[1] Clement of Rome (also called Clemens Romanus to distinguish him from Clement of Alexandria) was the third in succession after the apostle Peter as bishop of Rome (that is, the fourth pope). Clement is known mainly for the letter he wrote to the Corinthians in about AD 96. He is counted among the apostolic fathers. Little is known of Clement's life. What is known is from authors who wrote over a hundred years after his death, including Tertullian, Jerome, Irenaeus, Epiphanius, and Eusebius. His birth date is not known. He may have met Peter and Paul, and may have been ordained by Peter. Some associate him with the Clement in Paul's letters (Phil. 4:3). Clement is believed to have been named bishop of Rome (pope) in about AD 88, and held the position until about AD 98, when he died. Early sources noted that he died a natural death, perhaps in Greece; but another tradition tells of his martyrdom in Crimea in AD 102 by drowning when thrown overboard from a boat with a ship's anchor tied to him.

often beheld the latter disappear in the tumult to reappear again, however, more courageous, more dauntless than ever.[1]

I saw also about a hundred women prophesying as if in rapture. By them were men who mesmerized them. They filled me with loathing and horror and, as I thought I beheld among them the clairvoyant of Münster, I reflected that, at all events, the Father would not be with her.

While the ranks of the combatants around the dark abyss became thinner and thinner—until a whole city[2] had disappeared—the twelve new apostles constantly gained new followers; and from the other city (Rome, the true city of God) there issued as it were a luminous wedge that pierced the dark disc.

Above the little church stood a majestic lady in a flowing sky-blue mantle, a crown of stars on her head. From her streamed out light into the deep darkness. Wherever it penetrated, all things revived and flourished. In a large city I saw a church, once the smallest, become the greatest.[3] The new apostles entered into the light, and I thought I saw myself with others whom I recognized in the first rank.[4]

Now all is again flourishing. I saw a new, very resolute pope, and the black abyss gradually closing until the opening was so small that a water pail could cover it. Lastly, I saw again three troops or parishes uniting in the light under holy, enlightened men, and entering into the Church. The waters again gushed forth; all was renewed, all was living and flourishing, churches and convents were rebuilt. While that frightful drought prevailed I was taken over a verdant meadow full of those lovely white

---

[1] On another occasion Anne Catherine said: "I saw all things renewed and a church that reached from earth to heaven. I saw one of the twelve new apostles in the person of the young priest whom the unchaste bride wanted to marry. It was a very comprehensive vision and portrayed anew all that had been previously shown me regarding the Church's destiny. I was told that I should have to go again to the pope; but when all this will take place I cannot say."

[2] The false church with its followers.

[3] The little church of Notre-Dame des Victoires, Paris, in which the Arch-confraternity of the Most Holy and Immaculate Heart of Mary took its rise.

[4] That is, with others who like herself had contributed to the renewal of life.

flowers I once had to gather, and I came to a thorn hedge on which I scratched myself badly in the dark; but it also was full of buds and I pressed through joyously.

On the feast of Pentecost, May 21st, the pilgrim, who had witnessed her anguish and tears on the preceding evening, found her this morning radiant as a spouse of Christ, breathing but joy and holiness:

I have been in the cenacle with the apostles, and I have been fed in a way that I cannot express. Nourishment under the form of a wave of light flowed into my mouth. It was exceedingly sweet but I know not whence it came. I saw no hand, and I began to fear lest, perhaps, having broken my fast, I should not be able to receive holy communion in the morning. I was not here, and yet I distinctly heard the clock strike twelve, stroke for stroke. I counted each one.

I beheld the descent of the Holy Spirit on the disciples and how the same Holy Spirit on every anniversary of this feast spreads all over the earth wherever he finds pure hearts desirous of receiving him. I can describe this only by saying that I saw here and there in the darkness a parish, a church, a city, or one or more individuals suddenly illumined. The whole earth lay in darkness below me, and I saw by a flash of heavenly light here a flower-bed, there a tree, a bush, a fountain, an islet, not only lit up but rendered quite luminous. Through the mercy of God all that I saw last night was good; the works of darkness were not shown me.

All over the world I saw numberless infusions of the Spirit. Sometimes it was like a lightning stroke falling on a congregation in church, and I could tell who among them had received the grace. Or again, I beheld individuals praying in their homes suddenly endued with light and strength. The sight awoke in me great joy and confidence that the Church, amid her ever-increasing tribulations, will not succumb—for in all parts of the world I saw defenders raised up to her by the Holy Spirit. Yes, I felt that the oppression of the powers of this world serves but to increase her strength.

I saw in St. Peter's at Rome a grand feast celebrated with myriads of lights, and I saw the pope and many others receiving the strength of the Holy Spirit. I did not see the dark church last night, which is always a horror to me. I saw in different places the twelve enlightened men whom I see so often as twelve new apostles or prophets of the Church. I feel as if I know one of them, that he is near me. I saw the Holy Spirit poured out on some of our own land. I knew them all in my vision, but it is seldom that I can name them afterward. I think I saw the stern superior. I felt certain that the persecution of the Church here in our own country will turn out well, but great troubles await us.

Last night I had a vision of the pope. I saw St. Francis carrying the Church, and the Basilica of St. Peter borne on the shoulders of a little man who had something of the Jew in his countenance. It looked very perilous. Mary stood on the north side of the Church with her mantle extended over it. The little man was almost bent double. He is, as yet, a layman. I know who he is. The twelve men whom I always see as the twelve new apostles ought to have helped him, but they arrived too late. However, just as he was about to fall, they all ran up with myriads of angels to his assistance. It was only the pavement and the back part of the Church, for all the rest bad been demolished by the secret society, helped by the servants of the Church themselves. They bore it to another place and it seemed as if rows of palaces fell before it like fields of wheat in harvest time.

Finally, at Pentecost, 1821, early in a vision on the mountain of the prophets, Anne Catherine again mentions the twelve new apostles:

I have seen as usual the feast of Pentecost, and many pictures of the communication of the Holy Spirit throughout the whole world, also the twelve new apostles and their connection with the Church. I saw from several parishes, which received the Holy Spirit, a spiritual church formed. This was a new awakening of the Catholic Church, and I also saw numerous individuals receiving the Holy Spirit.

Music

I BEHELD maidens dancing. They stood facing each other in pairs, moving among each other in ever-changing figures and crossing lines. There was no leaping or hopping; it was more in the style of a minuet. Nonetheless there was considerable swaying and twisting of their whole bodies as they moved—not unlike some of the motions Jews make when at prayer. Some of the young women were playing musical instruments. They played flutes, triangles, and handbells. But most pleasant in sound, and also most remarkable in appearance, was a stringed instrument formed of a sort of wooden box whose tapering sides were spanned taut with strings that could be strummed. Within the box was a sort of bellows out of which a number of pipes emerged, some of which were straight and others bent over. At intervals while strumming, the bellows would be struck in various places, so that the harp-like sound of the strings would be augmented with horn-like tones. The instrument was played upon the knee, or sometimes a footstool situated between the knees.

On one occasion Anne Catherine said: I recall having seen how James the Less would sometimes play upon a harp. Nathaniel played a flute, as did Bartholomew also. These flutes were the sort that one plays by blowing air in from above. I would see them sometimes playing while at rest together at an inn or hostel. They often accompanied their playing with psalms. In fact, sometimes they would dance along as well, though it was more a gentle sliding, and not like our own dances.

Dame Philosophy and Philosophical Snakes

ON *one occasion Anne Catherine related the following vision upon the teachings of our times*:

My guide led me to a stately edifice: "Enter," he said, "and I shall show you the doctrines of men." We entered a spacious hall filled with pupils and professors. A heated dispute was going on—loud words, contradictory statements resounded on all sides. I saw into the hearts of the professors, and to my amazement I discovered in each a little black casket. In the center of the hall stood a female of imposing appearance who took a foremost part in the discussion. I paused a few moments with my guide to listen, when to my surprise I saw the audience disappearing, one by one. The hall itself began almost imperceptibly to fall to ruins; the floor was no longer safe. The professors mounted a storey higher, where they continued their debate with renewed ardor— but there too the building began to crumble. I trembled on seeing myself standing on a worm-eaten plank and begged my guide to save me. He reassured me and led me to a place of safety. Then I asked him the meaning of the little black casket. "It signifies," he said, "presumption and the spirit of contradiction. The female is philosophy, or, as they say, pure reason, which seeks to regulate all things by its own formulas. These professors follow her teachings and not those of truth, the precious treasure handed down by tradition."

Then my guide conducted me into another hall in which sat several professors in their chairs. All was very different here; the clearness and simplicity of their words charmed me, order and charity reigned, and many who had left the ruined halls took refuge here. My guide said: "Here is simple, unadulterated truth, which springs from humility and gives birth to love and all other blessings."

I HAVE had much to do for the church of this country. I have to work for the whole Church and am quite bewildered by the disorder and distress I see all around, and by my own pains and labors. I have had a vision on the fatal condition of students of the present day. I saw them going through the streets of Münster and Bonn with bundles of serpents in their hands. They drew them through their mouth, and sucked their heads, and I heard these words: "These are philosophical serpents!"

I have often seen that the simple, pious old schoolmasters, who are generally ignored as ignorant, form children to piety;

while the skillful masters and mistresses put nothing into their heads because—by their pride and self-sufficiency—they deprive their labor of its fruit and, so to speak, consume it themselves. It is the same as with the blessing attached to good works which, when done in public or through motives of policy, have little efficacy. Where charity and simplicity are wanting, there is no secret success.

Star-Flowers

THE *little daughter of Anne Catherine's brother, who came from the farm of Flamske near Coesfeld to visit her at Dülmen in the winter of 1820, was seized with violent convulsions every evening at the same time and beginning with distressing choking. These convulsions often lasted until midnight, and Anne Catherine, knowing as she did the cause and significance of this—and indeed of most other illnesses—was greatly affected by her niece's sufferings. She prayed many times to be told of a cure for them, and at last was able to describe a certain little flower known to her, which she had seen St. Luke pick and use to cure epilepsy.*[1]

As a result of her minute description of the little flower and of the places where it grew, her physician, Dr. Wesener[2] *found it; she recognized the plant he brought her as the one she had seen, which she called "star-flower" [see illustration from Brentano's notes below], and he identified it as* Cerastium arvense linnaei *or* Holosteum caryophylleum veterum *(field mouse-ear chickweed). It is remarkable that the old herbal Tabernamontani also refers to the use of this plant for epilepsy.*

On the afternoon of May 22, 1821, Anne Catherine said in her sleep:

Rue [which she had used before] and star-flower sprinkled with holy water should be pressed and the juice given to the child, surely that could do no harm? I have already been told three times to squeeze it myself and give it to her.

The writer, in the hope that she might communicate something more definite about this cure, had, unbeknownst to her, wrapped up at home some blossoms of this plant in paper, like a relic, and pinned the little packet to her dress in the evening. She woke up and said at once:

---

[1] See the subsection "Luke as Physician" in *People of the New Testament III.*

[2] Dr. Franz Wilhelm Wesener, district doctor of Dülmen, friend and physician to Anne Catherine.

That is not a relic, it is the star-flower.

She kept the little flower pinned to her dress during the night and on the morning of May 23, 1821, said:

I had no idea why I was lying last night in a field among nothing but star-flowers. I saw too all kinds of ways in which these flowers were used, and it was said to me: "If the healing power of this plant were known, it would not grow so plentifully around you." I saw pictures of it being used in very distant ages. I saw Luke wandering about picking these flowers. I saw too in a place like the one where Christ fed the five thousand many sick folk lying on these flowers in the open air, protected by a light shelter above them. These plants were spread out like litter for them to lie on; and arranged with the flowers in the center under their bodies, the stalks and leaves pointing outwards. They were suffering from gout, convulsions, and swellings, and had under them round cushions filled with the flowers. I saw their swollen feet being wrapped round with these flowers, and I saw the sick people eating the flowers and drinking water that had been poured on them. The flowers were larger than those here.

It was a picture of a long time ago; the people and the doctors wore long white woolen robes with girdles. I saw that the plants were always blessed before use. I saw also a plant of the same family—but more succulent and with rounder, juicier, smoother leaves, and pale blue blossoms of the same shape—that is very efficacious in children's convulsions. It grows in better soil and is not so common. I think it is called eyebright. I found it once near Dernekamp. It is stronger than the other.

Anne Catherine then gave the child three flowers to begin with; the second time she was to have five. She said:

I see the child's nature but cannot rightly describe it; inside she is like a torn garment that needs a new piece of stuff for each tear.

Dragons

ON *one occasion, when Anne Catherine was speaking of Datula and Pontianus*[1] *in connection with the region where Martha and Magdalene had earlier lived in Gaul, she reports that at that time a dragon was terrorizing the region around Tarascon, wreaking havoc with people and property, and that Martha went forth and slew it with the sign of the cross.*[2] *While speaking of these things, Anne Catherine was shown a map, on which she located Marsilia, saying that it was here that Martha had come to land. She added that Magdalene had slain a dragon also. It had stationed itself outside the mouth of her cave, and when she came upon it she cast it down. In truth, Anne Catherine saw this as some sort of demonic apparition.*

Anne Catherine saw dragons in other visions of historical scenes as well:

They were not in the form of a winged eidex or crocodile, but rounder, more in the form of a horse. Their backs were bowed downward, their necks thick but not so short as that of a horse, their heads broad and long. The jaws were hideous and their size magnified further when opened on account of folds of flaccid skin surrounding them. Rising out of the breast and shoulders were relatively diminutive bat-like wings. Their legs were not so large— in thickness rather like those of a cow—the upper limbs smaller and terminating in longish talons. Their tails were broad. During flight they would draw up their upper limbs tightly against their belly, while their legs trailed along behind. Their manner of flying was like a swooping or darting forward.

On one occasion Anne Catherine says the following regarding dragons:

I have seen them swooping along above high cedar forests. There is something horrifying and devilish about these creatures.[3] I saw no nests for their young. Mostly I came upon them in wild, deserted places, on terrifying cliffs or in vast caves. I have seen them also secreted in broad, hollow trees deep in remote forests, or sunning themselves on the steep banks of strange rivers. The

---

[1] See "Datula and Pontianus" in *Scenes from the Lives of the Saints.*
[2] See "Martha" in *People of the New Testament V.*
[3] She never saw them in any great numbers, however.

largest I saw were the size of a foal. Others were more the size of grown, or sometimes half-grown swine. They would attack only solitary men. Often I saw shoot forth from their throats a hot, fiery ray that would then diminish into a darkness of steam or mist.

In earlier times, and especially before the life of Christ Jesus, nature abounded here and there in many other such creatures. But in more recent times I no longer came upon them. Neither are their bones to be found upon the earth. Their heads were broad and blunt. Indeed, the whole creature was quite broad.

Satan

IN a certain city I saw over a gay party of ecclesiastics and seculars—men and women who were feasting and jesting—a heavy black fog stretching off into a region of darkness. In it sat satan under a hideous form, and around him as many devils as there were guests in the assembly below, all busily engaged in inciting the latter to sin, whispering to them and inflaming their passions. Although not entirely given over to lewdness, they were in a dangerous state of excitement, freely conversing in a light and wanton strain. The ecclesiastics belonged to the number of those whose motto is: "Live and let live!"—who argue thus: "In our day one must not be singular, one must not play the misanthrope; rather let us 'Rejoice with those that rejoice.'" And in such dispositions they daily celebrate holy mass!

I saw but one young girl in the party still perfectly innocent, and that was owing to her devotion to her patron, a saint whose name is well known and whom she was in the habit of invoking. I saw how they bantered with her and tried to lead her astray. But over her appeared a break in the darkness through which her patron shed light upon her and kept the evil spirits aloof.

Then satan from his dark circle called out to the saint, asking what he wanted and how he dared encroach upon his rights; he boasted with a contemptuous smile that all the priests below were his, since in their present state they said mass daily, thereby plunging deeper into his meshes.

The saint bade him retire, telling him that, through the merits of Christ Jesus, he had no right over the girl, whom he could not even approach. satan boastingly retorted that he would yet catch her, that he would make use of a stranger who had once made an impression upon her, and who would soon do the work.

Satan's figure was horrible: short arms with claws, long feet and knees turned outward so that he could not kneel even if he wished; his face was human, but cold, wicked, fearful, and he had certain appendages like wings. He was black and obscure, spreading darkness wherever he went. As I was surprised to hear him speaking of his rights, I was told that he really did acquire a positive right over every baptized person who, though endued with the power of Christ Jesus to resist him, yet freely and voluntarily delivers himself up to sin.

This vision was most impressive and affecting. I knew the people as well as the girl protected by her patron.

Satan knew nothing of the divinity of Jesus. He could not make out who he was, or in any way form a right assessment of him. He did hold Jesus to be a prophet, for he had early on remarked his holiness. He had likewise noted the holiness of his mother Mary, but she for her part paid him no mind, for there was nothing in her upon which he could lay hold with which to tempt her. For although Mary was the most beautiful of virgins, as also the most beautiful of brides, except for the occasion upon which eligible bachelors had been brought before her in the Temple—when a branch was passed among them to see whether it might bloom (this being an indication that her husband-to-be had been found), she had never had a single suitor.

Satan noticed that in dealing with his disciples Jesus did not always apply Jewish codes of conduct in the strictest manner, which led him to the erroneous view that he was no more than a man, for his followers occasioned disorder in such a way as to irritate the Jews. When he paid mind to Jesus's zeal, satan would try to anger Jesus under the form of one of his disciples; but when it was a question of Jesus's mercifuless, satan would try to touch Jesus instead by adopting the weak, bent-over form of an old man, and feign the conversation of an Essene.

Jesus

Two Genealogical Trees

I SAW the line of the descent of the messiah proceeding from David and dividing into two streams. The *right-hand* one went through Solomon down to Jacob, the father of Joseph, Mary's husband. This line ran in a higher direction. I saw the line of descent issuing most often from the mouth. It was of white, uncolored.

The figures in this line were taller than those of the left-hand line. Each one held a long flower stem—about an arm's length—with hanging leaves like those of palms: this stem was crowned with a great flower shaped like a bellflower [*campunella*], and had five stamens, yellow at the top, from which a fine dust was scattered. Halfway down this ancestral tree were three rejected shoots, blackened and withered. These flowers differed in size, vigor, and beauty. The flower borne by Joseph was the most beautiful and purest of all, with fresh and abundant petals. I saw that toward its extremity a ray united this line with the other.

I was given an explanation about the higher significance—full of mystery—of this line of descent [through Solomon]. It had in it more of the spirit and less of the flesh, and had some of the significance belonging to Solomon himself. But I cannot express this.

The *left-hand* line of descent went from David through Nathan down to Heli, which is the real name Joachim, Mary's father—for he did not receive the name of Joachim until later, just as Abram was not called Abraham until later. At the time I understood the reason for this but have forgotten it, but perhaps it will come back to me. In my visions I often hear Jesus called a son of Heli.[1]

---

[1] Brentano here adds a note: "In Luke 3:23 the expression 'who was a son of Heli,' applies to Jesus, and not to Joseph, as is said by many commentators,

197

I saw this whole line from David through Nathan flowing at a lower level: it generally issued more from the navel. This line had colors, with spots at some places, and then appeared more clear. I saw it colored red, yellow, or white, but never blue. The figures upon it were smaller than those of the line on the other side [that of Solomon]. They carried smaller branches, which hung down sideways and had little yellow-green leaves with serrated edges; their branches were crowned with reddish buds of the color of wild roses. Some were fresh, others limp. they were not flower buds but the beginnings of fruits, and always closed. ᘓ

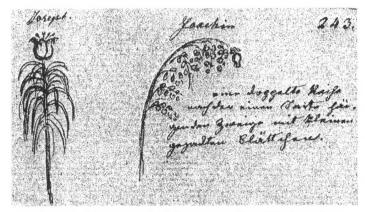

Above the blossom to the left is written "Joseph"; above the one to the right, "Joachim." Alongside the latter is written "A double row of little twigs hanging down on the same side with little serrated leaves."

Anne (the wife of Joachim) descended on her father's side from Levi, and on her mother's side from Benjamin. I saw in a vision the Ark of the Covenant being borne by her ancestors with great piety and devotion; I saw them receiving rays from the Mystery, which extended to their descendants, to Anne and to Mary. I always saw many priests in the house of Anne's parents, and also in Joachim's house; this was also the reason of their relationship with Zechariah and Elizabeth.

---

so that in this way [according to Brentano] the contradiction is resolved, for Luke is speaking of the race of Joachim, that is, of Heli."

In this line through Solomon there were several gaps separating its fruits more widely from each other. The figures were larger and more spiritual. Several times the lines met. At a point three or four generations before Heli (Joachim) the two lines crossed each other and rose up, ending with the Blessed Virgin.[1] At the point of crossing I think I already saw the blood of the Blessed Virgin beginning in the stream of descent.

At the time when Ismeria (Anne's mother) fell sick and was about to die, she called her household around her deathbed, gave them her parting advice, and appointed Anne as their future mistress. Then she spoke alone with Anne, saying that she must marry, for that she was a vessel of the Promise. About eighteen months after, Anne, then in her nineteenth year, married Heli, or Joachim. This she did in obedience to the spiritual direction of the prophet [the Essene Archos]. On account of the approach of the Savior's advent, she married Joachim of the House of David, for Mary was to belong to the House of David; otherwise she would have had to choose her spouse from among the Levites of the tribe of Aaron, as all of her race had done. She had had many suitors and, at the time of the prophet's decision, was not yet acquainted with Joachim. She chose him only upon supernatural direction. Joachim was poor and a relative of Joseph. Joseph's grandfather Matthan had descended from David through Solomon. He had two sons, Joses and Jacob. The latter was Joseph's father. When Matthan died, his widow married a second husband named Levi, descendant of David through Nathan. The fruit of this marriage was Matthat, the father of Heli, or Joachim.

---

[1] Brentano notes that Anne Catherine no doubt meant by this the connection between the line of David through Nathan and that through Solomon. In the third generation upwards from Joachim, Joseph's grandmother (who had married as her first husband Matthan, of the line of Solomon, and had by him two sons, one of whom was Jacob, the father of Joseph) took as her second husband Levi, of the line of Nathan, and had by him Matthat, the father of Heli or Joachim. Thus Joachim and Joseph were related to each other. It is remarkable that Raymundus Martini, in his *Pugio fidei* (p. 745, ed. Carp), also states that Joseph's grandmother after the death of Matthan married a second husband, from whom Joachim was descended. (See following paragraph.)

Some Advent Pictures

DURING *Advent, Anne Catherine had her usual visions of Mary and Joseph journeying from Nazareth to Bethlehem:*

I went to Bethlehem and thence journeyed a good distance to meet Mary and Joseph. I knew they would go into a stable and I hurried on joyously to meet them. Again I saw them coming with the ass, as peaceful and calm, as lovely as ever, and I was so glad to see it all once more as I had done in my childhood.

I went a long way back and found the stable, and on looking behind I saw Joseph and Mary far away with the ass, shining with light. It seemed as if a luminous disc surrounded the holy family as they moved forward in the darkness. Anne and Joachim had prepared all things for the Holy Virgin's delivery and they hoped she would come back in time to make use of them. But Mary knew she would not be delivered in her parents' house, and with wonderful humility took of all that had been prepared but two pieces, for she had an inexpressible feeling that she must and should be poor. She could have no outward show, for she had all within herself. She knew, or felt, or saw in some unknown way that, as through a woman sin had entered the world, so by a woman was the expiation to come, and it was in this sentiment that she exclaimed: "I am the handmaid of the Lord!" She always followed an interior voice which in moments of grace urged her irresistibly. This same voice has often called me to make long journeys, and never in vain.

Last night I was near Bethlehem in a low, square hut, a shepherd's hut, occupied by an old couple. They had partitioned off a corner for themselves on the left by a slanting black mud-wall. By the fireplace stood some crooks, and a few plates hung on the wall. The shepherd came out of his apartment and pointed to another just opposite, where sat Mary and Joseph in silence on the ground against the wall. Mary's hands were joined on her breast; she wore a white robe and veil. I stayed by them awhile reverently. At the back of the house was a bush.

I went to the promised land, as I had often done when a child, and I ran to meet Mary. I was in such a hurry, so eager for the coming of the Christ child, that I flew through Jerusalem and Bethlehem with streaming hair. I wanted to get them a good lodging for the night, and I found one not far from the first that I met on my entrance. I went into a shepherd's hut, back of which was a sheep-fold. The shepherd and his wife were both young.

I saw the holy family arrive late at night. The shepherd gently reproached Joseph for traveling at so late an hour with Mary, who sat sideways on the ass on a seat with a resting-place for her feet. She was very near the birth of the Christ child. They left the ass at the door, and I think the shepherd took it into the sheep-stable. They were treated kindly. They went into a separate apartment and made some arrangements. They had brought some small fine loaves with them but I never saw them eat much. I spoke quite simply with Mary and, as I had my work with me, I said to her: "I know well that you need nothing from me, but still I may make something for poor children. Be so good as to point out the most needy." She told me to go on quietly with my work and that she would do as I requested. Then I went over into a dark corner where no one could see me and worked away diligently. I finished many things, and watched the holy family preparing for their departure.

I journeyed quickly on to Bethlehem although I was quite fatigued, and I hurried to a shepherd's cottage, one of the best in sight of Bethlehem. I knew that Mary would arrive there that night. I saw her and Joseph in the distance. She was on the ass and shining with light. The interior of the cottage was like the others: on one side of the fireplace all sorts of vessels and pastoral utensils, on the other an apartment in which I thought Mary and Joseph would lodge. There was an orchard nearby and back of it the sheepfold, which was not enclosed, the roof supported only by stakes. The shepherd and his wife were young and very hospitable. When I first appeared they asked what I wanted, and I told them I had come to wait for Joseph and Mary, who would arrive there that day. They replied that that had happened long ago, and that it would never happen again. They were a little short with me. But I said that it happened every year, for the feast was kept in the Church. Then they grew quite clever and obliging.

I sat down in a corner with my work. They had to pass me often and they wanted to give me a light, but I assured them that I needed none, that I could see very well. The reason they said that the event was passed and would not again be repeated was that on entering the house I too had thought: "How is this? These people were here long ago and they are still here! They cannot still be alive!" Then I said to myself: "Why, what foolish questioning! Take things as you find them!" This reassured me, but the people had met my doubt by a similar one. It was like a mirror, reflecting these words: "Whatsoever you would that men should do unto you, do ye also unto them."

When Joseph and Mary arrived they were kindly received. Mary got off the ass, Joseph brought in his bundles, and both went into the little room on the right. Joseph sat down on his bundle and Mary on the ground against the wall. These young people were the first to offer them anything; they set before them a little wooden stool on which stood flat oval dishes. On one were small round loaves, on the other small fruit. Mary and Joseph did not touch them, though Joseph took some and went out with it—I think there was a beggar outside. The ass was tied before the door. Although they ate not, yet they received the gifts humbly and gratefully. I always wondered at their humility in taking whatever was given them.

I drew near to them timidly, rendered them homage, and begged the Blessed Virgin to ask her son at his birth not to let me do or desire anything but his most holy will. I spoke of my work, that she might tell me how to do it and distribute it. She bade me go on, soon all would be right. Then I sat down timidly in my little corner and sewed, but I did not stay until the holy family left.

My guide then took me through a wilderness some distance from Bethlehem toward the south, and it seemed to be in our own time. I saw a garden with trees shaped like a pyramid, their leaves fine and delicate, and there were lovely green plots with little flowers. In the center, on a column around which twined a luxuriant vine, stood a small eight-cornered church covered with the vine branches. At some distance only the leaves could be seen, but a nearer view disclosed bunches of grapes an ell long. It was wonderful how the branches supported their weight. The vine itself was as thick around as a small arm. From the eight sides of the little church, which had no doors and whose walls were transparent, ran pathways. In the church was an altar on which were three pictures of the holy season (Advent); one was Mary and Joseph's journey to Bethlehem; another the child Jesus in the crib; the third the Flight into Egypt. They seemed to be living representations. On the eight sides hovered twelve of the ancestors of Mary and Joseph who had celebrated these scenes. My guide told me that a church once stood here in which the relations of the holy family and their descendants always celebrated these holy feasts. It had been destroyed, but the feast will continue to be celebrated in the spiritual church until the end of time. Then he brought me back quickly.

My state on these days is very singular. I seem not to be on the earth. I see around, far and near, people and pictures, men dying of spiritual famine, evils everywhere; I see people here in our own country, or in the islands, or under tents, or in forests—I see them learning in one place, forgetting in another, but everywhere misery and blindness. When I look up to heaven, how poor and senseless seem these people! They are sunk in impurity, they interpret everything in a wrong sense. Then I try to push them on to God—it is all dark and obscure, and I feel a deep, deep disgust for life. Everything earthly is abominable, and violent hunger seizes me; but it is not disgusting, it is sweet!

I met Mary and Joseph near Bethlehem just about dusk. They were resting under a tree by the roadside. Mary got down from the ass and Joseph went alone into the city to seek a lodging in one of the nearest houses. The city had no gate here, the road passed through a broken part of the wall. Joseph hunted in vain for a lodging, for crowds of strangers were in Bethlehem. I stayed with the Mary.

When Joseph came back he told the Blessed Virgin that he could find no place near, and both returned to Bethlehem, Mary on foot and Joseph leading the ass. They went first to be enrolled. The man made some remarks to Joseph about bringing his wife, saying it was unnecessary, and Joseph blushed before Mary, fearing she might think he had a bad name here. The man said also that, as there was such a crowd in this quarter, they would do well to go elsewhere, and they would certainly find lodgings.

They went along timidly. The street was rather a country road than a street, for the houses stood on hills. On the opposite side, where they were far apart, there was a beautiful, widespreading tree, the trunk smooth, the branches forming a shelter. Joseph left Mary and the ass under this tree, and set off again in search of lodgings. Mary leaned at first against the tree, her loose robe falling in full folds around her, a white veil covering her head. The ass stood with his head turned toward the tree. Many passed on various errands, looked at Mary, but knew not that their Redeemer was so near! She waited so patiently, so quietly, so humbly! Ah! she had to wait a long time! At last she sat down, her feet crossed under her, her hands joined on her breast, her head bowed.

Joseph returned disappointed, for he had found no lodgings. Again he set out in another direction, and again Mary waited patiently; but he was unsuccessful as before. Then he remembered a place nearby where the shepherds sometimes sought shelter. They too could go there, and even if the shepherds came, they need not mind them.

They started, and turning to the left followed a lonely road that soon became hilly. Before a small rising stood a clump of trees, pines or cedars, and others with leaves like box. In the hill was a grotto or cave, the entrance closed by a gate of twigs. Joseph entered and began to clear away the rubbish, while Mary stayed outside with the ass. Joseph then brought her in. He was very much troubled. The grotto was but ten feet high, perhaps not that much, and the place where the manger stood was slightly raised. Mary sat down on a mat and rested against her bundle. It was perhaps nine o'clock when they entered this grotto. Joseph went out again and came back with a bundle of sticks and reeds, and a box with a handle containing live coals which he poured out at the entrance, and made a fire. They had everything necessary for that purpose, as well as various other utensils, though I did not see them cooking or eating.

Joseph again went out, and on his return he wept. It must now have been about midnight. For the first time I saw the Blessed Virgin kneeling in prayer, after which she lay down on the mat, her head on her arm, the bundle for a pillow. Joseph remained humbly at the entrance of the grotto. In the roof, a little to one side, were three round air holes with gratings. On the left of the grotto was another apartment cut out of the rock or hill, the entrance broader than the first and opening on the road that led to the fields where the shepherds were. There were small houses on the hills and sheds built of twigs or branches supported by four, six, and eight posts.

After this I had quite a different vision. I saw Bethlehem as it now is. One would not know it, so poor and desolate has it become. The crib is now in a chapel under the earth and mass is still read there; it is larger than it used to be and is covered with all kinds of white marble ornaments and figures. Above it stands a church like an old ruined convent. But mass is celebrated only in the grotto of the crib. I saw over it in the air a beautiful spiritual church. It was eight-cornered and had but one altar. Above it were choirs of saints. On the altar was a representation of the crib before which shepherds knelt, and through the air came little lambs like little white clouds in the picture. The officiating priest was a kind-looking old man with white hair and a long beard. He wore a very wide antique vestment, a cowl over his forehead and around his face. It was Jerome. Incense was used during the ceremony more frequently than with us. Holy communion was administered, and I saw, as among the apostles, a little body, like a tiny body of light, entering the mouth of the communicants. There were about six priests performing the ceremony, and when it was over they ranged before the altar, face to face as in choir, and chanted. Then the scene changed. Jerome remained alone, and the body of the church was filled with nuns of different orders. They ranged in three ranks as in choir and chanted. I saw the Annonciades, among them Jane,[1] who told me that from her childhood she had seen these mysteries thus represented and also the great good resulting from them to humankind. It was for this reason she had founded her order. She was now present with all her faithful sisters to continue the celebration of this feast almost forgotten by men. She exhorted me to reflect upon what had given birth to her charity and teach it also to my spiritual children. She told me many more things of the same kind that I intend to

[1] St. Jane of Valois.

leave after me to my sisters in religion. May God grant it! I saw also at the feast Frances and other nuns whom I knew.

On the evening of December 23rd, the pilgrim spent two hours at Anne Catherine's bedside while she lay in ecstasy.[1] *He wrote:*

"She experienced violent pains in her limbs and particularly in her wounds. She bore them joyously, though at times she was unable to repress her groans; her hands and feet quivered with pain, the former opening and closing convulsively. She has made all her presents, finished all her work, sorted and put away all the scraps and ends of thread that were left. When this was done she sank exhausted under her pains, which were to form her own Christmas gift at the Christ child's crib. These pains are always shown to her under the form of flowers."

She said: Dorothea is going with me to the crib; she has come for me. She told me that she had often been blamed for ornamenting the altar so profusely with flowers, but that she had always answered: "Flowers wither. God takes from them the color and fragrance that He once gave; so too may sin wither! May whatever is good be offered to Him, since it is from Him!" Dorothea used to be taken to the crib in spirit, and she offered everything to the Lord in sacrifice. The pilgrim too must take all his sufferings to the infant Jesus, all his weaknesses, all his faults, and he must take nothing back. He must begin all over and ask the child Jesus for a burning love, that he may taste the consolations of God. I see also St Jerome. He lived here a long time and obtained from God such a fire of love that it almost consumed him.

---

[1] The pilgrim was deeply touched by what he saw and heard. He began his entry in his journal by these words: "While I write I am saddened at the thought of the miseries by which we are surrounded. The darkness of our understanding prevents our calmly receiving and clearly recording the heavenly secrets revealed to us by this simple, childlike soul so favored by God. I can reproduce very imperfectly mere shadows, as it were, of those visions which prove the reality, in an ever eternal present, of God's relations with humankind obscured by sin. And even this has to be effected hastily and even stealthily. I cannot express what I feel! They who have for years stifled and mocked at this grace, they who recognize it and yet persecute her, who know neither how to seek nor how to appreciate it, will weep with me when the mirror that reflects it shall have been obscured by death! Infant Jesus, my Savior, give me patience!"

O, who can tell the beauty, the purity, the innocence of Mary! She knows everything and yet she seems to know nothing, so childlike is she. She lowers her eyes and when she looks up her glance penetrates like a ray, like a pure beam of light, like truth itself! It is because she is perfectly innocent, full of God, and without returns upon self. None can resist her glance.

I see the crib, and above it, celebrating the feast, are all the blessed who adored the child Jesus at his birth, all who ever venerated the holy place, and all who have gone there even only in devout desire. They celebrate in a wonderful Spiritual Church the eve of the Redeemer's birth; they represent the Church and all who desire the sacred spot to be honored, the holy season celebrated. Thus acts the Church Triumphant for the Church Militant; and thus should the Church Militant act for the Church Suffering. O how indescribably beautiful it is! What a blessed certainty! I see these Spiritual Churches all around, far and near, for no power can destroy the altar of the Lord. Where it is no longer visible, it stands invisibly, cared for by blessed spirits. Nothing is perishable that is done in the Church for the love of Jesus! Where men are no longer worthy to celebrate, the blessed do it in their stead, and all hearts that turn to the service of God are there present. They find a holy Church and a heavenly feast, though their corporal senses perceive it not; they receive the reward of their piety.

I see Mary in heaven on a magnificent throne offering to her divine Son—sometimes as a newborn babe, sometimes as a youth, and again as the crucified Savior—all hearts that have ever loved him, that have ever united in celebrating his feast.

Here Anne Catherine was radiant with joy, her speech, her glance, full of animation, and she expressed herself so intelligently and with so much ease even upon the most hidden and sublime subjects that the pilgrim was lost in amazement. His words but faintly reproduce those of this inspired soul, who spoke not so much in glowing colors as in fiery flames. She exclaimed:

See how all nature sparkles and exults in innocence and joy! It is like a dead man rising from the gloom and decay of the grave, which proves that he not only lives—youthful, blooming, and joyous—but that he is also immortal, innocent, and pure, the sinless image of his Maker! All is life, all is innocence and thankfulness! O, the beautiful hills around which the trees stretch their branches as if hastening to strew at the feet of their newborn Savior the perfumes, flowers, and fruits from him received! The flowers open their cups to present their varied forms, their colors, their perfumes, to the Lord who will so soon come to walk among them. The springs murmur their desires, and the fountains dance in joyous expectation, like children awaiting their Christmas gifts. The birds warble notes of joy and gladness, the lambs bleat and skip, all life is filled with peace and happiness. In the veins of all flow quicker, purer streams. Pious hearts, earnest, longing hearts, now throb instinctively at the approach of redemption. All nature is astir. Sinners are seized with sadness, repentance, hope; the incorrigible, the hardened, the future executioners of the Lord, are anxious and fearful; they cannot comprehend their own uneasiness as the fullness of time draws near.

The plenitude of salvation is in the pure, humble, merciful heart of Mary, praying over the Savior of the world incarnate in her womb, and who in a few hours—like light become flesh—will enter into life, into his own inheritance, will come among his own, who will receive him not. What all nature now proclaims before my eyes when its Creator comes to abide with it, is written in the books upon the mountain wherein truth will be preserved until the end of time. As in the race of David the Promise was preserved in Mary until the fullness of time—as this race was cared for, protected, purified, until the Blessed Virgin brought forth the light of the world—so that Holy Man [Christ Jesus] purifies and preserves all the treasures of Creation and the Promise, as also the essence and signification of all words and creatures until the fullness of time. He purifies all, erases what is false or pernicious, and causes the stream to flow as pure as when it first issued from God, as it now flows in all nature. Why do seekers seek and find it not? Here let them see that good ever engenders good, and evil brings forth evil if it be not averted by repentance and the blood of Christ Jesus. As the blessed in heaven, the pious on earth, and the poor souls [in purgatory] work together, helping, healing through Jesus Christ, so do I now see the same in all nature. It is inexpressible! Every simple-hearted man who follows Christ Jesus receives that gift, but it is through the marvelous grace of this season. The devil is chained in these days, he crawls, he struggles. The hideous demon is humbled, he can do nothing now. It is the unending grace of this holy season.

Two days later Anne Catherine related the following:

I saw Joseph going out in the evening with a basket and vessels, as if to get food. No words can express his simplicity, gentleness, and humility. I saw Mary kneeling in ecstasy in the same place as before, her hands slightly raised. The fire was still burning and on a shelf was a little lamp. The grotto was full of light. There were no shadows, but the lamp looked dull, like a torch in the sunlight, for its flame was material. Mary was alone. I thought then of all I wanted to bring to the crib of the expected Savior. I had a long journey to make through places I had often seen in the life of Christ Jesus, in all of which I saw care, trouble, anguish of soul. I saw Jews plotting in their synagogues and interrupting their service. I went also to a place in the environs where sacrifices were being offered in a pagan temple in which was a frightful idol with wide jaws. They put into it flesh offered in sacrifice, when the monster instantly fell to pieces. Fear and confusion seized the worshippers, who fled in all directions.

I went also into the country of Nazareth, to Anne's house, just one moment before the Savior's birth. I saw Anne and Joachim asleep in separate apartments. A light shone over Anne and she was told in a dream that Mary had brought forth a son. She awoke and hurried to Joachim, whom she met coming to her; he too had had the same dream. They prayed together praising God, their arms raised to heaven. The rest of their household likewise experienced something extraordinary. They came to Anne and Joachim, whom they found filled with joy. When they heard of the birth they thanked God with them for the newborn child. They did not know for certain that he was the Son of God, but they knew that it was a child of salvation, a child of promise. They had an intuitive assurance of it, although they could not express it. They were, besides, struck by the wonderful signs in nature and they looked upon that night as holy. I saw pious souls here and there around Nazareth rising up awakened by a sweet interior joy and, whether knowingly or otherwise, celebrating with prayer the entrance of the Word made flesh into the life of time.

My whole way on that marvelous night lay through the most varied scenes—people in all countries flocking together, some joyous, some prayerful, others uneasy and sad. My journey was rapid toward the east, though a little more to the south than when I went to the mountain of Elijah.

In an old city I saw a large open square surrounded by huge, half-ruined columns and magnificent buildings in which was extraordinary commotion. Men and women flocked together. Crowds were coming in from the country and all were gazing up at the sky. Some looked through tubes about eight feet long with an opening for the eye, others pointed out something in the air, and all uttered such exclamations as: "What a wonderful night!" They must have observed a sign in the heavens, perhaps a comet, which was without doubt the cause of their excitement, though I do not remember having seen anything of it.

I hastened on to a place where people with their priests were drawing water on the banks of their sacred river. They were more numerous than before—it seemed to be a feast. It was not night when I arrived, it was noonday.[1] I could not speak to all whom I knew. I spoke to some who understood me and were deeply moved. I told them they should no longer draw the sacred water but that they should turn to their Savior who was born. I know not how I said it, but they were surprised and impressed, and some, especially the most pious and reflective, were a little frightened, for there were very, very pure and deeply sensitive souls among them. These latter I saw going into their temples, in which I could see no idols, though there was something like an altar; they all knelt—men, women, and children. The mothers placed their little ones before them and held up their tiny hands as if in prayer. It was a truly touching sight!

I was led back to the crib. The Savior was born! The Holy Virgin sat in the same place, wrapped in a mantle and holding on her

---

[1] It must have been the hour there (India) corresponding to our midnight. Anne Catherine beheld Jesus's birth in Bethlehem at our midnight, and all the events there as night scenes; but on arriving in India, the time of nativity changes in her vision to the real time, the hour it really was at the Ganges when her soul arrived there. CB

lap the infant Jesus swathed in ample bands, even his face was covered. Both were immovable and seemed to be in ecstasy. Two shepherds were standing timidly at some distance, and some were looking down through the air holes in the roof. I adored in silence! When the shepherds went away, Joseph entered with food in a basket and carrying on his arm something like a coverlet. He set them down and drew near to Mary, who placed the infant in his arms. He held it with unspeakable joy, devotion, and humility. I saw that he did not know it to be the Second Person of the Divinity, although he felt that it was the child of promise, the child that would bring salvation into the world, that it was a holy child.

I knelt and begged the Mother of God to lead to her Son all who I knew had need of salvation, and immediately I saw in spirit those of whom I was thinking—my thought was the sign that she had heard my prayer. I thought of Judith on the mountain,[1] and all at once I saw her in her castle, in the hall in which the lamps hung, and there were many people present, among them some strangers. It looked like a religious reunion. They seemed to be consulting together about something and they were much agitated. I saw too that Judith remembered my apparition and that she both desired and feared to see me again. She thought if the messiah were really come, and if she could be quite sure of what the apparition had said to her, she would do what she had promised, in order to help her people.

It was day. Mary sat cross-legged in her usual place, busied apparently with a piece of linen. The child Jesus lay at her feet swathed, but his face and hands free. Joseph was at the entrance opposite the fireplace making something like a frame to hang vessels on, and I stood by the ass thinking: "Dear old man, you need not finish your work, you must soon go." Now came in two old women from Mary's country who seemed to be old acquaintances, for they were kindly received, though Mary did not rise. They brought quite a number of presents—little fruits, ducks, large birds with red, awl-shaped beaks, which they carried under their arms or by the wings, some small oval loaves about an inch thick, and lastly, some linen and other stuff. All were received with rare

[1] See "Judith of Africa" in *Scenes from the Lives of the Saints*.

humility and gratitude. They were silent, good, devout women. They were deeply affected as they gazed down upon the child, but they did not touch him. They withdrew without farewells or ceremony. I was looking at the ass; its back was very broad, and I said to myself: "Good beast, you have borne many burdens!" I wanted to feel it, to see if it were real, and I passed my hand over its back. It was as soft as silk, reminding me of the moss I had once felt.

Now came from the country of the shepherds, where the gardens and the balsam-hedges are, two married women with three little girls about eight years old. They seemed to be strangers, people of distinction, who had come in obedience to a miraculous call. Joseph received them very humbly. They brought presents of less size than the others, but of greater value; grain in a bowl, small fruits, a little cluster of thick three-cornered golden leaves on which was a stamp like a seal. I thought: "How wonderful! That looks just like the way they represent the eye of God! But no! How can I compare the eye of God with red earth!" Mary arose and placed the child in their arms. They held him awhile and prayed in silence with hearts raised to God, and then they kissed the child. Joseph and Mary conversed with them, and when they departed Joseph accompanied them a little distance. They appeared to have traveled some miles, and secretly, for they avoided being seen in the city. Joseph behaved with great humility during such visits, retiring and looking on from a distance.

When Joseph went out with the ladies, I prayed and confidently laid open my miseries to Mary. She consoled me, though her answers were very brief; for instance, three words upon three points. This manner of communicating is very difficult to explain. It is an intuitive perception something like the following. When Mary for example wanted to say: "These sufferings will strengthen you spiritually, you will not yield to them, they will make you more clear-sighted, will render you victorious," I perceived nothing but the meaning of these words under the figure of a palm-tree, which is said to become more elastic, more vigorous, by the pressure of a weight upon it. In the same way she told me something like the following: "The struggle with your sister will be painful, a sharp combat lies before you. Be comforted! With the trial and the suffering your supernatural strength will increase. The sharper your sufferings, the more clearly, the more profoundly, will you understand. Think of the profit you will derive from it!" I received this last instruction under the perception of the principle by which the purity of gold is increased under the hammer, or the polish of a mirror is produced. Then she told me that I must tell all, keep nothing back, even if it seemed to me of small importance. Everything has its end. I must not allow myself to be discouraged by the thought that I do not rightly comprehend. I must tell all, even if my words appear useless and unconnected. A change will come over many after my death, and the conviction of the truth of my state will contribute greatly thereto; consequently I must keep nothing back.

The Circumcision of Jesus

THE circumcision took place at dawn, eight days after the birth of Jesus. The Blessed Virgin was distressed and anxious. She had herself prepared the little cloths to catch the blood and to bandage the child and had kept them at her breast in a fold of her mantle. The octagonal stone slab was covered by the priests first with red and then with white. This was accompanied by prayers and ceremonies. One of the priests then placed himself in the chair, leaning back rather than sitting in it, while the Blessed Virgin, who was veiled and holding the infant Jesus in her arms at the back of the cave, handed the child to the maidservant together with the bandages. Joseph took him from the maidservant and gave him to the nurse who had come with the priests. She laid the little Jesus, covered with a veil, upon the cloth on the octagonal stone slab.

Prayers were again offered. Then the woman unwrapped the child from his swaddling clothes and placed him on the lap of the priest in the chair. Joseph bent down over the priest's shoulders and held the upper part of the child's body. Two priests knelt to right and left, each holding one of the child's feet: the one who was to perform the holy ceremony knelt before the child. The cover was removed from the stone to disclose the three boxes with healing ointments and lotions. The handle and the blade of the knife were both of stone. The smooth brown handle had a groove into which the blade could be shut down; the latter was of the yellow color of raw silk and did not seem to me to be sharp. The cut was made with the hook-shaped point of the blade, which when opened must have been nine inches long. The priest also made use of his sharp fingernails for the operation. Afterwards he sucked the wound and dabbed it with healing lotion and some soothing substance from the boxes. The part that was cut off he placed between two round discs of some precious material, shining and reddish-brown in color, and slightly hollowed out in the center, making a kind of flat box. This was handed to the Blessed Virgin.

The nurse now took the child, bandaged him, and wrapped him again in his swaddling clothes. Up till now these, which were red beneath and white above, had been wound around up to under the arms. Now the little arms were also wrapped around, and the veil was wrapped around his head instead of covering it. He was then again laid on the octagonal slab of stone, which was covered with its cloths, and more prayers were said over him. Although I know that the angel had told Joseph that the child was to be called Jesus, yet I remember that the priest did not at once approve of this name, and therefore fell to praying. I then saw a shining angel appear before the priest, holding before his eyes a tablet (like that on the cross) with the name of Jesus. I do not know whether he or any of the other priests saw this angel as I did, but he was awestruck, and I saw him writing this name by divine inspiration on a parchment.

The infant Jesus wept loudly after the sacred ceremony, and I saw that he was given back to Joseph. He laid him in the arms of the Blessed Virgin, who was standing with two women in the back of the cave. She wept as she took him, and withdrew into the corner where the crib was. Here she sat down, wrapped in her veil, and soothed the crying infant by giving him her breast. Joseph also gave her the little bloodstained cloths: the nurse kept the little bloody shreds of stuff that remained. Prayers were again said and hymns sung; the lamp was still burning, but day was breaking. After a while the Blessed Virgin came forward herself with the child and laid him down on the octagonal stone; the priests held out their hands to her, crossed over the child. After this she retired, taking the child with her. Before the priests left, taking with them all that they had brought, they ate a light meal in the arbor with Joseph and a few shepherds who had been standing at the entrance to the cave.

I learnt that all those who took part in this holy ceremony were good people, and that the priests were later enlightened and obtained salvation. During the whole morning generous presents were given to poor people who came to the door. During the ceremony the donkey was tied up farther away.

Today crowds of dirty, swarthy beggars went past the cave, carrying bundles, coming from the valley of the Shepherds. They seemed to be going to Jerusalem for some feast. They were very violent in demanding alms, and cursed and raged horribly at the crib because they were not satisfied with Joseph's presents. I do not know what was wrong with these people; I felt a great dislike for them. Today the nurse came again to the Blessed Virgin and bandaged the infant Jesus. In the night that followed I saw the child often restless with pain and crying a great deal. Mary and Joseph took him in their arms in turns, carrying him about and comforting him.

Regarding Circumcision

ANNE *Catherine was shown much concerning circumcision, but could retain only what follows:*

The overabundance that necessitated circumcision came after Noah (Noah, vine, circumcision, noble vines). This resulted from sin. It was not needful for human beings of earlier times. It was a sacrament of pure and ennobled begetting, and a preparation of the way for the flesh of the messiah, as from Mary. The circumcised Abraham was like a trimmed vine, a vine ennobled to bear grapes, and not only wood or leaves.

Before Noah, human beings were destroyed on account of their sins, depravity, and barrenness. They were like shoots growing into woodstocks, not grapes; or into straw, not barley. Noah was a good vine, preserved by God to people the earth.

The intoxication of Noah signified the propagation of his progeny, and the sin of Shem was his mocking of this. Also, angels brought to Noah in the ark a pure seed, like a vinestock, so that in the story of Noah, vine-planting and reproduction coincide, the one signifying the other. The covering of the father through the son appertains to this also.

After human beings had gone wild again, like rank growth, God singled out Abraham as the noblest vine of Noah's vineyard and placed him alone in a new vineyard, so that, through pruning, in time the blood of Christ and the holy sacrament might be brought forth. Later, He surrounded this vineyard with many fences and commandments of the law to protect it from going wild again, etc. Also, Noah was born circumcised, and three sons after him, but not the one who mocked him.

There were however certain Israelites who were born circumcised, so that but a slight incision was needed to remove a remnant of foreskin. These were children of grace. Moses was thus born, already circumcised. All servants of the Ark of the Covenant whom Moses picked were, by divine decree, such children of grace. But once he neglected this duty, and the one chosen was punished with death; and Moses received a rebuke. [She means Aaron's sons Nadab and Abihu, who brought impure fire.]

Most of the prophets were born without foreskin, and such children were given over as holy ones for schooling. They were called prophet children. David was such a one, as also many among the Essenes, and Joachim too, Mary's father. But not Jesus, for whom circumcision was his first martyrdom, which he bore for the sins of the world—for thereafter was circumcision rather to signify the state of those who believed in him, for by his death he removed the yoke of actual circumcision from them and brought them to a rebirth through water.

With the birth of the messiah was the purpose of circumcision fulfilled, and with redemption there came, with the rebirth of baptism, a spiritual circumcision of the heart, mouth, eyes, ears, etc.

I have often wondered that many learned Christians, who possess such deep inspiration, know nothing of such individuals who were born already circumcised.

I saw all of this previously even more deeply and clearly—and yes, the inner secret of it too—but I always forget it, for it seems so difficult to speak of it even when in all its purity and holiness it stands right before me.

The Baptism of Jesus

ON *one occasion Anne Catherine added some details to what she had earlier said[1] regarding the baptism in the Jordan:*

In a festive image I beheld the baptism of Jesus, which included something rather curious. Arching over him was something like a parasol, or church canopy. Jesus was standing in a cavity, or well, filled with water, communicating in turn by means of a canal to the river Jordan. Rising up from the middle of the well was a staff around which Jesus had wrapped his arms. John, positioned at the edge, poured water over his head.

Two others were assisting, one of whom (Saturnin) was holding Jesus's garments.[2] I don't know how the transparent, concave, shimmering canopy hovering above Jesus was supported.[3] The staff rose up through an opening therein and was crowned as with a green tree-top, bush, or wreath, upon which rested a dove.

[1] That is, in addition to what has hitherto been published of this event in various editions of her visions.

[2] Elsewhere Anne Catherine indicates that the other figure was the apostle Andrew.

[3] As an indication of a feast day, Anne Catherine often saw such a "flying carpet," in this case as the hovering canopy. CB

If I am not mistaken, I saw this same picture as a feast day image in the spiritual church [the church existing in the spiritual world], and that the bush and dove signified heaven. I see it only as a festive mystery, not a picture such as might happen today.

The following day Anne Catherine recalled that she had first seen this image of the baptism in a historical setting, surrounded by heavenly light and splendor, but that it had then risen up (she said "flown up") into a church that she described as the spiritual church of the baptism, which she had seen also in connection with John in the wilderness. Apart from this she saw also the great spiritual church, of which this image represented the baptismal font. She said she had forgotten the inner connection between these pictures.

The Voice of Jesus

THE tone of Jesus's ordinary voice was an agreeable tenor, perfectly pure in sound, without its counterpart in that of any human being. He could, without raising it, be distinctly heard above a great clamor. The lessons and prayers were chanted in the synagogue on a recitative tone, in the same manner as the choral singing and mass of the Christians, and sometimes the Jews sang alternately. Jesus read in this way the passages that he explained from holy scripture.

Last Passover
Supper and Passion in Brief

MAUNDY *Thursday, April 2, AD 33, being Nisan 13 in the Jewish calendar—was the day prior to the day of preparation for the Passover. According to Anne Catherine:*

Shortly before daybreak Jesus called Peter and John and gave them instructions concerning the preparation for the Passover feast in the cenacle (Luke 22:7–13). They went to Heli, the brother-in-law of the deceased Zechariah of Hebron, who had rented the cenacle, which belonged to Nicodemus and Joseph of Arimathea. Heli showed Peter and John the room for the Last Supper. The two apostles then went to the house of the deceased priest Simeon, and one of Simeon's sons accompanied them to the marketplace, where they obtained four lambs to be sacrificed for the meal. They also went to Veronica's house and fetched the chalice to be used that evening by Jesus at the institution of the holy communion.

Meanwhile Jesus spoke again of his imminent death, and—in taking leave of her—talked at length alone with his mother, the holy Virgin Mary. In Jerusalem Judas met again with the Pharisees and made the final arrangements for the betrayal of Jesus.

Around midday, after taking final leave of Mary his mother, the other holy women, and Lazarus, Jesus went to Jerusalem with the remaining nine apostles and a group of seven disciples. The disciples went to the cenacle to help with the preparations there, while Jesus walked with the nine apostles, teaching as he went, from the Mount of Olives to Mount Golgotha and back again to the valley of Jehosaphat. Here they were met by Peter and John, who summoned them to the Passover feast. Judas arrived just before the meal began. Jesus dined with the twelve apostles in the main hall of the cenacle; two groups of twelve disciples, each with a "house father," ate in separate side rooms. The house father of the first group, comprising older disciples, was Nathaniel, and that of the second group was Heliachim, a son of Cleophas and Mary Heli.

All subsequent events on this evening of the Last Supper, and the following events that night on the Mount of Olives, are described in each of the four gospels.

✝ ✝ ✝ ✝ ✝

ON *Good Friday, April 3, AD 33, as described by Anne Catherine, the moon was not quite full as Jesus, accompanied by the eleven apostles, walked through the valley of Jehosaphat up to the Mount of Olives. She recounted in detail the experiences undergone by Jesus in the garden of Gethsemane, where his suffering began. Here he lived through, in his soul, all the future suffering of the apostles, disciples, and friends of the early church; and he also underwent the temptation that he overcame with the words: "Not my will, but thine, be done" (Luke 22:42).*

Around midnight Judas arrived at the garden of Gethsemane accompanied by twenty soldiers and six officials. Judas went up to Jesus and kissed him, saying: "Hail, Master!" Jesus replied: "Judas, would you betray the Son of Man with a kiss?" (Luke 22:47–48). There then took place the capture of Jesus. Thus began Good Friday, the last day in the earthly life of Jesus Christ. The sequence of events summarizing his suffering (passion) and culminating in his death on the cross was given by Anne Catherine as follows:

The capture of Jesus shortly before midnight; Jesus presented to Annas around midnight; the trial by Caiaphas; Peter's denial; Jesus in the prison at Caiaphas's court; the sentencing of Jesus by Caiaphas; the suicide of Judas; Jesus presented to Pontius Pilate at around six o'clock that morning; Jesus presented to Herod Antipas; Jesus presented again to Pilate; the scourging of Jesus, which lasted about three-quarters of an hour and was over by about nine o'clock that morning; the crowning with thorns; Pilate handed over Jesus to be crucified and pronounced the death sentence upon him at about ten o'clock that morning; the carrying of the cross to Golgotha on the Mount; after Jesus had fallen three times under the weight of the cross, Simon of Cyrene was compelled to help him carry the cross; Veronica came to mop the blood and sweat from the face of Jesus with her veil; Jesus fell to the ground for the fourth and fifth times—the fifth time in the presence of the "weeping daughters" of Jerusalem; Jesus, on his way up Mount Golgotha, fell to the ground a sixth time, and then a seventh time shortly before reaching the summit—at this seventh time it was about 11:45 AM Jerusalem time; Jesus was disrobed for the crucifixion—at noon a reddish darkening appeared before the sun; Jesus was nailed to the cross at about 12:15 PM; then the cross was raised up; and at 12:30 PM the trumpets sounded forth from the Temple announcing the slaying of the Passover lambs; the two criminals were crucified—the repentant one to Jesus's right and the unrepentant one to his left; dice were cast for Jesus's clothes; Jesus, after being mocked, spoke the words: "Father, forgive them, for they know not what they do!"

Shortly after 12:30 PM, a darkening of the sun took place and the heavens grew darker and darker; the repentant criminal said: "Lord, let me come to a place where you may save me; remember me when you come into your kingdom," to which Jesus replied: "Truly, I say to you, today you will be with me in paradise!"; Jesus spoke the words to his mother, Mary, "Woman, behold, this is your son; he will be more your son than if you had given birth to him." And to John he said: "Behold! This is your mother!" Toward three o'clock that afternoon Jesus called out in a loud voice: "Eli, Eli, lama sabachtani!" which means: "My God, my God, why hast thou forsaken me!"; Jesus spoke the words: "I thirst!"; the centurion Abenadar reached a sponge soaked in vinegar up to Jesus's mouth; Jesus spoke the words: "It is fulfilled!" followed by the words: "Father, into Thy hands I commend my spirit!"; at these words Jesus died—it was just after three o'clock on that Good Friday afternoon, and an earthquake rent a gaping hole in the rock between Jesus's cross and that of the criminal to his left; the heavens were still darkened, and the radiant being of Jesus Christ descended into the gaping hole in the ground—thus began his descent into hell.

At the resurrection at dawn on Easter Sunday, April 5, AD 33, exactly 33½ years less 1⅓ days had elapsed since the birth of Jesus just before midnight on Saturday/Sunday, December 6/7, 2 BC.

Ecce Homo

WHENEVER in my meditations upon the sorrowful passion I hear this cry of the Jews: "His blood be upon us and upon our children!" the effect of that solemn self-malediction is made sensible to me in visions wonderful and terrible. I see over that vociferating multitude a gloomy sky covered with blood-red clouds, fiery scourges, and swords. It seems as if I see radiations from that curse piercing to the marrow of their bones—yes, touching even their children in the mother's womb.

I see the whole nation enveloped in darkness. I see that frightful cry bursting from their lips like so many lurid, angry flames—which rise and unite over their head and then recoil upon them, penetrating deeply into some but only floating around others. By these last were symbolized those that were converted after Jesus's death. Their number was not inconsiderable, for I saw Jesus and Mary, during all their frightful sufferings, praying continually for the salvation of the tormentors. For not one moment were the Savior and his mother angered by all their horrible maltreatment.

I see the entire passion of the Lord under symbols of the most malicious, the most barbarous torments, the basest and most insolent mockery; under symbols of rage and fury, and of the most horrible and sanguinary dispositions on the part of his enemies and their dependents; under symbols of ingratitude and denial on the part of many of his own followers; under symbols of the bitterest sufferings of soul and body. But I see Jesus enduring all, till his last gasp, in constant prayer, in constant love for his enemies, and constant supplication for their conversion. But by that very patience and love I see the rage and madness of his enemies still more inflamed. They become furious, because all their ill-treatment cannot draw from his uncomplaining lips one word that could justify their malice. Today at the Passover, when they are killing the paschal lamb, they know not that at the same time they are killing the real Lamb.

When in such contemplations I turn my thoughts upon the dispositions of the people and the judges, and then direct them to the most holy souls of Jesus and of Mary, all that takes place within them is shown me under various forms. It is true that the people themselves did not see it, but they felt all that those forms typify. I see then an innumerable throng of diabolical figures, each perfectly conformable to the vice that it symbolizes, and all in frightful activity among the people. I see them running hither and thither, inciting and confusing the multitude, whispering into their ears, slipping into their mouths. I see them driving numbers from the surging mass, uniting them into one band, and inciting them against Jesus, before whose love and patience they retire tremblingly and again disappear in the crowd. But in all their actions I see something desperate, perplexing, even self-destructive, a confused and irrational incentive, first here, then there.

Above and around Jesus, however, and near Mary and each one of the small number of holy persons present at this terrible scene, I behold innumerable saints in continual motion. I see them according to their various missions under manifold forms and raiment. Their actions appear sometimes to typify consolation afforded—as prayer or anointing, as feeding, clothing, and giving drink to the needy, or as other works of mercy.

In the same way I often see words of comfort or of warning issuing in various colored rays of light from the mouth of such apparitions; or, they carry in their hands messages in the form of scrolls of writing. I often see also (that is, if it is necessary for me to know it) the movements of souls and their interior passions, their suffering, their loving—all that the soul perceives. I see them penetrating, flashing through the breast and, indeed, through the whole body of human beings, sometimes in light of different colors, again in shadows. They appear under manifold forms, under colors and figures that undergo many changes, some sudden, others more deliberate; and then I understand it all.

But it is impossible to repeat it, for it is unending and, besides, I am so full of pain, suffering, and anxiety in consequence of my own sins and those of the whole world, so torn by the bitter passion of Jesus, that I know not how I am able to put together the little that I do relate. Many things, especially the apparitions and facts connected with the agency of angels and demons that have been contemplated by other souls when gazing in vision upon the passion of Christ, become intermixed when being related. They are fragments of similar interior, invisible, spiritual, visionary operations. They are retained in the memory according to the seer's own caliber of soul, sometimes in one way, sometimes in another, and are often erroneously joined together in the process of communication. Hence follow contradictory statements, since sundry things are entirely forgotten, others carelessly passed over, while some only are recorded.

Since every species of wickedness expended itself in tormenting Jesus, since all love has suffered in him, since he, as the Lamb of God, took upon himself the sins of the world—who could know, who could relate, those endless details of cruelty on the one side, of holiness on the other? If therefore the visions and meditations of many devout souls do not perfectly harmonize with one another, it is because those souls were not favored with similar graces of seeing, or facility of understanding and communicating.

Wound on the Shoulder

I ASKED *Anne Catherine once [said the Dean] if she had not also a wound upon her shoulder, for I think the Savior surely had his sacred shoulder wounded by the heavy cross. She answered:*

Yes, indeed! the divine Savior had a painful wound on his shoulder from the cross; but I have not the wound, although I have long felt its pain. I have venerated this wound from my childhood, because it is especially pleasing to our Savior. He revealed to me in the convent that this wound of which so little is thought caused him the greatest pain, and that when one honors it, he is as much pleased thereby as if that person had borne the cross for him up to Golgotha. At six or seven years old, when alone and meditating on the Lord's passion, I used to put a log of wood or some other weight on my shoulder and drag it along as far I was able.

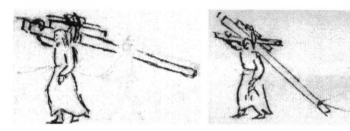

Cloth Used to
Lower Jesus from the Cross

WHEN he returned from the burial of Christ along with Joseph and the others, Nicodemus did not want to go to the cenacle, where some of the apostles were hidden, but instead preferred to go home alone. He had with him the winding sheet they had used to lower the body of Jesus from the cross. But the Jews had him under surveillance and soon captured him and locked him in a room, with the plan to leave him there during the Passover and then bring him before the court. But an angel came to him that night. There was no window in the room, but it was as though the angel lifted off the roof and raised him out over the walls.

Nicodemus went that night to the others in the cenacle, where they concealed him. Several days later, after he also had seen and recognized the Risen Christ, Joseph of Arimathea took Nicodemus to Arimathea and hid him there for a time, until such time as he (Joseph) could return and work together with Nicodemus as bursars for the community. It was then that the sheet that had been used in taking Jesus down from the cross passed into the hands of the Jews.

Veronica's Scarf and the Winding Sheet Upon Which Jesus Was Washed

IN the third year following Christ's ascension, Caesar called Veronica, Nicodemus, and the disciple Epaphras (a relative of Johanna Chusa) to Rome. He had earlier sent emissaries to Palestine and was eager to hear testimony of the events surrounding the death and resurrection of Jesus; and so it was that the three came to Rome. Veronica was brought to Caesar, who was ill. His bedchamber was raised up on steps, and a great curtain hung before it. The room was not large; there were no windows, but light filtered from above through shutters that could be opened or shut by pulling on cords. There was no light where Caesar lay, but only in the anteroom. Veronica had brought with her the scarf Jesus had pressed to his face while bearing his cross to Golgotha, as well as one of the winding sheets from the sepulcher. She laid the former out before Caesar. The countenance was visible on one side, and was arranged as in the picture here.

It consisted of a long strip of cloth, like a scarf, that Veronica had worn around her head and neck. The image of Jesus's face was not like a painting, but impressed into the cloth with blood; and it was also broader than a painting because of the wide swathe of fabric surrounding it. On the other cloth could be seen the bloody impression of the horribly scourged body of Jesus. It was the sheet upon which his body was washed before the burial.

It did not seem that Caesar was in any way moved at seeing these cloths, nor did he handle either. But he was healed by the sight of them. He wanted to keep Veronica by him, bestow gifts upon her, and give her a house with worthy servants as well, but she begged only to be allowed to return to Jerusalem in order that she might die there, where Jesus had died.[1]

Veronica and her companions returned to Jerusalem, and toward the end of the third year after her return she died, as it seems to me through confinement and torture on the part of her husband, who however was later converted to Christ by Joseph of Arimathea.[2]

The Mantle of Jesus

PILATE was called to Caesar, who was very provoked with him. Before he set out for Rome, Pilate took a small piece of Jesus's mantle (which he had received from the soldiers), placing it beneath his clothing against his breast. Upon his arrival, Pilate stood among some soldiers, waiting to see Caesar. All could sense Caesar's anger, which was clear for all to see as he finally approached Pilate. But as he came up to Pilate, Caesar grew suddenly mild and listened to him in a most friendly way. After he had left, however, Caesar's anger returned and he had Pilate summoned again—and once again Caesar softened as he came close to Pilate. It was then clear that this change in Caesar was caused by his proximity to the fragment of the mantle of Jesus that Pilate had hidden against his breast. But when I later saw Pilate again he was in some misery after receiving a sharp reprimand.

---

[1] Nothing more was said in this vision of what may have transpired at this time with Nicodemus and Epaphras.

[2] On an earlier occasion I seem to recall seeing that Veronica's kerchief remained with the holy women, and that Thaddeus took it with him to King Abgar, and that it came later to Constantinople and is now in Turin, where the burial sheet of Christ is.

Apparitions Upon the Death of Jesus

AMONG the dead who rose from their graves, and who were certainly a hundred in number at Jerusalem, there were no relations of Jesus. I saw in various parts of the holy land others of the dead appear and bear testimony to the divinity of Jesus. Thus I saw Sadoch, a most pious man, who had given all his property to the poor and to the Temple, appear to many persons in the neighborhood of Hebron. This Sadoch had lived a century before Jesus and was the founder of a community of Essenes: he had ardently sighed for the coming of the messiah and had had several revelations upon the subject. I saw some others of the dead appear to the hidden disciples of our Lord, and give them different warnings.

Terror and desolation reigned even in the most distant parts of Palestine, and it was not in Jerusalem only that frightful prodigies took place. At Thirza, the towers of the prison in which the captives delivered by Jesus had been confined fell down. In Galilee, where Jesus had traveled so much, I saw many buildings, and in particular the houses of those Pharisees who had been the foremost in persecuting our Savior, and who were then all at the festival, shaken to the ground, crushing their wives and children. Numerous accidents happened in the neighborhood of the Sea of Galilee. Many buildings fell down at Capernaum; and the wall of rocks that was in front of the beautiful garden of the centurion Zorobabel cracked across. The lake overflowed into the valley, and its waters descended as far as Capernaum, which was a mile and a half distant. Peter's house, and the dwelling of the Blessed Virgin in front of the town, remained standing. The lake was strongly convulsed; its shores crumbled in several places, and its shape was very much altered and became more like what it is at the present day. Great changes took place, particularly at the southeastern extremity, near Tarichea, because in this part there was a long causeway made of stones, between the lake and a sort of marsh, which gave a constant direction to the course of the Jordan when it left the lake. The whole of this causeway was destroyed by the earthquake. Many accidents happened on the eastern side of the lake, on the spot where the swine belonging to the inhabitants of Gergesa cast themselves in, and also at Gergesa, Gerasa, and in the entire district of Chorazin.

The mountain where the second multiplication of the loaves took place was shaken, and the stone upon which the miracle had been worked split in two. In Decapolis, whole towns crumbled to the earth; and in Asia, in several localities, the earthquake was severely felt, particularly to the east and northeast of Paneas. In Upper Galilee, many Pharisees found their houses in ruins when they returned from keeping the feast. A number of them, while yet at Jerusalem, received the news of what had happened and it was on that account that the enemies of Jesus made such very slight efforts against the Christian community at Pentecost.

A part of the temple of Garizim crumbled down. An idol stood there above a fountain in a small temple, the roof of which fell into the fountain with the idol. Half of the synagogue of Nazareth, out of which Jesus had been driven, fell down, as well as that part of the mountain from which his enemies had endeavoured to precipitate him. The bed of the Jordan was much changed by all these shocks, and its course altered in many places. At Machaerus, and at the other towns belonging to Herod, everything remained quiet, for that country was out of the sphere of repentance and of threats, like those men who did not fall to the ground in the garden of Olives, and consequently did not rise again.

In many other parts where there were evil spirits, I saw the latter disappear in large bodies amid the falling mountains and buildings. The earthquakes reminded me of the convulsions of the possessed, when the enemy feels that he must take to flight. At Gergesa, a part of the mountain from which the devils had cast themselves with the swine into a marsh fell into this same marsh; and I then saw a band of evil spirits cast themselves into the abyss, like a dark cloud.

It was at Nice, unless I am mistaken, that I saw a singular occurrence, of which I have only an imperfect remembrance. There was a port there with many vessels in it; and near this port stood a house with a high tower, in which I saw a pagan whose office was to watch these vessels. He had often to ascend this tower to observe what was going on at sea. Having heard a great noise over the vessels in the port, he hurriedly ascended the tower to discover what was taking place, and he saw several dark figures hovering over the port, who exclaimed to him in plaintive accents: "If thou desirest to preserve the vessels, cause them to be sailed out of this port, for we must return to the abyss: the great Pan is dead." They told him several other things; laid injunctions upon him to make known what they were then telling him upon his return from a certain voyage that he was soon to make, and to give a good reception to the messengers who would come to announce the doctrine of him who had just died.

The evil spirits were forced in this manner by the power of God to inform this good man of their defeat and announce it to the world. He had the vessels put in safety, and then an awful storm arose: the devils cast themselves howling into the sea and half the city fell down. His house remained standing. Soon afterwards he went on a great journey and announced the death of the great Pan, if that is the name by which our Savior had been called. Later he came to Rome, where much amazement was caused by what he related. His name was something like Thamus or Thramus.